Rudolf A. Haunschmied • Jan-Ruth Mills • Siegi Witzany-Durda

ST. GEORGEN-GUSEN-MAUTHAUSEN

This is a non-commercial publication.

It is dedicated to the memory of tens of thousands of forgotten KZ Gusen victims and the promotion of human sciences.

With the purchase of this book, you support the worldwide commemorational- and research endeavours of the Gusen Memorial Committee.

Donations welcome

IBAN: AT11 1500 0007 2105 8725
BIC: OBKLAT2L

Rudolf A. Haunschmied
Jan-Ruth Mills
Siegi Witzany-Durda

ST. GEORGEN-GUSEN-MAUTHAUSEN

Concentration Camp Mauthausen
Reconsidered

St. Georgen an der Gusen
December 2007

Bibliographical Information of the Deutsche Nationalbibliothek:
This publication is listed in the Deutsche Nationalbibliographie of the Deutsche
Nationalbibliothek; detailed bibliographical information can be accessed under
http://dnb.d-nb.de

Printing, Production and Layout: Books on Demand GmbH, Norderstedt
ISBN: 978-3-8334-7440-8

Contents

Foreword by Pierre Serge Choumoff

In 1993, having discovered the book published by the Market Community of St. Georgen an der Gusen for the 300-year anniversary of its foundation, I was chiefly impressed by Rudolf Haunschmied's study "Zum Gedenken 1938 – 1945". Detailed information was made available, some of it for the first time to my knowledge, about the GUSEN II (St-Georgen) tunnels network (with maps), built by my fellows. Previously the only publication available were Bernard Aldebert's gripping sketches that reveal the full truth of those tunnels, including production and assembly of Messerschmitt 262 [Me 262], the first jet fighter of the war.

I have been working with Rudolf Haunschmied since 1994 in the local-international "Gusen Memorial Committee (GMC)", created to organize the 50th anniversary of the liberation of the Gusen camps. Such cooperation was made possible for the first time by deepening cooperation between this Committee, including local representatives, the international community of survivors and the delegates of US liberators, including Harry Saunders, one of the last survivors of the Kosiek platoon having opened the gates of Mauthausen and Gusen on May 5, 1945. May I remember here that for the 20th anniversary only a committee of camp survivors gathered. Survivors and their families had taken up a collection to build the KZ Gusen Memorial around the remnants of the crematorium. The Memorial was dedicated that year.

In 1997 this Memorial has been given to the Bundesministerium of Inneres. Since that time the walls have been consolidated and the Visitor's Center has been added. Since 1995, however, the GMC has undertaken the task of gathering a substantial collection of memoirs, eyewitness accounts, artifacts and local records as well as records from archives worldwide.

This publication is one among many achievements resulting from the GMC's research.

The authors of this text, Rudi Haunschmied, Jan-Ruth Mills and Siegi Witzany-Durda, draw on previously unknown primary sources to construct a comprehensive narrative of the concentration camp complex Mauthausen and Gusen.

The text also discusses why this narrative was apparently lost to both historians and to the national consciousness of Austrians.

With my comrades I entrust the heritage of the Gusen Concentration Camps to Rudolf Haunschmied and the Gusen Memorial Committee because – as with this new study – they have demonstrated their ability to preserve and care for it in a far-sighted manner. With luck, it will draw, I hope, the proper attention by generations of historians.

Pierre Serge Choumoff

Vice-President of the International Mauthausen Committee
Officier de la Légion d´Honneur
Carrier of the "Grosse goldene Ehrenzeichen für Verdienste
um die Republik Österreich"

Inmate No. 25699 of Concentration Camp Mauthausen (April 1943)
Inmate No. 15014 of Concentration Camp Gusen I (April 1943)
Inmate No. 47836 of Concentration Camp Gusen/Mauthausen
(from 23 January 1944)

Foreword by Dusan Stefancic

Knowing that Mrs. Jan-Ruth Mills, Mrs. Siegi Witzany-Durda and Mr. Rudolf Haunschmied have prepared a new comprehensive study of the, until now unknown facts of the history of the Concentration Camp Gusen complex, I am of the opinion and consider this study an excellent and unique supplement to the written history of the Gusen camps. Moreover, since the work is based on an immense number of documents, collected by the authors from many sources and from archives from all around the world, as well as from documents received from the Gusen Memorial Committee and the numerous testimonies received from camp survivors (including my own statements), the study represents an important contribution to the history of the NS camp system.

I sincerely hope that my present lines about this new historical study about the Gusen camp complex researched and written by the above mentioned authors will encourage the upcoming generations to widen their research of KL Gusen and clear up the question remaining about the importance of KL Gusen. To many of us survivors it is obvious and clear that Gusen was not a simple side camp of Mauthausen but in fact a parallel camp of the Mauthausen system in many respects.

In this context Gusen must be treated as an independent unit and as such it must receive corresponding treatment from the Austrian government which should act with full cooperation with the Gusen Memorial Committee and bring knowledge of Gusen to the same international level as Mauthausen has today.

On behalf of my comrades and on my own behalf I fully support the Gusen Memorial Committee's demand to open Bergkristall and to incorporate the Gusen/St. Georgen camp complex in the future commemorative concepts of the Mauthausen State Memorial.

Dusan Stefancic

President of the Slovenian Mauthausen Committee
Union of the Associations of the War Veterans and Participants
of the National Liberation of Slovenia

Inmate No. 8482 of Concentration Camp Natzweiler/St-Marie aux Mines
(March 1944)
Inmate No. 91272 of Concentration Camps Mauthausen, Gusen I & Gusen II
(from August 1944)

Foreword by Henry Friedlander

I would like to congratulate the municipal government of St. Georgen an der Gusen for taking the initiative in 1989 to request the first study of the Nazi concentration camps operated in their vicinity from 1938 – 1945. Further congratulations are in order for requesting members of the Gusen Memorial Committee to extend that first study to the present volume using previously unpublished primary source documents, memoirs and eye-witness accounts.

This history is the first comprehensive study in any language to locate properly the administrative center of Deutsche Erd- und Steinwerke GmbH (DEST) in St. Georgen or to explore the history of armament manufacture at Gusen. The history of the Bergkristall Tunnel system and its production of Me 262s is documented here using primary sources for the first time, as well.

The current study broadens the focus on the well known Mauthausen Memorial to key locations in the nearby communities of Langenstein and St. Georgen that were essential for the development of the Mauthausen camp, as well. This allows a comprehensive overview of the real dimension of the Mauthausen Concentration Camp and reveals that the larger, more brutal Gusen camps provided key industrial infrastructure for the operation of the Mauthausen/Gusen system.

By extending the conventional approach to Nazi concentration camps dominated by Amtsgruppe D, the book introduces new militarily and economically important locations of the Mauthausen/Gusen system, particularly the regional DEST-Headquarters and the Bergkristall underground industries at St. Georgen.

By providing new perspectives on the history of the Mauthausen/Gusen complex, this volume also indicates an academic void that will need more in-depth research and discussion to provide a comprehensive understanding of the establishment, function and operation of the trifurcated St. Georgen-

11

Gusen-Mauthausen system and especially the post war policy dealing with the legacy of the two large concentration camp sites at Mauthausen and Gusen. Hopefully, this important work will be continued by historians in Austria and elsewhere.

Sincerely,

Henry Friedlander

Professor Emeritus of History in Judaic Studies
City University of New York
November 9, 2007

Preface of the Authors

This book is based on a study written by Rudolf A. Haunschmied, a native of St. Georgen an der Gusen, on request of the local municipal government that was published in 1989 under the title "1938/1945 – Zum Gedenken" in a history celebrating the 300-year anniversary of the extension of market rights at St. Georgen an der (a. d.) Gusen[1]. Interest in the recent history of the area developed as a new generation without personal involvement in the Second World War came of age. With enough distance from the events of this troubling period, they were able to face the past.

The 1989 text was intended to give the local people their first overview of war–related developments in St. Georgen an der Gusen. Most inhabitants of St. Georgen and its rural surroundings had no comprehensive knowledge about these years. Few eyewitnesses talked about their experiences. As most were "only" women, e.g. war widows or women who had remained in St. Georgen while their husbands were at the front, decades passed before scholars sought to interview them. In the years after the war hundreds of new families settled in recently-developed housing tracts. Many commuted to Linz to work in yet another remnant of the Third Reich, the nearby industries. These neighbors never heard the history of the concentration camps that existed in their new hometown from 1938 – 1945. Furthermore, because of the secrecy surrounding the armament projects for which the camps supplied labor during the war, surviving eyewitnesses knew only pieces of the puzzle, scattered impressions of the truth. Revealing too much knowledge was thought to be dangerous. Even in the late 1980s when elderly people were asked about their experiences, they still feared retribution should the Nazis return to power. Such terror, living in the minds of local people to this day, reveals the extent of the Nazi repression in the 1940s. In the decade immediately following the war, St. Georgen an der Gusen was under Soviet occupation, as was all of Upper Austria north of the Danube, along with Lower Austria. During this

---

[1]   Rudolf Haunschmied, „Zum Gedenken 1938/1945". 300 Jahre erweitertes Marktrecht St. Georgen a.d. Gusen – Geschichte Buch (St. Georgen/Gusen: Marktgemeinde St. Georgen an der Gusen, 1989)

period, many local people feared too much knowledge of Nazi crimes would mark them as fascist collaborators to the Soviets. The habit of secrecy born in fear outlasted the danger, long inhibiting the opening of a dialogue between local eyewitnesses and survivors of the camps.

In 2003, this revised English edition was again initiated by the municipality of St. Georgen/Gusen when it requested Miss Anna Innreiter, a student of the Auhof International School at Linz, to translate the 1989 text into English for the first time. Soon after, Rudolf A. Haunschmied, Jan-Ruth Mills, and Siegi Witzany-Durda decided to include new information gathered in the last fifteen years by the local-international Gusen Memorial Committee within Arbeitskreis für Heimat-, Denkmal- und Geschichtspflege St. Georgen/Gusen and a world-wide collaboration between the local population, survivors, liberators, and researchers.

This resulting publication is especially intended to serve a broader international research community as a reference guide to new and not yet fully researched aspects of the tragic reality in the St. Georgen-Gusen-Mauthausen region during the Nazi period in the second quarter of the 20th century. We intend for it to serve as a supplement to the well known but incomplete historical narratives of the State Memorial at Mauthausen and help future generations to understand the function and operation of Concentration Camp "Mauthausen" as the trifurcated system of the two concentration camps at Gusen and Mauthausen with infrastructure and administrational headquarters at St. Georgen/Gusen. It also provides key information to future generations of researchers to decipher the many camouflage codes that were used in the Third Reich to mislead the enemy and the public about truth and multiple purpose of the St. Georgen-Gusen-Mauthausen complex. These codes have worked well beyond their war-time intention, still focusing the attention of researchers and public on the Mauthausen part of the system while the St. Georgen and Gusen part continue to be overlooked.

We especially invite new inquiries to use this information to deepen research on the history of the Mauthausen/Gusen concentration camps in the future and thus promote a more comprehensive research on this very specific area in the history of the Holocaust. For this reason we have taken pains to provide exact locations for all primary documents where possible.

We would like to thank Dr. Jonathan Grant of Florida State University, Dr. Shlomo Aronson of Hebrew University Jerusalem, Prof. Dr. Uta Gerhardt of the University of Heidelberg, Prof. Dr. Michael Wildt of the Hamburger Institut für Sozialforschung, Mr. Pierre Serge Choumoff of the International Mauthausen Committee, Mr. Dusan Stefancic of the Slovenian Mauthausen Committee and Martha Gammer of the Gusen Memorial Committee for reading the drafts. Sherri Vance served as copy editor. Sincere thanks are also given to Victor Kielich, Karl Littner, Dusan Stefancic, and Joe C. for allowing us to use their unpublished firsthand accounts as former inmates of the Gusen concentration camps in this text. We also thank those survivors and witnesses who prefer to remain unnamed. We also thank Ms. Margarida Sala i Albareda of Museo d´Història de Catalunya (MHC), US Air Force Historian Dennis Mills, Mr. Joseph Caver of the Airforce Historical Research Center (AFHRC), Mr. Larry H. McDonald, Modern Military Archivist at the US National Archives at College Park, Maryland, Mr. Franz Walzer of Arbeitskreis für Heimat-, Denkmal- und Geschichtspflege St. Georgen/Gusen (AHDG), Ms. Louise Birch, Major Rtd. Charles R. Sandler, Mr. Reinhard Hanausch, Mr. Reinhard Kaspar and Mr. Franz Gindlstrasser for making authentic photographic records and illustrations available for this publication. The authors also thank the Market Community of St. Georgen/Gusen, the Provincial Government of Upper Austria and the Gusen Memorial Committee for funding the publication of this revised and enlarged English language edition.

Information and further photographs can also be found on the KZ Mauthausen-Gusen Info-Pages, a comprehensive website dedicated to the history of the concentration camps in the St. Georgen-Gusen-Mauthausen area with around 500,000 visitors each year and our digital archive.

www.gusen.org
http://ecc.pima.edu/~gusen

Preface of the Community of St. Georgen/Gusen to the 1989 Edition

1938/1945 In Remembrance

Few villages in Austria have so dark a chapter in their histories as the municipality of St. Georgen an der Gusen. Many young people living here are unaware of this dreadful history's significance.

These years permanently changed the village and its surroundings, but the precise consequences were only cursorily understood for more than half a century. Unfortunately the municipality's self-awareness could not be raised until today. Local people could not experience the unity or mutual support necessary to recover from and bear witness to the horrors perpetrated in their hometown.

Eyewitnesses to terrible scenes could tell no one what they had seen for fear of being arrested by the Gestapo. To this day, they feel uncomfortable when talking about their experiences.

The few fellow citizens of St. Georgen able to give firsthand accounts of these dramatic years are, for the most part, admirable older people who tell their stories with extreme difficulty, straining their powers of recollection. Long suppressed, terrible truths come to mind again, seemingly forgotten memories that nevertheless shaped their lives in the intervening years, and consequently, determined the development of the Market Municipality of St. Georgen.

We sincerely thank the eyewitnesses and former detainees of Concentration Camp Gusen for giving us information about that time.

The Municipal Council of St. Georgen/Gusen

Preface of the Community of St. Georgen/Gusen to the Revised and Enlarged English Edition

With publishing a first study in 1989, the Market Municipality of St. Georgen/ Gusen wanted to create a strong stimulus to clear lacunae in the history of our region during the National-Socialist period. As the politically responsible representative of the community, I was very thankful to Mr. Rudolf Haunschmied for his support in this goal. Later on, the Gusen Memorial Committee suggested an English language version of Mr. Haunschmied's earlier study. The new version would focus on the importance of the St. Georgen and Gusen area to the foundation and operation of the National-Socialist Concentration Camp System Mauthausen/Gusen. We willingly seized this suggestion and are proud that this publication is now available. With this publication we meet the steadily growing international demand for information on the history of our region during the National-Socialist period by interested people from all around the world.

Much as the 1989 publication was intended as introductory information for local residents, this widely enlarged English language edition should help interested people all around the world understand the tragic embedding of our region into the extermination policy and war industries of the National-Socialist Greater German Reich.

With this study, Rudolf Haunschmied, Jan-Ruth Mills and Siegi Witzany-Durda present a shocking supplement to the commonly accepted historical narrative of the former Concentration Camp Complex Mauthausen/Gusen. The significance of former SS infrastructure at St. Georgen and Gusen is documented through the use of previously unpublished primary sources and photographic material from archives all over the world.

We, the Municipality, are aware that the locations and remnants of the former concentration camps of our region have an importance that reaches far beyond our local community. They serve as places of commemoration and warning. For this reason, the market community of St. Georgen/Gusen actively supported local-international initiatives like "Plattform 75 Jahre Republik" or the Gusen Memorial Committee, which both grew in the region as a response to the study of 1989. Along with the establishment of twin towns and the Audiowalk Gusen (which was inaugurated in May 2007), we are also pleased to present this publication as an additional sign of the willingness of our community to nourish the memory to this inhuman period and to make it accessible to worldwide interest groups in English.

May this publication serve the memory of the countless victims of National-Socialist tyranny in our region and may it help future generations to conceive the incomprehensible and inhuman structures that were part of everyday life for the people of our region during the period between 1938 and 1945 and that traumatized generations of bystanders and witnesses for many decades, rendering them speechless. This history speaks for them, as well. However, as a community we wish more support and assistance from officials of the Republic of Austria and the Province of Upper Austria in bringing the legacy of the victims of this most horrible phase in our history into the future. We hope that a joint effort will make the "Bergkristall" tunnels at St. Georgen accessible to the public one day as a key element for the memorial landscape St. Georgen-Gusen-Mauthausen.

Mag. Rudolf Lehner

Councilor for Cultural Affairs of the Market Community
St. Georgen an der Gusen

Introduction

For a long time the village of St. Georgen an der Gusen was hidden in a safe location in the Riedmark, as the area north of the Danube River and east of Linz has been known since 1115 CE. In 1478, Upper Austrian territory was divided into four quarters (*Viertel*) named after rivers or mountain ranges. North of the Danube, two quarters were known as the *Mühlviertel* to the west and the *Machlandviertel* to the east, where St. Georgen lies. These two were combined to make the present Mühlviertel when Bavaria ceded the *Innviertel* (after the Inn River) to Austria in 1779. Along with the *Hausruckviertel* and *Traunviertel*, these quarters would eventually become Upper Austria with Linz as the provincial capital.[2]

By any name, here the Austrian granite highland merges with the Danube Plain in a conspicuous indentation of the prehistoric rock. During the Tertiary Period 18 to 25 million years ago, even before the Alps were formed by plate tectonics, this area was covered by the Thetis Sea, as were large areas of Austria. The receding waters left behind huge sand deposits. For some, the fossilized shark teeth, turtles, and similar artifacts of this lost sea would be scientific evidence of a remote history, while for others they would challenge beliefs about the nature of man and the origins of the universe. Regardless of what lay hidden beneath the surface, for many years the remote location undoubtedly contributed to St. Georgen's well-ordered life. While ethnic differences became a source of strife between Slavs and Germans, as well as Christians and Jews, in many parts of the Austro-Hungarian Empire, as a result of its cultural and economic isolation, St. Georgen remained a homogeneous community of Germanic Catholics.

Because of its proximity to Adolf Hitler's birthplace, Braunau am Inn, visitors to St. Georgen and neighboring Langenstein often assume the local population were entirely committed National Socialists. Hitler himself, in keeping with his racist ideology, saw the ethnic stability of Upper Austria in terms

---

[2]   Kriechbaum, Norbert. OÖ Landesarchiv, 6 June 2006, Personal Interview by Siegi Witzany-Durda

of "racial purity," and in 1931 ordered the Austrian Nazi Party headquarters moved to Linz, the provincial capital. However, even as the Nazis made significant gains in other provinces, Upper Austria remained primarily divided between three major parties: the Christian Social Party (CSP), predominantly Catholic bourgeoisie who increasingly called for an authoritarian state; the Greater Germany Party, pan-German nationalists calling for a German federation centered in Vienna (GDP); and the Social Democratic Party (SDP).[3]

Many former citizens of the Austro-Hungarian Empire lacked patriotic feelings for the "rump state" Austria, created at the end of World War One. Voters often felt more loyalty to their political parties than to the Republic.[4] Nor did the unrest that followed the war's end build confidence in the fledgling democracy. Returning troops and hungry citizens rioted and looted in the provincial capitals. When local police couldn't stop them, shop owners and industrialists hired former soldiers to defend their property. Outside the cities, armed farmers and peasants banded together to protect their crops from marauding city dwellers. Whether urban or rural, these armed militias became known as the *Heimwehren*, or "Home Armies."[5]

As labor unrest intensified during the interwar period, militias were used against striking workers in urban areas. In 1922, the Christian Social Party joined with industrialists, anti-Marxist, anti-Semitic and anti-Slavic groups to fund the Heimwehren. Valuing tradition and authority over individual rights, the primarily Catholic Christian Social Party (CSP)[6] hoped to unite the different militia groups into a movement capable of replacing "talkative parliament"[7] with an authoritarian government. The Heimwehr disrupted labor meetings, strikes, and functions of their political rivals, the SDP.[8]

---

[3] Pauley, Bruce F. "The Austrian Nazi Party before 1938." Parkinson, F. ed. Conquering the Past. Wayne State: Detroit 1989, 38-40

[4] Holmes, Blair R. "Austrian Monarchists, 1918 – 1938" Parkinson, F. ed. Conquering the Past. Wayne State: Detroit 1989, 95

[5] Carsten, Francis L. Fascist Movements in Austria. Sage: Beverly Hills 1977, 43

[6] Edmondson, C. Earl. The Heimwehr and Austrian Politics 1919 – 1936. Georgia:Athens 1978, 9 Carsten, 110

[7] Carsten, 60

[8] Ibid., 60

In 1923 the SDP formed the "Republikanische Schutzbund," the Republican Protection Force.[9] Local units of "Republikanischer Schutzbund" of Langenstein and Mauthausen (some 100 members and perhaps 500 workers) participated in the general strike called between July 16 and 18, 1927, called in response to the acquittal of men charged with murdering an eight-year-old boy and an unarmed man during a peaceful Socialist Democratic counter-demonstration. In Vienna, workers burned the Palace of Justice following the verdict.[10] Locally, the Schutzbund controlled the bridge and the ferry over the Danube at Mauthausen, all roads and the Danube's banks.[11]

The history of the militias in Upper Austria, generally, and in St. Georgen, specifically, remains a matter of some disagreement. Although the Upper Austrian Heimwehr would claim large numbers from 1921 on, these are frequently disputed and their leadership was fractious and inept.[12] But it is important to note that the Upper Austrian government was never closely aligned with the local Heimwehren and, despite frequent offers from Heimwehren leadership, generally relied on its own police to quell disturbances.[13] In *Fascist Movements in Austria*, Carsten notes that even during the upheaval during the 1927 riots, the Upper Austrian governor chose not to call on the Heimwehr as strike breakers or auxiliary police.[14] This seems to be true in St. Georgen and Langenstein as well: the government sent 64 police to Mauthausen to keep control of the situation in 1927. The local militias were not involved in earlier labor disputes in the Poschacher quarries in the 1920s, either.[15]

Despite the many inter-war photographs of St. Georgen which show a rather rosy, pretty bourgeois village where wealthy visitors from Linz enjoyed the public bath, this period was less than idyllic. Older residents from the lower class recall laborers marching in Holzschuhe (wooden clogs) to work in the

---

[9] Ibid., 64
[10] SPÖ Mauthausen (ed.), Der harte Weg. Geschichte der Arbeiterbewegung von Mauthausen [Der harte Weg]. Edition Geschichte der Heimat: Grünbach, 1989, 123. Carsten, 110
[11] Ibid., 124
[12] Carsten, 52 ff, Edmondson, 46
[13] Edmonson, 46
[14] Carsten, 111
[15] Der harte Weg, 124-130

nearby quarries at Gusen and four kilometers away at Mauthausen. Changes in the labor market when industrialized areas of the Austro-Hungarian Empire were ceded to successor states caused unrest locally.[16] However, Konrad Helmut reports that the homogeneity and stability of the working class in a region contributed to resisting an emotional decision to switch to National Socialism during times of crisis.[17] St. Georgen and neighboring Langenstein's major industries – agriculture and monumental stone production at the nearby Wienergaben and Gusen quarries – required little labor from outside the region. Unlike Linz, where German speakers resented Czech competition, there was little concern about "foreign" labor.

While the Nazi party succeeded in making inroads into the labor movement in other areas of Austria, several other factors prevented local people from embracing National Socialism.

While Carsten notes that without a doubt most Grossdeutsche Party members were racist antisemites, Catholics in Upper Austria were not: "In general it might be said that the *voelkisch* appeal was mainly successful among the students and certain disgruntled and dissatisfied urban groups, above all in Vienna and a few other towns. Elsewhere the influence of the Church and the Christian Social Party proved too strong a barrier – exactly as it had been during the pre-war period."[18]

Many Austrian Catholics were not attracted to NS racist propaganda as a result of the Habsburg monarchy's historical use of the universality of the Catholic communion to unify the linguistically and ethnically diverse peoples of the Austro-Hungarian Empire.[19] Archbishop of Vienna and Head of Austrian Catholic Church Theodor Cardinal Innitzer's initial cooperation

---

[16]   Horwitz, Gordon J. In the Shadow of Death. The Free Press: New York, 1990, 25
[17]   Konrad, Helmut, "Social Democracy's Drift toward Nazism before 1938." Parkinson, F. ed. Conquering the Past. Wayne State:Detroit 1989, 113
[18]   Carsten, 102 ff
[19]   Bukey, Evan Burr. Hitler's Austria: Popular Sentiment in the Nazi Era, 1938 – 1945. U North Carolina: Chapel Hill, 2000, 3

with the Nazis after the Anschluss is well documented:[20] Less well known is the response of Upper Austrian born Johannes Maria Gföllner, Bishop of the Diocese of Linz from 1915 – 1943. A staunch legitimist (Austrian monarchist) Bishop Gföllner remained critical of the Nazis.[21] In 1933, shortly before Hitler came to power in Germany, Gföllner wrote a pastoral letter on true and false nationalism. While the letter was published in his diocese, the Austrian bishops' conference did not support it. Gföllner rejected the National Socialist (NS) race theory as incompatible with Christianity, stating it was impossible to be both a good Catholic and a National Socialist. Strongly received, the letter saw eight editions and spread as far as the United States.[22]

Although, as Evan Burr Bukey reports, Gföllner also opposed the democratic Republic and preached against the "'atheistic' SD[P], Freemasons, Liberals, Methodists, Jehovah's Witnesses, Adventists, Jews, the YMCA, and even Rotary Clubs" along with "the foxtrot, tango and one-step shimmy,"[23] these do not diminish the importance of Gföllner's opposition to the racist ideology that taught that Jews and Slavs were subhuman. Sadly, anti-Judaism was nearly universally preached in Christian communities worldwide and had been used to justify violence against Jews for two millennia. However, Nazi plans to exterminate all Jews were a result of the racial anti-Semitism Gföllner preached against.[24] After the Anschluss, unlike Innitzer in Vienna, Gföllner refused to meet Hitler on his triumphant return to his native Lander. Gföllner also refused to sign the Concordat between the Austrian Catholic Church and National Socialists.[25]

One Upper Austrian Catholic, Franz Jägerstätter, the conscientious objector from St. Radegund who was beheaded in 1943, was inspired to martyrdom. In an article on Jägerstätter, Andreas Maislinger notes that Klemens von Klemperer, in studying the motivations of those who resisted Nazism to the death, found

---

[20] Schwarz, Robert. "Buerkel and Innitzer." Parkinson, F. ed. Conquering the Past. Wayne State: Detroit 1989, 138-140

[21] Bukey, Hitler's Home Town, 51

[22] Gföllner, Johannes Maria. *Hirtenbrief 1933:* Harry Slapnicka. 550 Stichworte zur Zeitgeschichte [550 Stichworte]. Edition Geschichte der Heimat. Grünbach, 2000, 92

[23] Bukey, Hitler's Home Town, 51

[24] Bauer, Yehuda. The History of the Holocaust. New York: Franklin Watts, 2001, 31

[25] Slapnicka, 550 Stichworte, 92 ff

that such sacrifice required both a political and a moral justification. Morality alone, Klemperer believed, would not prove a sufficient motivation to abandon ones family by sacrificing oneself.[26] Many local witnesses to the Concentration Camps Gusen I, II, and III, especially local women whose husbands were at the front (or in Dachau or Buchenwald in at least two cases) faced such a choice.

Like their bishop, the political hopes of many local Catholics focused on the past.[27] Maria F., born in 1915 on a small farm in Gutau, about thirty kilometers north of St. Georgen, laughingly recalled in an interview in 2000 how her mother would sigh and repeat "Mein Kaiser, mein Kaiser" whenever she looked at a picture on their wall at home of Francis Joseph I, the next-to-last ruler* of the Austro-Hungarian Empire.[28]

Although outright starvation in Austria became less common after severe food shortages ended in the late 1920s,[29] during the hard years of the depression, people still struggled to feed their children. Many Austrian farmers had divided their lands between their heirs for generations, until the resulting small farms could no longer support a single family. Maria F. recalls how her father worked as a field hand on farms neighboring his own. But even wealthier farmers could not always pay their workers.[30] Dire poverty led some local schoolchildren to allow themselves to be beaten up by classmates in exchange for a piece of dry bread.[31]

When Maria F. moved to St. Georgen after marrying in 1937, she recalls that fewer farmers were Nazis "because of their strong faith in God." But she said that "the young people believed in Hitler's promises that there would be

---

[26] Maislinger, Andreas. "Franz Jägerstätter." Parkinson, F. ed. Conquering the Past. Wayne State: Detroit 1989, 184

[27] Brook-Shepherd, Gordon. The Austrians. Carroll and Graf: New York, 1996

* Emperor Charles I reigned from 1916 – 1918 and was beatified by Pope John Paul II on 3 October 2004.

[28] Maria F., Personal Interview, 21 September 2000

[29] Black, Peter R. Ernst Kaltenbrunner: Ideological Soldier of the Third Reich. Princeton U, Princeton, 1984, 38

[30] Maria F., Personal Interview, 21 September 2000

[31] Interview 861207. Transcript in the possession of the author.

oranges and work and money. They thought they would get a better position if they joined the Nazis."[32]

The number of Austrian Nazis increased after Hitler took power in Germany, but Carsten reports that he found no explanation for the low numbers of Nazis during this period in Lander closest to Germany: Upper Austria, Salzburg, Tyrol.[33] By and large, workers and wage earners in Upper Austria were SDP, farmers, retailers, small businessmen and craftsmen were CSP. Professionals, civil servants and teachers belonged to the GDP.[34]

However, the presence of the "Deutscher Turnerbund" provided evidence of extreme nationalism in St. Georgen. In 1930 the local Turnerbund members who were from the upper economic strata of local society, bought a stable from a local inn on the St. Georgen market place and converted it into a gym.[35] Turnerbunde were gymnastic and athletic associations modeled after those supported by German nationalists from the 19th century on. Named after the Turnvater Jahn who had inspired the Prussian youth to revolt against Napoleon, these clubs glorified notions of national liberation. Very anti-Semitic as a whole, in other areas of Austria Turnerbunde distributed the publication *Bundesturnzeitung* which frequently blamed the loss of World War I on Jews and claimed Jews were living off of the reparations payments required by the post-war treaties.[36] This extreme pan-Germanic view was also reflected in former St. Georgen teacher Eduard Munninger's novel *Die Beichte des Ambros Hannsen*, in which he describes the end of the 17th century Protestant movement in the Riedmark. Published by a Nazi company in Goslar, Germany, the book's intensive pan-German propaganda won Munninger a 1937 German literary prize.[37] According to his niece, even Adolf Hitler received a personal copy when the novel was published.[38]

---

[32] Maria F., Personal Interview, 21 September 2000
[33] Carsten, 198
[34] Bukey, Hitlers' Home Town, 39
[35] Photographic documentation showing the Turnerbund members of St. Georgen converting the stable into the gym in 1931. Photographic collection. Arbeitskreis für Heimat-, Denkmal- und Geschichtspflege St. Georgen an der Gusen.
[36] Carsten, 91-93
[37] Haunschmied, 77
[38] Personal Interview, Gertraud D., 14 August 2007. With regard to Hitler's personal relation to the story see also footnote 314.

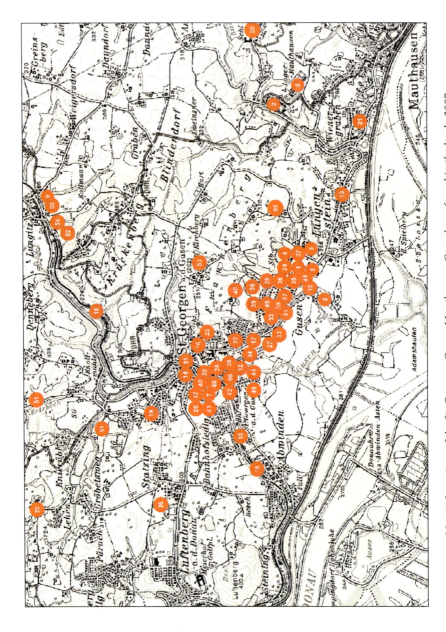

Map 1: Locations of the St. Georgen-Gusen-Mauthausen Complex referred in the book. 2007
Prepared by Rudolf A. Haunschmied (based on Austrian Map; BEV-No. EB2006/01347)

1 Appellplatz KL Gusen I (roll call square)
2 Wienergraben Quarry
3 Gusen Quarry
4 Kastenhof Quarry
5 KL Mauthausen
6 Jourhaus KL Gusen I
7 KL Sandpit
8 Village Gusen
9 Brickworks at Lungitz
10 Train Station St. Georgen
11 Bridge over Gusen River
12 Wimmingerbrücke Bridge
13 Town of Langenstein
14 Town of St. Georgen
15 SS Barracks Gusen
16 DEST Administrative Center
17 Hauderer Bezirksstrasse Road
18 Railway Line Linz – Ceske Budejovice
19 Rifle Range St. Georgen
20 Apfelsteiner Farm
21 Farmer Graf
22 (Deutsche Erd- und) Steinsiedlung

23 DEST Hostel with Kitchen
24 Stone Crusher
25 Meierhof Gusen
26 "Bergkristall" Underground Plant
27 "Schleppbahn" Railway Line
28 Regulated part of Gusen River
29 Overpass at the "Griesäcker"
30 Concrete Railway Bridge
31 Elevated Roadbed of former Main Road No. B3
32 Underpass of "Schleppbahn"
33 Archeological Find near Koglberg Hill
34 SS-Übernahmebahnhof (SS transfer station)
35 Barracks 13 – 16 and 21 – 24 at KL Gusen I
36 Spring in Weih
37 Steyr Factory Barracks
38 "Industriehof" KL Gusen I
39 Water Reservoir KL Gusen II
40 Wasner Farm
41 Brothel KL Gusen I

42 Bahnhofstrasse Road
43 Brunnenweg Road
44 "Bergkristall" Sewage Treatment Plant
45 SS Barracks for Luftwaffe Soldiers (26th and 27th guard company)
46 Brewery
47 Mariengrube Sand Pit
48 "Gusen-Steg" Bridge
49 Sand Mountain of "Kommando Kippe" at "Liebenau"
50 Makeshift Housing for Civilian Workers at Wimming
51 Makeshift Housing for Civilian Workers at Weingraben
52 KL Gusen III
53 Frankenberg Mountain
54 Bakery
55 Aircraft Parts Warehouse
56 "Kellerbau" Tunnels
57 Camp Gusen Cemetery
58 KL Gusen II
59 Pierbauer Quarry
60 Marbach Castles

While universities would prove important to the development of a Nazi Party presence in other areas of Austria, there were none close to the Mühlviertel.[39] Upper Austrian-born SS-Obergruppenführer Dr. Ernst Kaltenbrunner's biographer, Peter Black, traces the radicalizing effect of the pan-German nationalist dueling fraternities at Austrian universities. Members adopted the belief that political struggle was of racial nature – biological – and could only be resolved violently. The Austrian pan-German movement was fueled by educated elites who were against "liberalism, Marxian-socialism, democracy, constitutional law, Catholicism, Slavic nationalism, the Habsburg dynasty, a multinational state, industrialization and urbanization."[40] This grim mixture of hate and racism offered university students like Kaltenbrunner a way to identify with humble peasants and craftsmen central to the "völkische" ideal of German society without losing social status.[41]

In 1927, after graduating in law from the University of Graz, Kaltenbrunner took a job in Urfahr, across the Danube from Linz, intending to serve the peasants of the Mühlviertel. He joined and eventually worked for the Heimwehr which in Upper Austria was organized against the labor movement. To Kaltenbrunner's disappointment, while the amalgam of peasants, aristocrats, ex-army officers and students all hated Marxists, they were also legitimists strongly supported by the Christian Social Party. He quit the Heimwehr and joined the (Austrian) SS in 1932.[42]

Kaltenbrunner's paternalistic desire to "protect" the peasants and workers of the Mühlviertel from Jews, Slavs, socialism and democracy should not be confused with a corresponding desire on their part for such beneficence. Nor did all Austrians find the Austrian Nazi's desire to destroy the state and erase Austrian identity attractive.[43] Unlike other Lander where members of

---

[39] Johannes Kepler University Linz was founded 1966. While Anton Bruckner Private University for Music, Drama, and Dance and the Catholic-Theological Private University Linz have roots which go back many centuries, they do not claim to have been universities at this critical time in Austrian history.
[40] Black, Peter, 49
[41] Ibid., 49
[42] Ibid., 21-70
[43] Black, Peter, 66

the Christian Social, Social Democratic and Grossdeutsche Parties' inability to cooperate blocked efforts to govern the First Austrian Republic, the state leadership of Upper Austria created a tradition of cooperation, democracy and moderation.[44] As a result, the Christian Socialists, Social Democrats and even the Landbund (Peasants League) in Upper Austria remained committed to democracy long after party adherents in other regions abandoned the democratic process in favor of violently promoting narrow ideological goals.[45]

Examining the Austrian parliamentary election records, the Upper Austrian elections, and the local St. Georgen and Langenstein elections in the 1920s, one can see the SDP gained voters in St. Georgen and Upper Austria as a whole. The stability of the SDPs strength in Langenstein changed only in the community council election of 1929 in favor of an unlikely coalition, based on mutual anti-Marxism, between the CSP and the Landbund, a right wing, nationalist and anti-clerical party. Perhaps this was a protest vote over the violence in 1927. In any case, in the parliamentary election the next year, the SDP vote in St. Georgen increased significantly and that in Langenstein returned nearly to the previous level.

As several well documented studies of fascist and right-wing movements in Austria show, Austrian Nazi party membership had always been more attractive to the middle class. The first to join were low-level government workers followed increasingly by professionals, shopkeepers, university students, and intellectuals.[46] In St. Georgen, the three most important population groups were blue- and white-collar workers, farmers, and merchants in nearly equal numbers. Local party membership in 1945 reflects the national trend. Roughly ten percent of adults were members. Their professions are listed as railway workers, hair dressers, teachers, bakers, butchers, millers, smiths, carpenters, merchants. Only five local farmers were members.[47]

---

[44] Buckey, Hitler's Home Town, 60
[45] Carsten, 173, Buckey, Hitler's Home Town, 106
[46] Pauley, Bruce F. "The Austrian Nazi Party ...", 41; Carsten, 206
[47] Liste der Angehörigen der NSDAP und ihrer Wehrverbände und der Personen, die sich um die Aufnahme in die SS (Schutzstaffel) beworben haben, in der Ortsgemeinde St. Georgen a. d. Gusen. In the possession of the author.

Election Results 1923 – 1929 (Local, Regional & National)

Year	Election	Social Democrat	Land-bund	Christian Social	Greater German Party	National Socialist	Com-munist	Other	Total
1923	National Assembly (St. Georgen)	204** (27%)		363** (48%)	188** (25%)				755 (100%)
	National Assembly (Langenstein)	358** (58%)		201** (32.5%)	58** (9.5%)				617 (100%)
	National Assembly (Linz)	35,498 (43.5%)		31,268 (38.3%)	14,868 (18.2%)				81,634 (100%)
	National Assembly (Upper Austria)	122,189 (27.5%)		254,822 (57.2%)	67,895 (15.2%)			270 (90.1%)	445,176 (100%)
	National Assembly (Austria)	1,311,870 (39.6%)		1,490,870 (45.0%)	422,600 (12.8%)			87,266 (2.6%)	3,312,606 (100%)
1924	**Community Council (St. Georgen)**	**170** (21.4%)**		**280** (35.2%)**	**345** (43.4%)**				**795 (100%)**
	Community Council (Langenstein)	**373*** (59,7%)**		**251*** (40.2%)**					**624 (100%)**
1925	Landtag (St. Georgen)	168** (22.7%)		495** (67%)		75** (10%)	1** (0.14%)		739 (100%)
	Landtag (Langenstein)	322** (51.8%)		282** (45.3%)		1** (0,16%)	17** (2,7%)		622 (100%)
	Landtag (Linz)	32,445 (40%)		41,018 (50.8%)		4,856 (6%)	1,186 (1.5%)	1,262 (1.5%)	80,767 (100%)
	Landtag (Upper Austria)	113,456 (26%)		305,471 (70%)		12,127 (2.8%)	2,416 (0.6%)	2,996 (0.7%)	436,466 (100%)
1927	National Assembly (Linz)	32,482 (52.3%)	1,927 (3.0%)	27,712* (42.6%)		46 (0.1%)	242 (0.4%)	1,048 (1.6%)	64,990 (100%)
	National Assembly (Upper Austria)	141,113 (29.5%)	42,065 (8.8%)	290,018* (60.7%)				4,465 (0.9%)	477,661 (99.9%)
	National Assembly (Austria)	1,539,635 (39.6%)	230,157 (6.3%)	1,756,761* (48.2%)				114,976 (3.2%)	3,641,526 (100%)
1929	**Community Council (St. Georgen)**	**191** (24.2%)**		**314** (39.6%)**	**288** (36.2%)**				**793 (100%)**
	Community Council (Langenstein)	**299*** (44.2%)**	**377*** (55.8%)**						**676*** (100%)**

* Source for Linz, Upper Austria and Austria: Bukey, Evan Burr. *Hitler's Home Town: Linz Austria 1908 – 1945* (Bloomington: Indiana University Press, 1986), 42 – 43
** Source: Numbers provided by Martha Gammer (GMC) based on local community archives
*** Source: Johann Prinz. *Das karge Leben – 80 Jahre Sozialdemokratie in Langenstein*. 1999, 144

Table 1: *Election Results 1923 – 1929 (Local, Regional, National)*
Prepared by Jan-Ruth Mills

While German Nazi Party membership was closed after Hitler's rise to power in 1934, Austrian Nazi party membership remained open (although illegal for a time), and increased in most regions after the Anschluss in 1938.[48] Yet, as the attached chart shows, Nazis received 6% of the vote in St. Georgen and less than 1 percent in Lagenstein in the parliamentary election of 1930. By contrast, 10% of Viennese voted NS in 1932.[49] Locally, the percentage actually went down in the provincial elections the next year (1931), when less than five percent of St. Georgen residents voted NS and no residents of Langenstein voted NS. Although the Nazis received a larger percentage of the votes in St. Georgen than in Upper Austria as a whole, these figures dispel the myth that the Gusen concentration camps were built in these communities as a reward for overwhelming support of National Socialism.

Tension between right and left continued to mount in Austria as a whole. The Christian Social Party blamed parliamentary democracy for the increase in labor unrest and violence. They believed the plurality necessary for a multi-party democracy was a sign of weakness. Their dislike of the Austrian constitution was well known. Signed in 1920, it gave more power to the National Assembly than to the executive, or president. Dissatisfaction with Christian Social Chancellor Engelbert Dollfuss' government rose as well. In the spring of 1933, the three National Assembly Presidents resigned – a move which should have resulted in elections, according to the Austrian constitution. Instead, Chancellor Dollfuss suspended the National Assembly. Since the Austrian constitution gave the executive no such powers, Dollfuss tried to justify his actions by using a special war-powers provision of the 1917 Austro-Hungarian constitution.[50]

The Social Democrats brought the illegality of Dolffuss' actions before the Austrian constitutional court. Before they could rule, however, Dollfuss asked the members to resign. He then declared the court invalid.[51]

---

[48]   Carsten, 206
[49]   Slapnicka, Harry. „Oberösterreich zwischen Bürgerkrieg und Anschluss, 1927 – 1938", Oberösterr. Landesverlag, 1975, page 44 ff. Provided by Martha Gammer
[50]   Carsten, 231
[51]   Ibid., 231

Election Results 1930s (Local, Regional & National)

Parliamentary Elections 1930

	Votes	Christian Social Party	Social Democrats	Schober Block	Land-bund	Heimat-block	NS Workers Party	Other
Austria*	3,687,082	1,314,468 (35.7)	1,516,913 (41.1)	427,962 (11.6)		227,197 (6.2)		200,542 (5.4)
Upper Austria*	479,274	217,674 (45.4)	135,933 (28.4)	34,964 (7.3)	36,31 (7.7)	39,724 (8.3)	11,562 (2.4)	1,293
Wahlkreis Linz*	91,461	23,881 (26.1)	39,977 (43.7)	10,906 (11.6)	1,923 (2.1)	10,520 (11.5)	3418 (3.7)	
Luftenberg and Puerach**	567	212 (37.4)	267 (47.1)	10 (1.8)	56 (9.9)	13 (2.3)	9 (1.6)	
Langenstein***	677	244 (36.04)	373 (55.09)	12 (2)	45 (7)	2 (.3)	1 (.15)	
St. Georgen***	810	312 (38.51)	280 (34.56)	108 (13.33)	50 (6.17)	13 (1.6)	47 (5.8)	

Provincial Government (Landtag) Elections 1931

	Votes	Christian Social Party	Social Democrats	Schober Block	Land-bund	Heimat-block	National Social-ists	Nationaler Wirt-schafts-block	Com-munist
Upper Austria*	457,563	239,923 (52.4)	128,374 (28.0)	50,836 (11.1)		18,818 (4.1)		15,770 (3.5)	3,431 (0.8)
Wahlkreis Linz*	87, 737	27,976 (31.9)	39,558 (45.1)	7,945 (9.1)		7,1110 (8.1)	67 (10.1)	4,412 5.0	736 (0.8)
Luftenberg and Puerach**	610	251 (41.2)	291 (47.7)				1 (0.16)	67 (10.98)	
Langenstein***	646	239 (37)	362 (56)					45 (7)	
St. Georgen***	741	365 (49.25)	210 (28.34)				32 (4.31)	134 (18.08)	

*   Source for Linz, Upper Austria and Austria: Bukey, Evan Burr. Hitler's Home Town: Linz Austria 1908 – 1945 (Bloomington: Indiana University Press, 1986), 42 – 43

**   Source: Heimatbuch Luftenberg an der Donau, 1991, p. 296 – 297

***   Source: Numbers provided by Martha Gammer (GMC) based on local community archives

Table 2: Election Results-1930s (Local, Regional, National)
Prepared by Jan-Ruth Mills

Dollfuss outlawed the Schutzbund and abolished all opposing political parties. Conservative parties joined into the one legal party, the "Vaterländische Front" (Fatherland Front). Now illegal, the Nazis continued to oppose Dollfuss with violence and calls for new elections.[52]

By May a new constitution gave the executive all power. Attempts to reorganize Austrian society according to estates (a historically anti-democratic system) resulted in chaos. Like Hitler in Germany, Dollfuss demanded "unconditional obedience."[53] But Dollfuss failed to establish clear lines of authority in either the Fatherland Front or the government.[54]

As a result, Austrian society fragmented further. Using a destructive combination of high explosives and hate-filled propaganda, the German-trained Austrian SS gained popularity. They claimed the incarceration of their members as proof that Jews controlled the government and were imprisoning Germans in revenge for the ghettoes in the Middle Ages.[55]

In St. Georgen, the Social Democrats also had their own sports association, ASKOE (Arbeitersport-Klub of Austria).[56] On 8 September 1929 the Schutzbund had opened a rifle range in Mauthausen, increasing concerns that violent clashes with the Heimwehr were imminent. Although the Social Democratic mayor of Langenstein, Johann Steinmüller, would be voted out of office by 1934, he continued to serve the party as head of the local "Kinderfreunde" youth organization.[57]

Intensified interest in the Roman Catholic Church is reflected in the increase in religious instruction in St. Georgen's school from two classes to three,

---

[52] Pauley, Bruce. From Prejudice to Persecution, Chapel Hill: University of North Carolina Press, 1992; Carsten, 233

[53] Carsten, 238

[54] Ibid., 236-241

[55] Ibid., 249-250

[56] Der harte Weg, 101

[57] Der harte Weg, 134

approved by local school authorities.[58] So, despite indications that educators nationally were attracted to Nazism, this was not the case in St. Georgen.

No local incident shows the division in the community clearer than the moment in 1934 when Stationmaster Zdenko K., a fanatical National Socialist and illegal Ortsgruppenleiter of St. Georgen, shot down the crucifix hanging on a wall in the office of the St. Georgen railway station. Another St. Georgen railway worker, Heinrich B., reported the incident. Zdenko K. was cited for interrogation by higher railway authorities in Linz, but the matter would not be resolved so easily. Both men's lives would remain violently entangled not only in local but national history.[59]

In February 1934 police searched the Social Democratic Party offices in Linz. The Schutzbund revolted in protest. The uprising spread to Vienna, eventually erupting into a civil war. The socialists fought not only against the Heimwehr, but the Austrian Army and military police. Although they would lose the war, they earned the distinction of fighting the only armed battle against a dictatorship in pre-war Central Europe.[60] The stonemason Johann Steinmüller, former Social Democratic mayor of Langenstein from 1920 to 1927, fought with the SDP and was imprisoned for two weeks as a result.[61]

After the war, Dollfuss' attempt to shore up his power by negotiating with the Nazis did not diminish their violence or their plans to destroy Austria. On 25 July 1934 the National Socialists attempted a putsch. Members of the illegal SS-Standarte 89 stormed the Chancellor's office in Vienna and shot him dead. After a few days the police put down the putsch, and Minister of Education Kurt von Schuschnigg came into power.[62] Seven SS were executed,

---

[58] „Das kirchliche Leben während der NS-Zeit (1938 – 1945)". 700 Jahre Kirche zum Hl. Georg in St. Georgen/Gusen [Pfarrbuch St. Georgen] (St. Georgen a.d. Gusen: Pfarre St. Georgen a.d. Gusen, 1988), 41

[59] Pfarrbuch St. Georgen, 39-40

[60] Carsten, 235

[61] Horwitz, 27

[62] Maleta, Alfred. Der Weg zum „Anschluss" 1938 – Daten und Fakten. (Vienna: Karl v. Vogelsang-Institut, 1988), 98 ff.

and many others were imprisoned.[63] Nine illegal Nazis from the St. Georgen police district were jailed for six weeks after with this putsch.[64]

Ironically, only three days before Dollfuss' death, a railway colleague of St. Georgen Ortsgruppenleiter Zdenko K. met with Chancellor Dollfuss to ask him to intervene. Losing hope after Dollfuss' death at the hands of his fellow SS, Zdenko K. hanged himself. Heinrich B. must have thought the matter concluded, but would find out otherwise four years later on the night of the Anschluss when Zdenko K.'s widow, a fanatic Nazi in her own right, urged the newly-legal Nazi authorities to take their revenge.[65]

Other members of the illegal Austrian Legion of the SS who were driven out of Austria collected at the Sammelstelle (assembly point) of Concentration Camp Dachau outside Munich, Germany, where many of the SS who would eventually hold life-and-death power in St. Georgen, Gusen and Mauthausen were trained. This group of Austrian Nazis subordinated themselves to the German Reich while those still underground in Austria remained loosely organized, holding on to a belief that they could exploit their connection to German Nazism for their own nationalistic purposes.[66]

One important figure in this regard is St. Georgen born SS-Standartenführer Franz Peterseil. A leading illegal Nazi from the first hours in 1928 and carrier of the SS-Blutorden (Blood Order of 1923), by 1937 he was appointed Chief of the (illegal) "Upper Austrian" SA-Brigade No. 4. On 12 March 1938 an illness prevented Peterseil from hearing Hitler's first speech in his hometown Linz, so Hitler and Himmler paid him a bedside visit. By 14 April 1938, Peterseil was a member of the Reichstag. He left the SA on 19 August 1938, and on 9 November 1938 he was appointed SS-Standartenführer of SS-Abschnitt

---

[63] Black, 75
[64] Bericht des Gendarmeriepostenkommandos St. Georgen/Gusen an die Sicherheitsdirektion Linz. Unveröffentlichtes Manuskript für das von der Bundesregierung herausgegebene Rot/weiß/rot Buch 1946, Dokumentationsarchiv des österreichischen Widerstandes (DÖW No. 8359). Vienna, undated
[65] Pfarrbuch St. Georgen, 39-40
[66] Koehl, Robert Lewis. The Black Corps: The Structure and Power Struggles of the Nazi SS (Madison: University of Wisconsin Press, 1983), 104-105

(Division) VIII Linz. In 1940 he was promoted to a "Gauinspekteur" and became the deputy of the Gauleiter (governor) of Oberdonau (Upper Austria). Although it is clear that Peterseil helped organize the gassings at Hartheim Castle and that he commanded the "Gausturm" that hunted hundreds of Mauthausen inmates who escaped in February 1945, his role in the takeover of the stone quarries east of St. Georgen in 1938 (or earlier) remains unclear. One of Peterseil's colleagues in the Reichstag and former comrade of SS Division VIII was SS-Standartenführer Dr. Ernst Kaltenbrunner.[67]

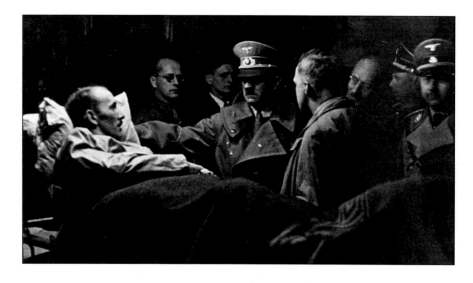

Figure 1: Bedside visit of Adolf Hitler and Heinrich Himmler to Franz Peterseil, 1938
Source: Franz Gindlstrasser

As an illegal Nazi, Peterseil had attended secret meetings some four kilometers north of St. Georgen in the village of Niederthal. The meetings were held in sand cellars similar to the cellars which would attract the attention of SS engineers.[68]

---

[67] Gindelstrasser, Franz. Franz Peterseil – Eine nationalsozialistische Karriere (Grünbach: Buchverlag Franz Steinmassl – Edition Geschichte der Heimat, 2003), 6 ff
[68] Ibid., 64

As did most villages in the Mühlviertel region, St. Georgen produced its own beer, kept cool in the summer in a cellar, or *Keller* in German. In 1878, local brewery owner Martin Boublik constructed a "Märzenkeller" reaching 25 meters into the sandstone mountain. The back part, an ice cellar about 8 meters high, had an area of about 36 square meters. In the spring of 1880, he built a Malztenne ("malt floor," or building where malt was produced) near the brewery. The same year, about 4 meters behind that building, Boublik built another malt floor into the sand in Cellar No. IV. In 1882 the St. Georgener Bierhalle (Ale-House of St. Georgen) was added to the brewery on the same level. Mr. Boublik continued to produce and sell beer at the St. Georgen Brewery until 1918 when he sold it to the Upper Austrian beer tycoon, Anton Poschacher, who used the old brewery as a beer warehouse.[69]

Innocuous as these first incursions into the sand hill would seem, sixty years later their stability would attract Nazi engineers looking to build underground factory space to protect armament manufacturing from aerial bombardment. The first tunnel system in Gusen would be known as *Kellerbau*, or Cellar Construction. The second, *Bergkristall*, Rock-Crystal, would be built in six months by alternating three 8-hour shifts of 6,600 slave laborers, according to a September 1945 Combined Intelligence Objectives Sub-Committee (CIOS) report titled "Messerschmitt Plant at ST. GEORGEN, Austria [capitals in original]."[70] By March 1945, the CIOS report states over 520,000 square feet (48.910 square meters) of underground factory space would shelter a finished factory. "This is a large underground plant for the production of jet-propelled Messerschmitt airplanes. Complete planes (except for wings) were being manufactured here on an assembly-line system."[71]

For several reasons, both Holocaust and military historians have had difficulty constructing an accurate narrative of the Gusen camps which provided labor for the tunnel construction. The intense secrecy of the tunnel

---

[69]   Gemeindearchiv St. Georgen a.d. Gusen (Archive of the Municipality of St. Georgen a.d. Gusen).
[70]   „Messerschmitt Plant at St. Georgen, Austria," German Underground Installations: Part One of Three, Section Three, pages 8-15. CIOS Section, Intelligence Division APO 887, September 1945 NARA Record Group 319, Entry 82, Assistant Chief of Staff G-2, (Intelligence); Administrative Division, Document Library Branch; Publications („P") Files, 1946 – 51, Boxes 2151-2152.
[71]   Ibid.

construction at Bergkristall caused even well informed Gusen I prisoners such as survivor Pierre Louis Le Chène, husband of historian Evelyn Le Chène, to assume Kellerbau was the only tunnel system built at Gusen.[72] While Le Chène's *Mauthausen* is to this day a valuable resource, her U.S. sources, such as the Cohen Report, could not provide her with the documentation regarding Gusen II or Bergkristall.

The secrecy the SS practiced regarding the Bergkristall tunnels also created an array of code names that made connecting documents with locations and projects difficult. The United States Strategic Bombing Survey's post-war misinterpretations of data about the German jet industry and the Study's failure to conduct rigorous inquiries into labor conditions at the dispersed armament factories contributed to the obscurity. When asked about SS enterprises in post-war interviews, Albert Speer (whom Hitler appointed Reich Minister of Armaments on 2 February 1942 and who headed Me 262 underground dispersal until 1 March 1944)[73], characterized SS businessmen as laughable and too stupid to produce soft drinks. Concentration camp labour produced only "primitive"[74] items, he said, although he does mention an underground plant "near Nordhausen built under Kammler's Höhlenprogramm, where the SS were making 300 fighter fuselages a month while Himmler was telling everybody that the plant was making 300 'aircraft.'"[75]

Historians would continue to see "300 'aircraft'" a month as an inflated figure for decades.[76] The United States Strategic Bombing Survey (USSBS), published on 30 September 1945, the same month as the CIOS report quoted above, perhaps did not have access or clearance to use all the information available on underground factories and so relied on the testimony of war criminals. It is unfortunate that historians have assumed the USSBS to be a complete inventory of all important aircraft factories within the Third Reich

---

[72] Le Chène, 203-207
[73] Allen, Michael. The Business of Genocide [Business] (The University of North Carolina Press, Chapel Hill, 2004), 232
[74] Interrogation Reports: War Crimes Proceedings at Nuremberg Speer Interviews NARA M 1270 Roll 29
[75] Ibid.
[76] Murray, Williamson. Strategy for Defeat: The Luftwaffe, 1933 – 45 (Airpower Research Institute, 1983), 272-275

and a complete narrative of their development, which the Survey itself never claimed to be.

Whether USSBS's inaccuracy was caused by classification of U.S. post war intelligence reports about Bergkristall and jet production is beyond the scope of this book. However, another factor obscuring this history is the fact that these tunnels and towns were in Soviet territory during the Cold War, thus complicating investigations into inconsistencies in the narrative constructed about these camps directly after the war.

When Nazi defendants mention St. Georgen in their Nuremberg trial testimony, it is in reference to the "granite works in St. Georgen" in order to avoid association with crimes committed at KZ Mauthausen, which had gained a reputation for brutality even before the trials because of the use of slave labor in the Wienergraben.[77] However, Wolfgang Sanner, Manager of A.E.G. Berlin, Secretary of the Labour Drafting Deparment at the CC Mauthausen, in a 10 May 1945 report on "Forced Labor" at Mauthausen, would identify Deutsche Erd- und Steinwerke G.m.b.H at *St. Georgen a.d. Gusen* as the firm responsible for the quarry and war plant at Mauthausen as well as Gusen, where DEST was also responsible for "Quarry and arming [sic]plant, Aerplane Factory Messerschmidt [sic] and underground mines for arming purposes." This document also links the Concentration Camp at "Gusen" to SS Führungsstab B9 [sic] Dipl.-Ing. Karl Fiebinger with forced labor for "Buildings below surface for secret war material plant." Also listed with Fiebinger in association with forced labor and underground plants at Gusen is Dr.-Ing. Kammler.[78]

In addition, without a proper understanding of the use of slave labor in the tunnel construction and armament manufacture contained therein, the histories of Mauthausen Concentration Camp Complex have also overlooked the Gusen camps' importance to aircraft production. Histories which rely on Hans Marsálek's seminal work *Die Geschichte des Konzentrationslagers*

---

[77] Nuremberg Military Tribunal, Volume 5, pages 488, 573 and 1242, http://www.mazal.org/archive/
    nmt/05/, 10 March 2003.
[78] NARA AG 254 Detention and Internment Camps USGCC Record Group 260 39.40.17.02, 6

Mauthausen have followed his lead in limiting discussions of the KZ Gusen camps located in St. Georgen and neighboring Langenstein to the SS exploitation of the Gusen stone quarries. Marsálek's brief references to the use of slave labor in the armament industries cannot account for the 20,000 prisoners liberated from Gusen I, II and III on May 5, 1945, nor for the nearly 40,000 deaths between 1939 and May 1945.

Michael Thad Allen's *The Business of Genocide,* an enormously helpful discussion of the professional communities (SS and the civil servants and industrialists within the Reich Ministry for Armaments and Munitions) describes the story of the struggle between Speer, the SS, and Kammler over production of the Me 262 as "well known,"[79] but does not pursue the connection between Deutsche Erd- und Steinwerke GmbH (DEST), KZ Gusen, and Bergkristall. A full examination of the interweaving of commercial ventures, ideology and air armament interests in the last years of the war is needed to fully understand the history of the Gusen Camps and the towns that witnessed them. While Allen refers readers to Paul Jaskot's *The Architecture of Oppression*[80] for an outline of the development of the exploitation of slave labor in the building industry at Mauthausen, Jaskot seldom mentions KZ Gusen I as it relates to the quarrying and refining of building stones.

But just as Jaskot explains that art history's focus on the aesthetics of the product (in this case the monumental buildings) without considering the process of production, fails to explain the political history of the art, so Reinhard Hanausch, a historian of Messerschmitt GmbH Regensburg's use of slave labour, similarly argues that too many military histories focus on the Me 262 as a "miracle of technology" or maintain "a misty eyed focus on the great man, Messerschmitt himself" without considering social and economic history, particularly labour history, involved in the production of this first jet.[81] We hope this book will make important connections between the

---

[79]   Allen, Business, 203
[80]   Jaskot, Paul B. The Architecture of Oppression. London: Routledge, 2000
[81]   Hanausch, Reinhard. Sklavenarbeit für den Düsenjäger. KZ-Produktion und Zwangsarbeit bei den Regensburger Messerschmitt-Werken 1939 – 45 (unpublished). See also Begegnungen mit ehemaligen ZwangsarbeiterInnen (Regensburg: Buntehunde, 2003)

disparate elements that caused DEST and Messerschmitt GmbH Regensburg to connect in a fury of destructive production.

The fact that many Austrian academic historians have been, for decades, reluctant to research or discuss the Holocaust or slave labor in Austria may find an explanation in Herbert Steiner's "The Role of Austrian Resistance with Special Reference to the Labor Movement." Steiner speculates that professional and intellectual Austrians who did not witness the camps themselves are reluctant to discuss the Holocaust because so many benefited materially or professionally by the vacancies created when 100,000 Austrian Jews were forced to leave their homes and/or professions in large urban areas.[82]

There is no doubt that some residents of St. Georgen benefited from the Gusen camps. Horwitz describes how many local merchants and private business owners welcomed opportunities to be involved in supplying and constructing Mauthausen and Gusen I.[83] This study will reveal more of the details of that construction. But from the night of the Anschluss those who might have voiced objection had the example of Heinrich B., who was dragged from his home in St. Georgen and beaten by the Sturmabteilung (SA) for having reported Zdenko K. four years earlier. Deported to Dachau and then Flossenbürg, he was imprisoned for four years.[84]

Such violence would have been known by the whole town if not by morning then by the end of Sunday Mass on the following day. In discussions of these communities and what they might or might not have done, one might do well to keep in mind how small St. Georgen and Langenstein were. In 1939, each had 1,429 and 1,239 residents, respectively. By 1940, there were 600 guards at

---

[82]   Steiner, Herbert. „The Role of Austrian Resistance with Special Reference to the Labor Movement" (The Journal of Modern History Volume 64, Supplement: Resistance Against the Third Reich, Dec. 1992), 128

[83]   Horwitz, 27

[84]   Protokoll aufgenommen am 1. Juli 1945 über Veranlassung der Amerikanischen Militärregierung (Mil.Polz.) in St. Georgen a.d. Gusen wegen der erfolgten Massregelung, Verhaftung und Internierung des Weichenstellers Heinrich B. in das Konzentrationslager Dachau verfügt von Frau Anna K. derzeit in Graz. In the possession of the author. Pfarrbuch St. Georgen, 39-40

Gusen I.[85] On average, eleven to thirteen SS-guard companies were stationed at CC Gusen,[86] adding up to about 3,000 men. In addition, many officers' families relocated to St. Georgen.

All Austria's attitude toward concentration camps is frequently assumed to be exemplified by the townspeople of Gmunden, in the Traunviertel, who applauded Gauleiter August Eigruber's 1938 announcement that a concentration camp system would be built in Upper Austria.[87] While Austria had concentration camps prior to the Nazi takeover, they were nowhere near as brutal as the Nazi camps would be. Witness the fact that Ernst Kaltenbrunner, after his arrest for high treason in 1934, went on a hunger strike to protest conditions at the Kaisersteinbruch Concentration Camp.[88]

As Horwitz reports, the Governor of the District of Perg (where Mauthausen, St. Georgen and Langenstein are located) was not confident about his constituents' reaction to camps planned for his district. On hearing the plans for a concentration camp at Mauthausen, he wrote to Himmler, warning that the local people were "preponderantly former Marxists and clericals who would exploit the establishment of a concentration camp as welcome cause for inciting against the NSDAP. For this reason, one might find another location for it."[89] Himmler, of course, had methods of dealing with dissent. But how much dissent was there to National Socialism in St. Georgen and Langenstein? We have seen that the local "clericals" might well have been committed Catholics and that "former" Marxists may well have had police records and reputations as anti-fascists.

Horwitz reports that in 1939 Langenstein's former mayor Social Democrat Johann Steinmüller was sent to Buchenwald for 8 months for complaining in a Mauthausen tavern that inmates were being shot to death in Gusen and that local people were upset about the treatment of prisoners. Horwitz

---

[85] Mob.-Stärkenachweisung der K.L. durch den Inspekteur der Konzentrationslager vom 12. Februar 1940. BArch, NS 4/Ma/36/22.
[86] Marsálek, Gusen, 10.
[87] Bukey, Evan Burr. Hitler's Austria; 38; Horwitz, 28
[88] Black, 74
[89] Quoted in Horwitz, 31

questions the depth of the "uproar" and the sincerity of concern for prisoners based, apparently, on the lack of other arrests and imprisonments.[90] In fact, Johann Steinmüller, who lived at Gusen village No. 14, was fired earlier that day, 7 July 1939, for passing a jug full of water to prisoners during a break. He actually spent 39 months in Buchenwald and then Dachau before returning to his family on 19 September 1942.[91]

But, as Heinrich B.'s story shows, residents were already familiar with the consequences for voicing opposition to the SS. Steinmüller's dissent, as well as the earlier act of giving water to the thirsty, must be seen in this context as well as the fact that, as Horwitz notes, the waitress was all too willing to testify against him.

What did this mean for the future prisoners and the possibility of rescue? The escape and rescue of Esther Zychlinski neè Feinkoch is illustrative for several reasons. The young Hungarian Jewish woman was transferred from Auschwitz in 1945 to a provisional camp outside Mauthausen main camp. The wire fence surrounding the 300 to 500 women turned out not to be electrified. Seeing a hole in the wet ground under the fence, she escaped into the forest. She walked until she came to the Schatz family farmhouse in St. Georgen/Frankenberg where she knocked on the window and asked for a piece of bread. The Schatz family hid her in their house, treating the nineteen year old (who looked like thirteen) like their own daughter. After the war she joined young Jewish survivors who sailed to Palestine. Onboard, she found her brother, the only other survivor from their family.[92]

The Schatz family's ability to rescue Zychlinski depended on her successful escape. Any contact between prisoners and local residents was highly suspect. Civilians could not enter the camps or approach prisoners unless they, too, were under SS surveillance. Unlike the hundreds of Russian POWs who escaped from CC Mauthausen in February 1945 and were hunted down

---

[90] Ibid., 39
[91] Pfarrbuch St. Georgen, 43
[92] Schatz, Maria, Speech given at 2006 Gusen Memorial, translated and summarised by Siegi Witzany

by Gauinspekteur Peterseil's "Gausturm," Ms. Zychlinksi escaped without alerting the guards. Other escapes, even of a single prisoner, initiated long searches which could last for days and only ended when the prisoner was brought back to camp. No doubt local Nazi Party members and SS like Peterseil as well as their families and sympathizing neighbors would have assisted actively or passively in the searches, but these same people posed a threat to the Schatz family as well as to Esther Zychlinkski. In these small towns, local Nazis knew which of their neighbors had a history of Social Democratic activism, who was a "clerical," who was a "former Marxist" and who a National Socialist. There was no great distance between camp and town, between SS barracks and school, between a place of assembly of Gusen II and the parish church.

In winter 1938/39, Rudolf P. remodelled the brewery that his family bought a few years earlier into apartments, which he then rented. After Maria F. married in 1937, her husband worked in the sand production industry in St. Georgen. She eventually moved into an apartment in the former brewery from which, over the coming years, she witnessed the construction of the Bergkristall tunnel system built near her home and the two local sandpits, the "KL" and the "Mariengrube".

Interviewed in 2000 at 86, she measured every word as she recalled her life in St. Georgen during the war, working as a domestic servant for the SS families in town. While she talked, delicate earrings in her paper-thin earlobes responded to her confident manner until she described a frequent visitor to an employer's house, Commandant of CC Mauthausen and CC Gusen SS-Standartenführer Ziereis. At Ziereis' name she leaned closer and dropped to a whisper as if being overheard were still dangerous. And when she recounted the murderous crimes the SS and capos committed against concentration camp prisoners, crimes she and her children saw committed in the yard below her apartment windows, her age-clouded blue eyes filled with tears. Even after sixty years of hard work since the end of the war, she says, "I can still see these things in my heart."[93]

---

[93] Personal Interview, 21 September 2000

The "Deutsche Erd- und Steinwerke GmbH" – an SS Enterprise

On 12 March 1938, the day of the Anschluss, Hitler arrived in Linz and announced German soldiers had come to "help" Austria. For St. Georgen natives, the first sign of assistance was the dismissal of the elected mayor who, along with the mayor of Mauthausen, was replaced by a National Socialist. Although Nazi propaganda had promised no changes would be made in religious instruction in the schools, teachers were portentously told to choose between their jobs and singing in the church choir. On March 14, school children were required to greet teachers with the "Hitler Gruss," the "Heil Hitler" greeting accompanied by raising the right arm outstretched straight forward to the level of the eyes.[94]

Hitler promoted Dr. Ernst Kaltenbrunner, who had headed the illegal Austrian SS since 1935, to SS-Brigadeführer (Brigade General) after the Anschluss and then appointed him State Secretary for Security Matters in the new National-Socialist cabinet of Seyss-Inquart as well as Higher SS and Police Leader (HSSPF) to the governors of Vienna, Lower Danube, and Upper Danube, in Wehrkreis (Corps Area) XVII (after Austria was reorganized into Alps and Danube Districts).[95]

Within days, Reichsführer SS Heinrich Himmler visited Mauthausen and Gusen, accompanied by his SS Chief of Administration Oswald Pohl.[96] While people often associate the SS with poorly-educated concentration camp guards, as others have discussed, on this day Himmler and his entourage represented a lesser known aspect of the SS – businessmen assessing an opportunity: could the local quarries be successfully exploited using slave labor from as-yet-to-be-built concentration camps? Himmler's mission was twofold: to

---

[94] Pfarrbuch St. Georgen, 41-42
[95] Marsálek, Mauthausen [English], 188. ([English] will indicate use of the translation by Max R. Garcia survivor of KZ Buna, KZ Auschwitz, KZ Mauthausen, KZ Melk, KZ Ebensee); Black, 104
[96] Oswald Pohl, born on 30 June 1892, was sentenced to death by the American Military Court and executed on 8 June 1951. Marsálek, Die Geschichte des Konzentrationslagers Mauthausen – Dokumentation [Mauthausen], 26

secure building materials for Hitler's monumental building projects and to create a place for concentration camp labor in the construction process.[97]

The scope of Himmler's mission, and his commitment to it, can only be understood in relation to the immensity of the plans to radically change the infrastructure, landscape, architecture and economy of the German "Reich" and ultimately the world. As historian Jochen Thies explains, the Third Reich's building plans, though never realized, most clearly reveal its long term goals: the return not only to classical architectural elements in the imposing structures meant to signal domination of the German "master race," but also the shift to a slave economy in service of that "race." Hitler began drafting changes to his favored cities (Berlin, Nuremberg, Hamburg, Munich and Linz) as early as 1925. These plans were expanded and refined by hundreds of German and Austrian architects, among them Albert Speer, whom Hitler appointed "General Supervisor for the Redevelopment of the Reich" in 1937.[98]

As the years passed, the plans grew in their frightening absurdity. A 136-meter-high train station would be built in Munich. The Nuremberg Party Congress complex, covering sixty square kilometers, would be finished by 1943. Along with the now famous plans for the five "Führer-Städte," cities with special associations for Adolf Hitler, (here "Führer" should not be translated as "leader," rather it indicates the special importance of these cities to the career of Adolf Hitler – the Führer), over fifty other German cities were to be extensively "redeveloped" with features such as 100-meter-wide north-south and east-west axes. Jochen Thies states the estimated costs, on the basis of 1937 – 1938, would have exceeded 100 billion Reichsmarks. Hitler remained obsessed with these plans to the end of his days, brooding over a cardboard and wood model of Linz in the bunker beneath his Chancellery in Berlin before committing suicide there. Yet, even as these plans were made, shortages of materials, labor and money were widely acknowledged.[99] As

---

[97] Marsálek, Mauthausen, 3; Allen, 21 ff.

[98] Prof. Dr. Ing. Albert Speer, born on 19 March 1905 in Mannheim. On 30 September 1946 he was sentenced to 20 years of imprisonment in Nuremberg. Marsálek, Mauthausen, 27.

[99] Thies, Jochen "Hitler's European Building Programs" Journal of European History, Vol. 13, No. 3 (July 1978), 413-431

Paul Jaskot shows in *The Architecture of Oppression,* this was particularly true in the building industry, not only because of the increased demand for monumental stone, but because Hermann Göring's Four Year Plan directed manpower into the Reich's military which Fritz Todt also supported with building resources in his position as General Plenipotentiary for the Regulation of the Building Economy (Generalbevollmächtigter für die Regelung der Bauwirtschaft).[100]

Although the mania with building and rebuilding would be taken up by city and town counsels throughout the Reich, for Himmler the building projects meant influence over national economic policy through SS ownership of stone quarries and brickworks and SS control of the supply of concentration camp labor. Building plan estimates would call for three million slave laborers by 1943.[101] Jaskot argues that despite a persistent belief that Himmler wanted to develop SS businesses to make the Waffen SS economically independent (as architect and Armament Minister Albert Speer claimed after the war), the shortage of choice building materials, granite and marble, combined with the shortage of labor was threatening the elite's aesthetic choices. This motivated Himmler to try to influence political economic policy by making the concentration camp system and slave labor an integral part of the building economy, even in the peacetime presumed to follow a German victory. The solution was to use slave labor to produce the materials for the very buildings from which the regime would manifest its power.[102]

In *The Business of Genocide,* an analysis of how the corporate culture of the SS facilitated mass murder, Michael Thad Allen argues that Himmler's commitment to the building economy was rooted in his megalomaniacal goal of remaking the world economy in the service of National Socialism (which is to say, of the German "master race").

To this ideological end, problems with supply were, like concerns about profits, part and parcel of doing business in the old capitalist model. Radical

---

[100] Jaskot, 17
[101] Thies, 418-419
[102] Jaskot, 15-18

fascism would change the face of business as it changed the face of capitalism's former urban centers. Obtaining a market share of the building materials industry was part of a revolutionary economic strategy.[103]

As Himmler and Pohl toured the vicinity of Mauthausen and St. Georgen in March 1938 and inspected the stone quarries, they could not know that their hulking monument schemes would be inverted by the business structure they would create and by the engineers of total war into 50,000 square meters of "underground factory-floor space" built in a violent frenzy beneath the very landscape they were evaluating.[104] Other than the quality of the granite, their other concern on this day, a ready labor supply, was being resolved in a brutal fashion. Within 24 hours after Nazi troops arrived in Austria and were greeted by hysterical crowds, tens of thousands of other Austrians were arrested, including Heinrich B. in St. Georgen. The illegal local SA waited four long years to extract revenge for his having reported Zdenko K. for shooting the crucifix off the wall of the St. Georgen train station in 1934. Thousands more would soon join them: members of Catholic youth organizations, Socialists, Communists, Fatherland Front representatives, labor organizers including the illegal Austrian Labor Movement, and Austrian Jews.[105]

On their visit in mid-March, Himmler and Pohl determined concentration camps could be built in the village of Marbach, above Mauthausen, and Langenstein, near the Gusen quarries. On 24 March 1938, Pohl returned with SS-Brigadeführer (Brigade General) Theodor Eicke, former Commandant of Dachau and now Inspector of Concentration Camps,[106] to solidify the plans which Hitler and Speer had instigated[107] to provide labor for their building projects. On 29 April 1938, after months of planning, the SS and German Police, which Himmler also headed from within the Department of Interior, founded the company "DEUTSCHE ERD- UND STEINWERKE GmbH"

---

[103] Allen, Business, 14 ff
[104] German Underground Installations: Part One of Three, CIOS Section, Intelligence Division, Office, Chief Engineer, USFET, APO 887, September 1945. NARA RG 319, „P"-File, Joint Intelligence Objective Agency, Br. No. 1, Part 1 of 3.
[105] Steiner, 131
[106] Marsálek [English], 14; Jaskot, 35
[107] Allen, Business, 59

(DEST) in Berlin[108], SS-Obersturmbannführer Arthur Ahrens became "Geschäftsführer" (Chief Executive Officer) of DEST in April 1938.[109]

Not only was DEST intended to supply the monumental building industry with bricks and granite stones, but Himmler and Pohl also wanted it to be a shining example of mass production accomplished with modern technology orchestrated from a centralized, corporate structure. Within a year, however, Pohl would fire the man at the top, Ahrens, for incompetence. SS-Standartenführer Dr. Walter Salpeter, DEST Deputy Manager, would rely on SS-Hauptsturmführer Karl Mummenthey[110] to straighten out the accounting problems Ahrens created. Mummenthey worked on the legal staff within the SS-Verwaltungsamt, the Adminstrative Office created by Chief Adminstrative Officer Pohl within the Administrative Office to which Himmler appointed Pohl in 1936. The SS-Verwaltungsamt office accounted for all party funds and is understood by Allen to be part of a change within the SS from a de-centralized bureaucracy to a "nationwide, impersonal modern administration." As Allen details, despite early dismal financial returns, DEST would survive as a business to become the base of operations for many concentration camps throughout the Reich because of the ability of managers (like Pohl, Mummenthey, and Salpeter, and, later, SS-Obergruppenführer Dr.-Ing. [General and PhD. Engineer] Hans Kammler) to incorporate extermination and labor into a modern business structure. Essential to their dark success was the hard won cooperation of the individual concentration-camp administrations to force prisoners to work productively *enough* for DEST before dying, since murder would remain the shared ultimate goal of all segments of the SS.[111] What the history of the Concentration Camps Gusen I, II, and III can reveal is how the process by which the business structure set up to

---

[108]   Marsálek, Mauthausen, 3; Jaskot, 14; Beglaubigte Abschrift aus dem Handelsregister des Amtsgerichts in Berlin, Abteilung B 53864, Bezirksgericht (local court) Mauthausen, Grundbuch (land register) [Grundbuch Mauthausen], TZ 586/38

[109]   Marsálek, 3; Jaskot, 21; Allen, Business, 60

[110]   Karl Mummenthey, born 11 July 1906. Mummenthey, an SS member since 1934, had studied law after vocational training school and served a bank apprenticeship before joining the legal department in the SS-Verwaltungsamt. On 3 November 1947, he was sentenced to lifelong imprisonment in Nuremberg. Later on the life sentence was reduced to 20 years. Marsálek, Mauthausen, 18 and 27

[111]   Allen, Business, 27, 60-63, 85

produce building materials to construct a Nazi empire in Poland and Russia was easily reorganized to produce underground factory space and provide labor for building the Me 262 (and other sophisticated weapons).

DEST's first order of business was the construction of the soon-to-fail brickworks at Concentration Camp Sachsenhausen and another more successful one at Concentration Camp Buchenwald. DEST also quickly acquired or leased quarries at Flossenbürg, Mauthausen and Gusen, and set about building nearby slave labor camps. On 16 May 1938, barely three weeks after DEST was established and barely a month after the Anschluss, thirty civilians began working in the quarries of Mauthausen. However, while the Wienergraben Quarry was only leased from the City of Vienna in the early years, on 25 May 1938 Ahrens arranged for DEST to purchase property in Gusen from Mr. Anton Poschacher for the projected Concentration Camp at Langenstein (CC Gusen).[112] This was only four weeks after the foundation of DEST and a little more than two months after the annexation of Austria to Nazi-Germany. Clearly, DEST saw the importance of the two quarries near the village of Gusen, the Gusen and the Kastenhof quarries, from the start. This may not be evident to researchers because DEST used the company name "Granitwerke Mauthausen," which some have assumed refers only to the Wienergraben Quarry, for its activities at Gusen as well as Mauthausen.

Only one month later Pohl talked with financial experts of the Deutsche Arbeitsfront (German Work Front) about financing the construction of concentration camps in the Ostmark (the Nazi term for Austria). Prison labor from these SS concentration camps would be leased to DEST at a set rate per prisoner per day to produce building material for the Reich's projects in Berlin, Nuremberg, Munich and Linz. In order to provide DEST with ready capital to begin operating, Albert Speer negotiated the first large orders for building materials with DEST on 30 June 1938.[113] Speer paid 9.5 million

---

[112] DEST, Bilanz 1939. Aufstellung über erworbene Grundstücke. BArch, NS 3/1345/29 and Grundbuch Mauthausen, TZ 586/38
[113] Marsálek, Mauthausen [English], 17-18. Footnote #20 also reports the German Red Cross invested 8 million Reichsmarks.

Reichsmarks in advance for bricks and stones, and the German Work Front loaned DEST 700,000 Reichsmarks.[114]

According to Allen, DEST (like other SS companies) was supposed to "manifest ideals of Volksgemeinschaft," the national community. The company's profits were to serve cultural and ideological ends. In this scheme, slave labor could serve the state by punishing and re-educating the state's enemies even though the very existence of these slaves was destructive to it. Although always a factor when evaluating a prisoner's supposed threat to the "German race," eugenics would increasingly determine a prisoner's fate. The punishment of these individuals through labor would successfully achieve the integration of slavery into a modern corporate structure in the service of the Reich or the German race. Pohl even argued that SS companies should get a special tax status as this non-capitalistic goal would cause some SS concerns to lose money, perhaps for years, while they "educated" prisoners.[115] In fact, DEST considered itself a public enterprise by 2 February 1939 and as such did not pay the usual fees and taxes when purchasing land on a large scale in the area of St. Georgen-Gusen-Mauthausen.[116]

As new concentration camps were built near stone quarries and brickworks, the number of concentration camp guards from the Totenkopfverbände (or Death's Head Units under SS-Gruppenführer Theodor Eicke, the Inspector of Concentration Camps) doubled in 1938 from 4,833 to 8,484.[117] When the Ministry of the Interior became a source of funding for the Death's Head Divisions in 1938, Oswald Pohl relieved Eicke of the financial oversight of the camps, thus increasing the influence Pohl already had over SS enterprises as Chairman of DEST and as Chief Administrator of the SS.[118]

Eicke had less interest than one might assume in running concentration camps. Although Himmler appointed him to the Inspectorate of

---

[114] Allen, "The Business of Genocide" Business and Industry in Nazi Germany. Eds Francis R. Nicosia and Jonathan Huener (New York: Berghahn Books, 2004), 88
[115] Allen, Business, 81-83
[116] Grundbuch Mauthausen, TZ 28/39
[117] Thies, 418
[118] Allen, Business, 57

Concentration Camps (IKL) as a reward for restructuring the administration of Dachau, Eicke cared more about establishing a militarized division.* Nevertheless, Eicke made changes in the camp system which reflected, at least conceptually, Pohl's preference for centralized management. Eicke closed the smaller locally-operated camps spread throughout the Reich and built permanent camps centrally administered from the IKL at Sachsenhausen north of Berlin.[119] But Allen suggests Eicke was relieved to relinquish mundane business concerns to Pohl, who took them on with an ideologically-driven fervor characteristic of the managers, lawyers and other businessmen Himmler had recruited to the SS in the 1930s (many of whom came from white collar and even military backgrounds). Feeling betrayed by prewar capitalism, these men felt passionately about transforming business according to Nazi ideology.[120]

Although Eicke was equally passionate and committed to Nazi ideology, he despised the detailed record keeping necessary for the effective administration of a complex organization. Eicke was much better at training his men to hate inmates as genetically inferior material who must be "educated" through abuse and hard labor. In this, he agreed perfectly with his more sedentary but better schooled Allgemeine (General) SS superiors. However, if the men under Eicke's command could not accept the demands of concentration camp life, they could be transferred to the Allgemeine SS.[121] As a result of Eicke's focus on brutality rather than detail, however, the concentration camps would remain notoriously plagued by mismanagement and graft, particularly in regards to supplying prisoners with food and meeting their other physical needs. As a consequence of starvation and "education," slave laborers would prove to be less than ideally productive workers and death rates within the prison workforce would remain high, facts that would be the

---

* Until the Death's Head Division was organized in 1939, the Death's Head units, battalions and regiments which Eicke commanded were armed paramilitary forces trained as body guards (for political terror) and as concentration camp guards but not for front line combat (Sydnor, Charles. Soldiers of Destruction, (Princeton: Princeton University, 1990), 21-36).
[119] Sydnor, 17-25
[120] Allen, Business, 21-35
[121] Sydnor, 17-25; Allen, 21-45

real source of conflict between the SS business managers and concentration camp administrators.[122]

This clash of differing corporate cultures between DEST and the Totenkopf-verbände always resulted in more suffering for prisoners, but the racial elitism and anti-religious training that Eicke gave his men to steel them against regret for their crimes would prove detrimental to some St. Georgen residents as well. There were, of course, numerous local SS and Nazi party members who welcomed an SS presence and/or immediately benefited from the construction of the concentration camps at Mauthausen and Gusen.[123] But Eicke trained his men to hate Christianity as "idolatrous and paganistic" and see incense [used in the Catholic Mass] as "destructive of the German soul just as Jews are to the race."[124] In 1938, Eicke furthered his men's distance from normal civilian life by lengthening their term of service from four to twelve years. He also demanded that they renounce Christianity, a move that alienated many from their families.[125] This anti-Christian sentiment existed in St. Georgen, as well, as the incident regarding the train station crucifix demonstrates.

On 1 July 1938 the 4. SS-Totenkopfstandarte (Fourth Death's Head Regiment) "Ostmark" was founded with the preliminary designation "Steyr" at Oranien-burg and stationed at Linz-Ebelsberg until the war began in September 1939. From there, several men would be sent to guard CC Mauthausen until the K.L.-Verstärkung Mauthausen (Concentration Camp Reinforcements Maut-hausen) became operational on 31 August 1939.[126] Another connection to DEST was the fact that this regiment became one of the company's first key customers: DEST delivered construction material for the huge SS-barracks at Linz-Ebelsberg[127] (which are still in use today as Army barracks for the Austrian Army).

---

[122]   Allen, Business, 45
[123]   Personal Interviews, Maria F., September 2000 and Joe C., 7 May 2004
[124]   Sydnor, 29 Footnote 68
[125]   Sydnor, 27-31
[126]   Labitzke, Lars. SS-Totenkopfsturmbann K.L. Mauthausen/Gusen. Unpublished. In the possession of the author.
[127]   DEST-Bilanz 1939, BArch NS 3/1345

On 8 August 1938 the first 300 prisoners arrived at Mauthausen from Concentration Camp Dachau. They built the first barracks in the Wienergraben Valley. SS-Sturmbannführer Albert Sauer, who had been trained by Eicke himself at Camps Sulza and Sachsenhausen, arrived with eighty SS guards and several non-commissioned officers.[128]

In the early years, the SS unit at Mauthausen was simply called "KL-Verstärkung Mauthausen" (Concentration Camp Reinforcements Mauthausen).[129] Within a few months, 14 barracks were completed. More detainees arrived in October. The exploitation of labor in local quarries began in January 1939: DEST employed 375 prisoners and 171 civilian employees at the Mauthausen and Gusen quarries.[130] The DEST balance sheet for 1939 already reports RM 20.254,20 paid for work carried out by concentration camp prisoners at the Gusen quarries. The equivalent figure for the Wienergraben Quarry at Mauthausen was RM 43.024,50 for the same period.[131] The 1,000 prisoners then working in the Wienergraben camp increased to 2,666 prisoners by the end of 1939.[132] While work at the Gusen quarries began with fewer prisoners, it is important to note that DEST invested substantially more in property and material for the Gusen quarries than in the Wienergraben Quarry from the start. On 30 January 1941, in his notes following a visit with Mummenthey, Wienergraben Quarry manager Johannes Grimm wrote, "I felt as if I had been slapped in the face when I was told that Mauthausen was 'the sleeping beauty' of the German Earth and Stone Works."[133] He complains that the relationship between management and the administration is confusing and the lack of "comradely cooperation" with which it would be possible "to alter the bad opinion of Mauthausen which exists in Berlin. In any case

---

[128] SS Captain Albert Sauer, born on 17 August 1898 in Misdroy, later on became chief of Sturmbann II/24 in Wilhelmshaven. Truppenstammrolle und Bestätigung der Diensthebung durch das SS-Personalamt vom 15. April 1939. BArch (ehemals BDC), SSO, Sauer, Albert, 17.08.1898.

[129] Labitzke, npag.

[130] Stärkemeldung der Granitwerke Mauthausen. Records of the United States Nuremberg War Criminal Trials, United States vs. Oswald Pohl et al. (Case IV), January 13, 1947-August 11, 1948, NARA microform publication M890/13/0968 (NI-541).

[131] DEST, Bilanz 1939, Aufstellung über die in den Jahren 1938 und 1939 eingesetzten Häftlinge und Bewertung derselben. BArch, NS 3/1345/58

[132] Marsálek, Mauthausen, 17 ff, 218

[133] NARA II, Record Group 549, Entry 290, JAG Cases Tried Box 336

I could not help receiving the impression in Berlin that they were not very pleased with us in Mauthausen." [134] Grimm also reports difficulties with water supply and notes that the request was denied for a funicular railway between Schotterbrecher (stone crusher) Wienergraben and the cog railway Gusen-Kastenhof. [135] Grimm would, however, retain enough confidence to be appointed in August 1944 to be in charge of prisoners at Bergkristall. [136].

Very quickly, the Gusen and Kastenhof quarries returned DEST's investment and proved to be the company's primary quarries in terms of both production and profit. [137] The DEST inventory for 1939 reports earnings of RM 58.712,10 for the two quarries at Gusen in comparison to only RM 13.980,90 for Wienergraben Quarry (at Concentration Camp Mauthausen). [138] DEST's 1939 balance sheet also shows significant investments in the old Gusen Quarry and the newer Kastenhof Quarry near the village of Gusen. For the Gusen Quarry, the company purchased an electrical transformer, a smithy, air compressors, garages for locomotives, and a pump station. Prison labor was also used to construct several halls for stone masons, office barracks, housing barracks, and two houses. For the Kastenhof Quarry, DEST purchased and constructed one barracks for civilian employees, two barracks for stone masons, and three barracks for tooling as well as an additional barracks. [139]

Given this primacy from the company's early days, there is surprisingly little information about the Gusen quarries or CC Gusen, built less than four kilometers away from CC Mauthausen. Holocaust historians, most notably Hans Marsálek, have focussed attention on the history of CC Mauthausen and the Wienergraben Quarry. While Jaskot discusses the political and aesthetic implications of "fortress" Mauthausen (built to resemble a fortress but without real defensive features), there is no discussion of the implications of the markedly less monumental and less imposing architecture of the Jourhaus,

---

[134] Grimm, Johannes, 925-Gm/2480, Record Group 549 Entry 290 59/12/3 Box 336
[135] Ibid.
[136] Ibid.
[137] Jaskot 43, end note 90
[138] DEST, Inventur 1939, Bestandsaufnahme der Halb- und Fertigerzeugnisse. BArch NS 3/1345/34.
[139] DEST, Bilanz 1939, Aufstellung über das Anlagevermögen der Deutschen Erd- und Steinwerke G.m.b.H. Berlin. BArch NS 3/1345/14 ff.

the entrance to CC Gusen I. Most books follow Marsálek's lead, providing detailed information about other subcamps of Mauthausen, such as Ebensee or Melk, but little, if any, information about the camps or the tunnel systems in St. Georgen and Gusen.

Figure 2: Contemporary photograph of the "Jourhaus"
(the former main entrance into CC Gusen I is used as a family house today), Spring 2007
Source: Rudolf A. Haunschmied

The Construction of Concentration Camp Gusen I

[CC Gusen was referred to as CC Gusen I after another subcamp, Gusen II, was established in 1944.]

When the school year began in St. Georgen in 1938, the headmaster and several teachers had been replaced with National Socialists. If clandestine Nazis did not dominate the town's administration before the Anschluss, overt Nazis did afterward. Prayer was abolished from classrooms and substituted with the Wochenspruch (proverb of the week and a song), always reflecting NS ideology and sometimes including an actual prayer to Hitler. The title "Religious Instruction" was not to be used for classes either: it was now "Confessional Instruction." Prior to the Anschluss, Religious Instruction was at the top of the list of subjects on students' school reports, as it is again today. In 1938, it was put at the end of the list and substituted by Leibeserziehung (Physical Education), a clear illustration of the new values and priorities. The Religious Instruction teacher (usually a priest) was excluded from teachers' conferences. By the beginning of the 1939/40 school year, Religious Instruction was no longer obligatory but voluntary. Crosses were removed from classrooms. Priests who made remarks critical of the regime were forbidden to go on teaching, another way to "dry up" Religious Instruction through lack of staff.[140]

On 1 April 1939 Albert Sauer was officially relieved of command of Mauthausen for laziness (in a position for which the bar for efficiency was set notoriously low) by SS-Sturmbannführer Franz Ziereis.[141] As commandant, Ziereis became responsible for nearly all other concentration camps to be built in Austria.[142] Ziereis had joined the SS-Totenkopfstandarte (regiment) "Thüringen" on 1 December 1938 and was awarded the "Ehrendegen" (Sword of Honour) by the Reichsführer SS Himmler. He inherited and would oversee

---

[140] Pfarrbuch St. Georgen, 39-40
[141] Truppenstammrolle und Bestätigung der Dienstenthebung durch das SS-Personalamt im SS-Hauptamt vom 15. April 1939. BArch (ehemals BDC), SSO, Sauer, Albert, 17.08.1898.
[142] Franz Ziereis, born on 18 May 1905 in Munich, was a skilled carpenter. Marsálek, Mauthausen, 200.

the construction of camps modeled after Eicke's adminstration at Dachau. Mauthausen and the new camp at Gusen, would be divided into five administrative offices:

1) Office of the camp commandant (Sauer and then Ziereis at Mauthausen), his adjutant, and his Schutzhaftlagerführer in charge of protective detention camps (in the case of CC Gusen, this was SS-Obersturmführer [Lieutenant] Georg Bachmayer[143] at first). This office also contained law-court officials, postal censors and motor pool.

2) Political section headed by the Gestapo or Kripo (Criminal Police) with offices for prisoner identification, construction of jails, registry and crematorium.

3) Office for the detention camp. This office assigned and coordinated the officers and non-commissioned officers (NCOs) in charge of the prisoners. These camp administration titles were not SS military ranks, but the SS military rank to which the jobs were usually assigned are indicated.

   a. **Arbeitsdienstführer,** Work Command Leader, an NCO responsible for work commands after morning roll call and before return to the camp at the end of each shift.[144]
   b. **Blockführer,** Block Leader, usually an SS-Scharführer (technical [staff-] sergeant) in command of a "block" or barracks (250 inmates). Reported to the Rapportführer.
   c. **Rapportführer,** Roll Call Leader, usually an SS-Oberscharführer (master sergeant [C.S.M.]) who reported to the Schutzhaftlagerführer in the case of a subcamp.

---

[143] SS-Obersturmführer (Lieutenant) Georg Bachmayer was another SS officer trained under Eicke at Dachau in a position of power at CC Gusen. Reportedly a shoemaker, he belonged to the 1. Totenkopfstandarte „Oberbayern." Bachmayer was the Schutzhaftlagerführer I (Officer in Charge of the Protective Detention Camp) of the Concentration Camp Mauthausen and as such oversaw CC Mauthausen's sub camp. Marsálek Mauthausen, 200; Erwin Gostner, 1000 Tage im KZ – Dachau-Mauthausen-Gusen (Innsbruck: Edition Löwenzahn, 1986), 156

[144] Marsálek, Mauthausen [English], 347

4) Camp chief administrative officer and his staff which handled prisoner personal property, food supply and laundry, also the engineer's office.

5) Medical office: Standortarzt, camp doctor, doctor for SS men, Standortzahnarzt (dentist), dentist for SS men and pharmacy.[145]

The engineer's office, (Bauleitung – Construction Directorate renamed the Neubauleitung – New Construction Directorate in 1939) was part of the camp administrative structure and subordinate to the commandant until 1941. That year SS-Standartenführer Dr.-Ing. Kammler made the office responsible to him (rather than to the SS Death's Head concentration camp commanders whom Kammler outranked within the SS), and also recruited engineers who outranked the camp administrative staff.[146] This change significantly impacted St. Georgen and the prisoners in CC Mauthausen/Gusen.

Only the commandant's staff could actually enter the camp, and what they did there, as well as how they were disciplined for any infractions, was entirely up to the camp commandant. Most guards served on the watchtowers, along the camps' perimeters, or guarded the work details.[147] In postwar trials, such as US vs. Schuettauf, et al., Waffen SS guards would use the fact that they were not allowed to enter the protective custody camp as an alibi, denying that they had ever beaten a prisoner or seen a prisoner beaten. The Waffen SS guards also claimed that they had no authority to beat prisoners in the quarries or responsibility to oversee work done there.[148] When local people came into contact with prisoners, they were accompanied by these exterior guards, not the camp command staff. As Sydnor and Allen detail and as survivors and local witnesses attest, these exterior guards were as often as not undereducated cruel misfits.[149]

---

[145]   Sydnor 19; Marsálek, Mauthausen [English], 183-184; Labitzke, npag.
[146]   Allen, Business, 83-84
[147]   Marsálek, Mauthausen [English], 183
[148]   United States vs. Shuettauf, et al. Case No. 000-50-5-3 NARA Record Group 153 Entry 143 270/1/14-15/6-1 Box 12, 343, 210, 220 ... http://ecc.pima.edu/~gusen/Schuettauf/Index_to_Schuettauf_Summaries.htm
[149]   Sydnor, 26-27; Allen, Business, 39-40

On 17 August 1938 Hitler declared the SS Death's Head Units, along with other SS units, to be separate from both the army and the police and placed them under Himmler's control during peacetime for guarding and running concentration camps. Himmler was allowed, however, to arm and to train them as military units. When Germany invaded Poland on 1 September 1939, Eicke's three original Death's Head Regiments ("Oberbayern," "Brandenburg," and "Thüringen") were deployed behind the Wehrmacht and under its command. Waging a terror campaign against Polish civilians, they confiscated livestock and crops, destroyed property, and murdered large numbers of Polish intellectuals, statesmen, aristocrats, Jews and businessmen. Acting as the police authority in occupied Poznan, Lodz, and Warsaw, they remained under Eicke's direction until October, at the time these regiments were withdrawn to form the Death's Head Division which would see front line combat under Wehrmacht command. Death's Head SS units continued to have a presence in Poland, however, guarding concentration camps and terrorizing civilians. As an additional incentive to maintain discipline within Eicke's new combat division, the punishment for poor comportment or morale was a transfer to a concentration camp guard unit.[150]

From the start of construction on Concentration Camp Mauthausen, the SS used sand from St. Georgen. On 4 August 1939, the SS-Neubauleitung KZ-Lager Mauthausen (SS New Construction Directorate for Concentration Camp Mauthausen) acquired unlimited prospect rights to the "KL" Sandpit there.[151] The fact that the SS-Neubauleitung secured rights to this sandpit so early would facilitate the swift conversion of St. Georgen from the production of building materials to underground factory space and Me 262s after Kammler became head of both the Construction Directorates (within HAHB Office II) and the Jägerstab, the special staff for constructing fighter jets. Only five years after securing rights to the sand, the main entrance to "Bergkristall" would be built in the "KL" Sandpit by thousands of starving and beaten men whom the SS would assemble not 100 meters from the parish church.

---

[150] Sydnor, 32-59
[151] Treaty between the Reichsführer SS and owner on 4 August 1939. In the possession of the author.

On 1 October 1939 the construction of Concentration Camp Gusen (CC Gusen) began in Langenstein[152] at the foot of Frankenberg Mountain, near the Meierhof, the traditional residence of the steward of nearby Castle Spielberg. Historically a good deal of land belonged to the castle. In 1911, this estate was split between the heirs, who continued to farm until the Third Reich and DEST purchased much of the land for the Gusen camps and the DEST installations associated with them.

SS-Hauptscharführer Anton Streitwieser oversaw the camp's construction and reported to Ziereis' Schutzhaftlagerführer SS-Obersturmführer Georg Bachmayer. Like Bachmayer, Streitwieser was trained by Eicke at Dachau, where he shot a prisoner before being transferred to Sachsenhausen and then Esterwegen. After 27 November 1938, he headed the motor pool in Camp Mauthausen, where he shot the prisoner Anton Eder. Shortly thereafter he was promoted to a master sergeant and transferred to CC Gusen as the Rapportführer.[153]

One indication of the separate administrative structures of CC Mauthausen and CC Gusen overlooked by historians was the establishment of separate SS guard units at both camps. On 7 November 1939, SS-Hauptsturmführer Markus Habben became commander of SS-Totenkopfsturmbann (SS-T.Stuba) Gusen. This appointment made CC Gusen's SS T-Stuba (the SS-guard battalion) widely independent from Mauthausen remarkably early in the camps' development. On 9 January 1940 the 2./SS-T-Stuba Dachau (2nd SS-guard company of KL Dachau) was moved directly to Gusen and became 1./SS-T-Stuba Gusen, the first SS-guard company at CC Gusen.[154]

Although the SS guard units were already billeted in Gusen by January 1940, until March of that year approximately 400 prisoners marched daily from the Wienergraben Camp at Mauthausen to the Gusen quarries in order to

---

[152] Perz, Bertrand. Projekt Quarz: Steyr-Daimler-Puch und das Konzentrationslager Melk. Industrie, Zwangsarbeit und Konzentrationslager in Österreich. Vol. 3. (Vienna: Verlag für Gesellschaftskritik, 1990), 229
[153] Marsálek, Mauthausen, 205.
[154] Lars Labitzke, npag.

complete the first three prisoner barracks and several SS barracks.[155] (The village of Gusen is about 850 meters southwest of the quarries). Quartering prisoners in these barracks spared the SS guards who oversaw the work commands and the daily trudge to and from the Gusen and Kastenhof quarries from CC Mauthausen. In addition to deaths from exhaustion, illness and starvation, many inmates of CC Gusen died along this route, making the name "Gusen" a symbol of horror for the inmates caught early in the bifurcated system of Concentration Camps Mauthausen and Gusen.

However, the prisoners were not relieved of the trudge for humanitarian reasons. Until prisoners could be housed at an officially opened camp, for reasons of "security" the Inspectorate of Concentration Camps (IKL) required that they work no further away from an established camp than they could manage to walk "to and from" in one day.[156] The Inspectorate of Concentration Camps did not interfere in a positive way with the treatment of prisoners, their care, or the conditions of their labor and should not be seen as in any way advocating for their welfare.[157] The SS Death's Head guard units who watched the detainees starve to death or drop in their tracks along the march had been trained to hate, humiliate and punish prisoners according to regulations Eicke wrote while reorganizing Dachau in 1933. Guards could murder prisoners for a variety of broadly defined infractions such as "political organizing" and "approaching a guard."[158] Allen points out that Eicke's guidelines ritualized punishment rather more than they protected prisoners.[159] According to Hans Marsálek, the regulations at Mauthausen (adopted from Eicke's) "limited" guards to giving prisoners from 5 to 75 strokes of a whip in the presence of a doctor. However, Marsálek notes, there is no record of medical staff being called to "professionally" witness lashings. Furthermore, four weeks were supposed to elapse between beatings if the prisoner

[155] Sagel-Grande, Irene, et.al. Justiz und NS-Verbrechen. Sammlung Deutscher Strafurteile wegen Nationalsozialistischer Tötungsverbrechen 1945 – 1966. Bd. XVII: Die vom 04.11.1960 bis zum 21.11.1961 ergangenen Strafurteile. Lfd. Nr. 500-523. Ks 1ab/61 Strafverfahren gegen Chmielewski Karl. (Amsterdam: University Press Amsterdam, 1977), 160

[156] Le Chène, 37; Allen, Business, 170

[157] Allen, Michael "The Banality of Evil Reconsidered: SS Mid-Level Managers of Extermination through Work" Central European History 30 (1997), 266

[158] Marsálek, Mauthausen, 42

[159] Allen, Business, 37

received more than 25 strokes, but since little record was kept of whippings, it is unlikely that this rule was adhered to either. The one rule that seems to have been applied consistently, according to survivors, was that the prisoner was required to count the strokes loudly. If the prisoner failed to do so, the beating would begin again.[160]

Nor did punishment always fit into a recognizable category such as "lashing." Polish born survivor Joe C., a man so sweet the brutality he witnessed at CC Gusen from June to November 1940 still retains the power to leave him breathless and stunned after 65 years, demonstrated how a guard beat him for slacking on a masonry command for which Joe had volunteered. "The guard told me to keep my arms out like this," Joe said, raising straight arms to crucifixion height. "Then he hit me in the ribs. My God, I wanted to put my arms down, but I wasn't supposed to. He kept hitting me and hitting me." His fists thudded into my ribs then flew up to straightened arms in a frenzy of memory, as if he could now be guard, prisoner and witness all at once. "Somehow I managed to keep my arms up while he hit me like this. It hurt so badly. And I had dysentery from the poor food and from eating dandelions and other plants, which we thought would help us; after all, animals live off of grass, we thought. So we would eat leaves with our bread. But after straining to keep my arms up, I lost control of my bowels. I thought, oh, now he will beat me to death. But maybe he saw that I was sick or maybe he just wanted to move away from the smell. I don't know why, but he left me alone after that."[161]

Different groups of prisoners were also subject to different levels and duration of punishment. Joe C, who was assigned to Barracks 10, reports that Polish Jews in Barracks 11 were beaten through the night. "The screams coming from there were horrible. What those poor people suffered. Soon they were all dead," Joe recalls, shaking his head, his eyes closed against the memory of the sound. Brutality toward prisoners afforded guards an opportunity to display

---

[160] Marsálek, Mauthausen, 42; see also Martin Lax with Michael B. Lax, Caraseu: A Holocaust Remembrance (Cleveland: The Pilgrim Press, 1996), 95-97 and Kielich and Jan Ruth Mills, The Way of Thorns, unpublished manuscript, 40-43
[161] Personal Interview, Joe C., 7 May 2004

their commitment to Nazi ideology on the bodies of their victims,[162] and so there was a ranking and chronology to the suffering. Although Jews of any nationality always received the worst treatment, prisoners of other nationalities would suffer according to their position in the Nazi race ideology as well as the progress of the war into Western Europe after 1940 and into the Soviet Union after 1941.[163] Of course, for an individual who lost a loved one or upon whose body a blow fell, such generalizations are surely meaningless.

On 9 March 1940, 480 Polish prisoners were brought to the main camp at Mauthausen. At the beginning of April, they joined the German and Austrian prisoners who had been marching to Gusen daily to form the first 800 resident detainees of CC Gusen. This increase in Polish prisoners coincided with the removal from Poland of the intelligentsia and the resistance movement in spring 1940. Many Polish citizens like Joe C. who had no connection to the Polish resistance were swept up in the terror. One such teenager, Victor Kielich, would survive four years as a CC Gusen prisoner. Kielich was arrested on 25 February 1940 for failing to turn in his boyscout uniform when the Nazi occupational forces required all military uniforms be surrendered. Like many others who were not killed immediately on arrest, Victor was sent to Fort VII in Poznan, a concentration camp operated by the SS in Poland, before being transferred to Mauthausen and then finally to Gusen on 6 January 1941.[164] Thus, the number of prisoners in CC Gusen increased rapidly. By spring 1941, the total reached 4,000.[165]

After 27 May 1940 only Polish prisoners worked in commands at the Gusen quarries and the Lungitz brickworks, causing CC Gusen to be called the "Polenlager" (Camp for the Polish) before the war in the West brought additional prisoners from France and the Low Countries. 1,522 prisoners died in 1940 from the harsh working conditions, the lack of food, and the brutality of SS-guard units.[166] Prisoners arrived either at the train station in

---

[162] Allen, Business, 40
[163] Marsálek, Mauthausen, 45
[164] Kielich Victor and Jan Ruth Mills, The Way of Thorns, unpublished manuscript
[165] Marsálek, Mauthausen, 132
[166] Marsálek, Hans. Konzentrationslager Gusen – Ein Nebenlager des Konzentrationslagers Mauthausen (Vienna: Österreichische Lagergemeinschaft Mauthausen, 1987), 5 ff.

Mauthausen or the station in St. Georgen after journeys of several days. On 1 June 1940, the first of these trains arrived in St. Georgen. As was to become routine, the prisoners were beaten from the trains. The SS set barking dogs upon prisoners they drove through the village of St. Georgen to CC Gusen, shouting at them all the way. These transports, most often arriving during the night, were conducted in this manner until the end of 1941. The detainees were chased through the village. While the native population had been warned that these camps contained the worst sorts of prisoners, murderers and thieves,[167] prisoners were seen making the sign of the cross as they passed the crucifix of the bridge over the Gusen River.[168] Witnesses also tell about prisoners disembarking at night at the railway station of St. Georgen to be marched across the Wimmingerbrücke [Bridge] located a few hundred meters south of the village's center.

In 1939, the population of Langenstein was 1,239, and that of neighbouring St. Georgen was 1,429. The influx of prisoners and SS was overwhelming. In spring 1940 the total number of SS command staff and administrators at both concentration camps added up to 190 officers, non-commissioned officers and other staff. While there were, by this time, 600 SS guards at CC Gusen, there were only 460 guards of corresponding rank at CC Mauthausen. The "Wachblock KL [CC] Gusen" during this early period consisted of 4 SS guard companies with 150 men each, living in the barracks built parallel to the road after 1938.[169]

---

[167] Personal Interview, Willy and Irmi Nowy, September 2000

[168] Klinger, Otto. Volkschulchronik St. Georgen (Chronicle of the Primary School of St. Georgen), 143.

[169] One such guard company consisted beneath the ordinary guards of: 1 Kompanieführer (company commander) in the rank of a SS-Hauptsturmführer (captain), 1 Zugführer (platoon commander) in the rank of a SS-Obersturmführer (lieutenant), 1 Stabsscharführer (R.Q.M.S.) in the rank of an SS-Hauptscharführer (C.S.M.), 4 Unterführer (non-commissioned officers) in the rank of a SS-Oberscharführer (C.Q.M.S.) and 15 Unterführer (non-commissioned officers) in the rank of SS-Scharführer (Staff-Sergeant). Mob.-Stärkenachweisung der K.L. durch den Inspekteur der Konzentrationslager vom 12. Februar 1940. BArch, NS 4/Ma/36/22.

Figure 3: *Arriving new inmates change clothes at CC Gusen I Roll Call Square, After 1942
Source: Museu d'Història de Catalunya*

In March 1940 the first permanent barracks for prisoners were finished. A temporary fence, charged with high voltage, surrounded the camp.[170] Also in March 1940, Bachmayer was relieved of responsibility for CC Gusen by SS-Hauptsturmführer (R)[*] Karl Chmielewski[171] who became Schutzhaft-lagerführer I of the camp, inspecting the camp and overseeing the work in the quarries, according to Erwin Gostner. Gostner, an Austrian sent to Mauthausen via Dachau in 1938, worked on the command that built CC

---

[170] Marsálek, Gusen, 5 ff

[*] This (R) signifies that Chmielewski was from a reserve unit and so was not an entirely equal rank to a Hauptsturmführer from a regular SS unit. Another indicator was „(F)", meaning „Fachführer" – a person in SS-rank responsible for certain tasks that needed special education, e.g. business administration at DEST or the CC administrations.

[171] Chmielewski came from CC Sachsenhausen and is credited with helping to build CC Herzogen-busch (Vught) after 1942. Chmielewski left Gusen on 21 January 1943 for Concentration Camp Herzogenbusch (Vught) in the Netherlands. His wife and children remained at St. Georgen. He returned to contact his family after the war before going underground. Sagel-Grande, 154 and 163; Meldeunterlagen (registration) für Carl Walter Chmielewski. Gemeindearchiv St. Georgen a. d. Gusen.

Gusen in 1939/1940. His memoirs *1000 Tage im KZ – Dachau-Mauthausen-Gusen,* published in September 1945, are a remarkably early German source by a survivor for the development of concentration camps in Germany and Austria during the war's first years.[172]

Oberscharführer Anton Streitwieser, who had overseen the initial construction of CC Gusen, now reported to Chmielewski as Rapportführer.[173] Under Streitwieser, Bachmayer, or Chmielewski, prisoners who constructed CC Gusen endured unbelievable hardships. In June of 1940, when Joe C. arrived after a nightmarish train journey from Poland, CC Gusen had only twelve barracks, mud streets, open latrines and a line of twenty faucets for washing. Commandant Chmielewski greeted the men in Joe's transport with, "You will never see Poland again." Every day, Joe C. and other prisoners were marched through the gates of the Jourhaus, the administrative building at CC Gusen, to the quarry. They returned carrying large stones on their shoulders. If the capos thought a prisoner was trying to carry too light a stone, they chose one heavier than the man could bear and then beat him for stumbling under the weight. Prisoners returned to the camp through a back gate in the wire fence, near where Barracks 24 and 16 would eventually be built. They dropped the stones at what eventually would be Roll Call Square and then circled back through the Jourhaus to the quarry, returning through the back gate with another huge stone tearing at the skin of their shoulder blades through their thin uniforms. Meanwhile, other prisoners crushed the stones with sledgehammers, spreading the gravel across the square and between the barracks. Ten or so men would then push, or pull, huge steel rollers to smooth the stones. Increasingly finer sized stones were placed on top and then flattened with the roller until a smooth surface was achieved and the mud streets

---

[172] Gostner, Erwin. 1000 Tage im KZ – Dachau-Mauthausen-Gusen (Innsbruck: Edition Löwenzahn, 1986), 156

[173] SS Oberscharführer (C.Q.M.S) Anton Stretiwieser, born 3 July 1916 in Surbein, left Gusen I in mid 1941 and spent a year at the front. He returned to CC Mauthausen in October 1942 as Schutzhaftlagerführer III (Third Officer in Charge for the Protective Detention Camp). After another year of training, he commanded several satellite camps of Mauthausen in eastern Austria from March 1944. He escaped from US custody after the war and disappeared. In 1953 he was presumed dead, but then arrested again in 1956. Between this arrest and the 1967 trial in which he was sentenced to life imprisonment, he was at liberty several times. He died in the Bochum prison hospital on 17 July 1972. Marsálek, Mauthausen, 205.

paved. Eventually washrooms were constructed, but while prisoners had only the row of faucets pouring water directly onto the soil underfoot while they washed, capos often beat them on returning to the barracks for tracking mud inside. Hundreds died in the camp construction alone due to overwork and the meager rations they tried to supplement with dandelions and weeds.[174]

Figure 4: Leading SS officers in front of new arrivals at CC Gusen I. From left to right: SS-Ostuf Karl Heimann (Commander 3rd Guard Company at Gusen), SS-Ustuf Karl Schulz (Head of Political Section CC Mauthausen), unknown, SS-Hstuf Karl Chmielewski (Commandant of CC Gusen), October 1941
Source: Museu d´Història de Catalunya

Some residents "leased" prisoners for manual labor and came to see first hand that they were not "criminals." Joe C. recalls that the SS asked the men assembled on Roll Call Square one day if anyone knew how to mow hay. He volunteered with several others and was escorted under guard to a farm. To his great relief, at lunch the farmer's wife brought ham "on a tray, with a white

---

[174]   Personal Interview, Joe C., 7 May 2004

napkin, as if she were serving guests." However, residents who did provide "leased" prisoners extra food also had to bribe the SS guards, usually with cigarettes and schnapps: excessive attention given to prisoners would have been suspicious. Joe C. learned from this experience to volunteer for other such jobs and credits the extra food he received on these occasions with saving his life.[175] It is important to note that no surviving Jewish prisoners interviewed by the authors to date were allowed to work outside the camp and so were cut off from this important, though rare, source of food.

Figure 5: Inmates paving roll call square at CC Gusen I, 1940
Source: Museu d´Història de Catalunya

On average, eleven to thirteen SS-guard companies were positioned in CC Gusen,[176] adding up to about 3,000 men. At the end of 1941, CC Gusen had about 1,000 prisoners more than CC Mauthausen. Significantly, from this

---

[175] Personal Interview, 7 May 2004
[176] Marsálek, Gusen, 10.

time on (with the exception of 1943) there were always several thousand more inmates working at CC Gusen than in the "main camp" at Mauthausen. From the end of 1941 on, the number of detainees at CC Gusen averaged 8,500, the same number of inmates originally projected to run DEST production at CC Gusen.[177]

In the beginning both CC Mauthausen and CC Gusen were administered from a specially-authorized local SS headquarters located in the Wiener-graben Valley,[178] where four barracks had been built in 1938. The first twenty wooden prisoner barracks built where CC Mauthausen is today were not completed until the end of 1939. Ziereis' office was very likely in these barracks as well since land for the Mauthausen fortress was purchased after March 1939 according to the land register.[179] According to Michel Fabréguet, Ziereis' office was housed in a wooden barracks at Mauthausen until it was moved in the winter of 1941/1942 into the stone structure we see today. The other main construction work at CC Mauthausen was completed from 1940 to 1941, and the electric fence was completed in spring 1941. Construction of the huge stone walls around the camp started in the second half of 1941 and was finished in 1942. Fabréguet also writes that the construction of the "camp hospital," begun in September 1940, was still a "carcass" at the end of 1943. It was not in operation until summer 1944. Construction of the gas chamber began in autumn 1941 and was completed in spring 1942.[180] This timeline shows Mauthausen was a construction site for many years, while CC Gusen's more primitive structure allowed it to develop more quickly.

Understanding the difference between the SS command structure and DEST's administrative structure could mean the difference between life and death for a prisoner. From early spring until the winter of 1941, CC Gusen prisoner Victor Kielich worked in the plasterers' command constructing SS barracks

---

[177] Marsálek, Mauthausen, 132 ff.
[178] Chronik des k.K. Gendarmeriepostens Sankt Georgen an der Gusen (Chronicle of the Rural Police Command at St. Georgen).
[179] Grundbuch Mauthausen, TZ 68/41.
[180] Fabréguet, Michel. „Entwicklung und Veränderung der Funktionen des Konzentrationslagers Mauthausen 1938 – 1945". Die nationalsozialistischen Konzentrationslager, Vol. 1 (Göttingen: S. Fischer Verlag GmbH, 1998), 193 ff.

and administrative offices to the right of the Jourhaus of Gusen I. This allowed him to escape the deadly quarries, where he had worked as an unskilled laborer producing building material for DEST. Prison laborers in the quarries were a focus of hatred for SS guards and capos who felt duty bound to work or beat them to death. As Allen has explained, as far as the camp commandant was concerned, deaths in the quarries were as much a service to the state as any stone production achieved for DEST. The plasterers' command, on the other hand, worked for the camp's SS Construction Directorate, the civil engineer in charge of construction for the camp who answered directly to the camp commandant. Victor received better treatment while at work and some extra food in this command not because he was valued as a human being, but because the project was valued by the civil engineer in charge. The skills of most workers in the quarry could be replaced overnight, but experienced plasterers were harder to train.[181] Along with better treatment on the job, working on the plasterers' command afforded Victor other opportunities to improve his lot because his prisoner-supervisors, the capo in charge of the command and the qualified plasterer responsible for the project, were given considerable leeway as long as the job was done:

> After several weeks, I got familiar with the layout of the SS barracks. Our supervisor, whose name eludes me, but whom I will call "Jan," was a twenty-five-year-old Polish prisoner who kept a tight rein on the others, mainly older Polish tradesmen. During working hours Capo Emil disappeared to play cards with his mates, always returning to get us back to the camp on time. I gradually came to know the command as I brought them the sand and cement I mixed on the ground outside the barracks. Working on the building site gave me a chance to pick up cigarette butts the SS guards threw away. Of course, I had to share with Jan, who often sent me wandering through the SS barracks streets looking for butts. Whenever I met friendly guards, I offered to clean their boots or chop firewood. Some sympathetic and generous older family men would pay me with a few cigarettes or some bread.

---

[181]   Kielich and Mills, 127

Figure 6: *Contemporary photograph of SS-administrative building at Gusen*
(facing destruction soon), Spring 2007
Source: Rudolf A. Haunschmied

While this shows that not all SS guards were equally committed to brutality
for all prisoners, some weeks later Victor was caught scavenging for bread
crusts in the SS rubbish bin by a less friendly guard just days after the capo of
the entire builders' command, Walter Junge, had beaten him for not ladling
soup properly. Victor tells what happened:

> Not long after I got this terrible thrashing, an SS guard caught me inside the
> rubbish box. Although the box was mainly for paper and cigarette butts, it
> was still a good source of food despite its distance from the SS kitchen. Sit-
> ting inside, I did not hear the guard approach with his rubbish bag. As he
> opened the lid, I was on my knees scratching to find bits of crusts. He picked
> up a stick and called for me to get out of the bin, but when I tried to get out

through one of the top openings, he hit my head, and I fell back into the bin. I tried the other opening. But he played cat and mouse with me; each time I lifted my head, he hit me again.

Eventually, he allowed me to escape. With a badly bleeding cut by my ear, I ran back to my command in the basement where I cleaned myself and hid out with "Jan" for the rest of the day.

During that evening's roll call when Victor took his place among the thousands of men standing with others from their barracks to be counted by the capos (the number then relayed up the chain of command from the Blockführer to Rapportführer to Schutzhaftlagerführer Chmielewski), no privilege distinguished one prisoner from another:

When we returned to camp, a prisoner was discovered missing during roll call. It was not my day. My beaten face, head, and ear ached terribly, exposed to the cold wind. Capos and barracks-chiefs beat prisoners at random while we stood in the blustery cold. The SS searched inside and outside the camp with their dogs until they found the prisoner and brought him back. The poor man could hardly walk from the Jourhaus across the Roll Call Square while an SS dog shredded his clothes. None of my friends knew him. He surely did not live to see daylight.[182]

Clearly, skilled prisoners could be beaten and even killed during this random violence. In *The Business of Genocide,* Allen explains that in the summer of 1941, Oswald Pohl appointed Austrian Georg Burböck to resolve the problems caused by camp commandants who placed punishment above production. Allen credits Burböck, a former "technical-administrative expert for the Austrian Post," with facilitating the first selections for murder in a blundered attempt to provide industry with statistical data about the size of the available workforce and their skills. Burböck created a position in each concentration camp, the Labor Action Leader (Arbeitseinsatzführer), subordinate to the commandant, who was supposed to negotiate with the

---

[182] Ibid., 38

commandant and DEST (as well as other SS industries) regarding allocation of labor. In pursuit of this goal, he attempted to instigate a file system
in which every prisoner's skills and suitability for work was kept ready for
evaluation. Ideally, the Neubauleitung (New Construction Directorate) of CC
Gusen could have phoned a Labor Action Leader at CC Mauthausen each
spring and ask for a score of plasterers, for instance. But since few commandants were interested in this administrative task that smacked of the "fat lazy
bureaucrats" Eicke had warned them not to become, they cared little about
preserving skilled workers beyond their immediate usefullness. Instead, they
took the opportunity to use data on a prisoner's health to determine who had
crossed the line between being "fit for work" (who might still make himself
useful to the state by providing labor) and "unfit for work" (who was simply
draining the state's resources).[183] Had Victor been unable to recover quickly
from the beating in the trash bin, he might have crossed just that line. As
Allen points out, "health, criminality, race and industrial efficiency" were
all seen as synonymous in Nazi ideology. Regardless of skills, or in many
cases even health, if a worker was determined to be "arbeitsunfähig," or
unfit, he was handed over to the doctors in charge of "Operation 14 f 13,"
the euthanasia program originally intended for the mentally ill among the
civilian population.[184]

Thus, selections of prisoners for murder began at CC Gusen I. Victor Kielich
recalls:

> Sometime in the spring of 1941 the barracks-secretary announced that a
> transport would go to a sanatorium soon and asked prisoners who wished to
> go to register immediately. Many prisoners in bad health signed up hoping to
> improve their lot. I had been moved from Barracks 13 to Barracks 15 because
> the camp had to make room for the quarantine barracks for Republican
> Spaniards. My new friend from Barracks 15, Bronek, registered to go to the
> sanatorium although he was still very agile. I was tempted, but a sanatorium
> sounded too good to be true. From time to time registered prisoners were
> called up for physical examinations in Barracks 4 near Roll Call Square.

---

[183] Allen, Business, 124
[184] Allen, Business, 117-123

One evening, Bronek grew curious about the goings on in Barracks 4. We found a window only partially covered by the curtain. To our horror, we saw the SS doctor drawing all sorts of marks on the prisoners' naked bodies before sending them to the other half of the barracks. After a while, we understood about the "sanatorium." Many regretted having registered as their health had improved, but it was too late. So it was for Bronek. When his number was called, he and I again walked to Barracks 4, knowing this time he would undergo an "examination." Crossing the threshold, he became a statistic.[185]

French survivor of CC Mauthausen and Gusen I Pierre Serge Choumoff documents in *Nazi Mass Murder* that five thousand prisoners from Mauthausen and Gusen were so designated and taken to be gassed at Hartheim Castle, known as "Facility C" after the killing center in the former sanatorium was established in November 1940. Many of them were tricked in just the manner described, but others were simply selected. From 1941 – 1942, 1,239 CC Gusen prisoners were murdered there. In 1941 alone, the total number of registered murders at Hartheim was 8,599. Public protests against the murder of civilian invalids and civilian developmentally disabled caused Hitler to supposedly halt this practice in August 1941. But what came to be called "wild euthanasia" followed: patients were killed by poison injections, starvation or – especially at Gusen – bathing to death.[186] In the winter of 1941, Victor, now living in Barracks 19 recalls, "Next door was an open-air shower that had been built recently for the extermination of Jews, invalids, or unwanted prisoners by keeping them under a jet of freezing water until they collapsed. A few days after I had had my bath in the kitchen [Victor was whipped and nearly drowned on Chmielewski's orders], SS-Oberscharführer Helmut Kluge, together with several ruthless capos, drowned the last surviving Jews."[187]

---

[185] Kielich and Mills, 36
[186] Eugen Kogon, Hermann Langbein, Pierre Serge Choumoff. Nazi Mass Murder. (New Haven: Yale University Press, 1993), 16-50
[187] Kielich and Mills, 41

Gusen vs. Mauthausen + Satellites

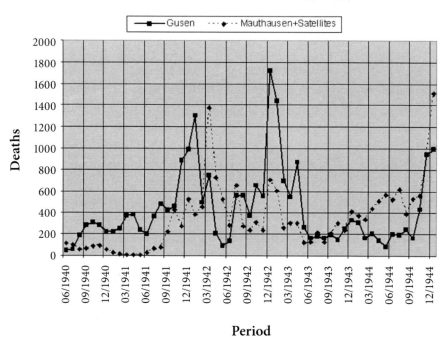

Diagram 1: Deaths Gusen vs. Mauthausen
Prepared by Rudolf A. Haunschmied
Source: Marsalek Mauthausen (1980), 155 – 158

Another method of mass murder was placing prisoners under a "quarantine," a practice which seldom had anything to do with protecting healthy prisoners from unhealthy ones. Rather, the practice often isolated unwanted populations in certain areas of the camp where they received even less food in an attempt to murder them. The use of this medical term is an indication of how clearly certain "races" were equated with vermin and disease. Anti-Fascist Spanish prisoners who had been held in concentration camps in France before the Nazi invasion were transported to CC Mauthausen beginning in August 1940 and to CC Gusen beginning in January 1941. Of the 3,846 who arrived in 1941, only 444 survived to January 1944.[188] Victor recalls that a few weeks before Christmas 1941, "any Spaniards who survived the hunger and diseases in the quarantine barracks were now working in the quarry."[189]

On 27 April 1943, the SS Business Administrative Office (WVHA) tried to limit "Operation 14 f 13" to mentally ill patients because of the drastic labor shortage, but camp doctors were allowed to continue to kill the terminally ill,[190] a troubled concept in an extermination-and-labor camp. The practice continued regardless of labor shortages. Even possessing a necessary skill would not protect the most hated prisoners, as Karl Littner, a native of Oswiecim, Poland, attests. Swept into the slave labor system in 1940, Littner survived the liquidation of the Srodula Ghetto in 1943 only to be imprisoned in Auschwitz-Birkenau, a mile or so away from his hometown. From there he was sent with 600 other Jews to Fünfteichen, a subcamp of Gross-Rosen, where he worked until January of 1945 as a welder, a skill which would be much in demand in the underground Messerschmitt factory in St. Georgen when Littner arrived there. But his skills did not change the conditions of his transfer to CC Gusen II. Along with 30,000 other Jews, he embarked on a Death March that January. At the end of a two week walk during which thousands died, they were loaded into open coal cars near Weimar-Buchenwald. Thousands more died before the train reached Mauthausen. As Littner recalls:

---

[188]   Pike, David Winegate. Spaniards in the Holocaust (New York: Routledge, 2001), 97
[189]   Kielich and Mills, 43
[190]   Kogon, Langbein, and Choumoff, 34-40

Blue from the cold wind lashing us, ten shivering skeletal looking Muselman stepped forward from the column at a time to run across the snow-covered road to the "showers." Standing under the cold water just long enough to get wet and fill our shoes with water, we were chased back to join the waiting column. So many dropped dead in the snow, the road was piled with Jewish corpses. Mr. Gutentag, a medical doctor from Chszanow, a city not far from Oswiecim, shook next to me, steam rising from his gray, shaking body. Nearly frozen myself I asked him, how could human beings survive such an ordeal? His teeth clattering, obviously convulsing from pain, he strained to say, "Medically I cannot explain how a human being can survive this." Those were his last words. He fell dead on a mound of snow.[191]

By 1942, the Jourhaus at CC Gusen was surrounded by a stone wall with six granite watch towers built by Spanish prisoners. Although Paul Jaskot analyzes the development of SS architecture, he does not discuss the Jourhaus, the entrance of Gusen I, and the stone wall and watchtowers are not discussed in terms of the form and function of SS architecture. Of the "fortresses" of CC Flossenbürg and CC Mauthausen, he writes that the style "exemplifies the projection of an authoritative institutional identity as well as the perceived need to punish and exploit the enlarged labor force." Form, Jaskot writes, was also influenced by the availability of building materials. However, the Jourhaus of Gusen I, also built during what Jaskot calls the "period of military optimism" is a simple, two story structure, unassuming enough to be used currently as a private residence.

This clear lack of "institutional identity" troubles Jaskot's chronology of the development of SS architecture from fortress-like labor camps to "the later extremes of the death camps." The architecture of the Jourhaus seems to suggest the extremes of the later death camps, despite having been completed before the "fortress" Mauthausen, and just a few kilometers away, despite the availability of what Jaskot refers to as the higher quality granite of the Gusen and Kastenhof quarries.[192] Perhaps this extreme form reflects that the extermination-and-labor function of the Gusen camps was understood even

---

[191] Littner, Karl. *Life Hanging by a Spider's Web*, unpublished manuscript, npag
[192] Jaskot, 126-133

before the January 1941 order designating it a "camp of no return" along with CC Mauthausen. The decree issued by SS General Heydrich divided concentration camps into three categories of severity, placing CC Mauthausen and CC Gusen in Category III, the worst. While concentration camps dedicated to the destruction of Jews were under construction in 1941, transport to CC Mauthausen and CC Gusen was officially understood as a death sentence.[193]

---

[193]   Marsálek, Mauthausen [English], 33 ff

St. Georgen Becomes an Administrative Center of DEST

In March of 1939, DEST was put under Oswald Pohl's control. Further-more, the office within the SS Administrative Office which Pohl had led since becoming SS Chief Administrative Officer in 1936, Administration IV, was made into a Main Office, the Administration and Business Office, Verwaltungs- und Wirtschaftshauptamt (VuWHA). Pohl was also appointed Ministerial Director of the Chief of German Police, a title which actually signified appointment to the Interior Ministry.[194]

While these and other bureaucratic changes that Himmler made within the SS are very difficult to keep in mind, the importance for the history of the Mauthausen/Gusen Camps is that Pohl's influence over SS businesses, prison labor and construction increased. Pohl split his Main Office into three sections. Office I controlled budgets and payroll for all of the SS. Office II controlled all SS construction, and so had more influence over concentration camps as inmates were increasingly used to construct SS business sites, such as DEST offices and housing at St. Georgen. Office III Wirtschaft had control over business and industrial tasks, including machines, labor, and finances.

Another Main Office for Budgets and Building (Hauptamt Haushalt und Bauten or HAHB) was created separate from Office III Wirtschaft to alleviate any possible conflict of funding between industry, business, and building. It was to the Building Office II of HAHB that Dr.-Ing. Hans Kammler would be hired in June 1941 to assist RFSS Himmler with constructing concentration camps and the vast building projects envisioned for the German settlements in Poland and Russia.[195]

Two years before Kammler would become essential to the construction of Berg-kristall, as a result of his responsibilities in HAHB he was given opportunities to acquaint himself with St. Georgen's geography and with CC Gusen I, two factors which would be essential in designating St. Georgen as the site for the underground tunnels. His knowledge of these factors and the changes he made

---

[194]   Ibid., 14
[195]   Allen, Business, 83-84, 129

in the engineers' offices within the local camps enabled him to transform the production goals of DEST at St. Georgen from building materials to underground factory space and jet fighters.

In *The Architecture of Oppression,* Jaskot notes that by 1939 "all approval of building design, distribution of funds and ordering of materials for the concentration camps was managed by SS Hauptamt Haushalt und Bauten, Hauptabteilung C" (which absorbed HAHB Office II in mid-1942[196]) to which Kammler was appointed in 1941 to straighten out chronic mismanagement.[197] Allen stresses that Oswald Pohl "courted Dr.-Ing. Hans Kammler, an engineer from the German air force, who would quickly prove to be one of the most capable and dedicated men ever to make his career under Himmler." Kammler was admired for his fanatical commitment to Himmler's monstrous plans to transform Poland and Russia with settlements designed to promote "Germandom" and enslave the native peoples.[198]

Kammler held his position at Hauptamt Haushalt und Bauten, Hauptabteilung C throughout the war, even after being appointed to oversee most of the underground dispersal projects of the Reich, including St. Georgen, Ebensee and Redl-Zipf. In fact, in the administration of his duties for HAHB C, Kammler had to discuss any building plans with the concentration camp administration (who would provide the labor) as well as the representatives of DEST (who would provide materials and support). While the HAHB, Hauptabteilung C would not be directly connected to the construction of DEST housing or administrative buildings in St. Georgen, in its relationship to construction at Concentration Camps Mauthausen and Gusen, Kammler's office had a key role in the hierarchy of the building process which determined how "specific decisions about camp buildings were made in relation to particular geographies, functions, available forced labor and materials." Jaskot notes that Kammler's obsession with administrative detail and his assignment to reform the businesses practices of the office

---

[196] Ibid., 149 Allen explains that in mid-1942, Pohl joined the Main Office for Budgets and Building and the Administration and Business Main Office's SS businesses into the Wirtschaftsverwaltungshauptamt (WVHA), the Business Administration Main Office which he then split. But here we are concerned with Office Group C-Construction. 154-158

[197] Jaskot, 129

[198] Allen, Business, 141

drove him to review, and in the case of KL Flossenbürg, to retroactively approve plans made by the office, concentration camp personnel and DEST prior to his arrival.[199] Kammler not only had access to the same geographical, structural and labor information regarding all buildings associated with Concentration Camps Mauthausen and Gusen, he also had a similar responsibility to evaluate his predecessors' plans. In addition, he had demonstrated fanatical interest in planning communities which would promote National Socialist ideals.[200]

In St. Georgen and Langenstein, the additional residents caused a housing short-age. Many local families had all but one room in their homes requisitioned by the SS. In Langenstein, St. Georgen and Mauthausen, local craftsmen – even with the labor of slaves – could not build barracks and private homes fast enough to accommodate the growing number of SS and other personnel. In August of 1939, when Maria F.'s husband left for the war, he told her Poland would be defeated quickly and he could be expected home in a fortnight. She moved back to her parents' home in Gutau to deliver her second son and to wait for her husband. When the war continued into the fall, Rudolf P., her husband's former employer, gave her a job in his brick factory and rented an apartment to her in what had been the brewery next to his house. She moved her baby and two year old son into two rooms. "The apartment was good," she recalls. "There was a kitchen/living area and a bedroom. And Rudolf P. did not charge me much rent. If I milked his cow, I could have a litre of milk for the children."[201]

In winter 1939/40, in addition to building CC Gusen and CC Mauthausen, DEST sought to provide accommodations for the two camps' administrators and supervisors. During a "local consultation" which included the camp leadership and Linz architect Paul Theer, St. Georgen's eastern exit was chosen from three possibilities for the construction of the housing project "Stein und Erde" (Stone and Earth). On 13 February 1940 the SS finalized an agreement with the Governor of Oberdonau for a comprehensive building program for St. Georgen a. d. Gusen.[202]

---

[199] Jaskot, 129-130
[200] Allen, Business, 54
[201] Interview, May 7 2001
[202] Schreiben des Landeshauptmannes von Oberdonau vom 20. Februar 1940 an das Siedlungsamt Linz, den Bürgermeister von St. Georgen, den DEST-Werkleiter SS-Hauptsturmführer Spichalsky

The SS's first goal was the construction of "50 homes in the style of public housing with the possibility of extensions in the event of families with many children" for blue- and white-collar workers and employees of the quarry industry in CC Gusen and CC Mauthausen. Later, public buildings for the settlement (e.g. a kindergarten and shops) were to be constructed, dispersed among the groups of buildings to form an organized unit.[203] These plans reflect the determination of the SS to impose their ideals of social order on the community outside the walls of the camps as well as inside the walls. Designs of SS communities intended for the occupied territories were also meant to promote SS unity and reinforce their German identity.[204]

At this time the only impediments to extending St. Georgen towards Gusen were the expansion of the Hauderer-Bezirksstrasse (the historic main road on the northern bank of the Danube River) to a major road and the construction of a supplemental railway line of the Reichsbahn (the German rail system) between St. Georgen and the town of Mauthausen. (Note here the geographical proximity and mutual interest for planners from both DEST and HAHB in the railway benefiting both CC Mauthausen and the surrounding area by connecting the line between Mauthausen and Gaisbach to the line between St. Georgen and Gaisbach.) The route between Mauthausen and Gaisbach remained operational until the end of the war when it was used as the demarcation between US troops and the Red Army in the weeks after liberation. During the Soviet occupation, it was dismantled, and as recent research shows, this railway would have played a key role in the SS's plans to rebuild the CC Auschwitz incinerators in spring 1945 in Altaist-Hartl – a small village some 10 km north of CC Mauthausen/Gusen.[205]

---

and Architekt Theer. Gemeindearchiv St. Georgen a. d. Gusen.

[203] Kanzlei-Anmerkung des Landeshauptmanns von Oberdonau Z/RO. I.H. 46/1-1940, XIa of 13 February 1940. Gemeindearchiv St. Georgen a.d. Gusen.

[204] Allen, Business, 52

[205] Perz, Bertrand and Florian Freund. „Auschwitz neu? – Pläne und Massnahmen zur Wiedererrichtung der Krematorien von Auschwitz-Birkenau in der Umgebung des KZ Mauthausen im Februar 1945", Dachauer Hefte, Nr. 20 (Sonderdruck), without date.

Figure 7: DEST Headquarters at St. Georgen (Building 1), 1942
Source: AHDG; Collection Franz Walzer

Real estate negotiations began in April 1940 and, by August 1940, the planning of the DEST administrative center was completed. The administrative center consisted of two main buildings: an administrative building with two apartments and a residential building with two shops and seven apartments. Detainees of CC Gusen built these structures within the town of St. Georgen proper. Thus the SS with its company, DEST, overwhelmed and controlled St. Georgen a. d. Gusen, transforming the town into a center of business for "Granitwerke Mauthausen." So the seat of "Granitwerke Mauthausen" was, ironically, at St. Georgen a.d. Gusen and not at Mauthausen. As a result DEST archival material dealing with "Mauthausen" very often actually refers to the headquarters at St. Georgen, causing confusion and further inhibiting the understanding of the history of this region.

Figure 8: *DEST Headquarters at St. Georgen (Building 2), 1942*
Source: AHDG; Collection Franz Walzer

The interests of the native population of St. Georgen became irrelevant to the agenda of the SS. On 12 December 1940 the District President of Perg, whose authority had been ignored, awarded a building permit to DEST for the already-completed DEST buildings. Since Berlin ignored Austrian laws on building and trade when constructing and operating the concentration camps and DEST facilities at St. Georgen, Gusen and Mauthausen, any legal complications were personally smoothed out by SS-Obergruppenführer and General of the Police and Waffen-SS Kaltenbrunner who personally intervened as the "Higher SS- and Police Leader 'Donau' of Vienna." He arranged for regional authorities to retroactively legalize most of the buildings. Kaltenbrunner thus served as a "point man" for the regional DEST and concentration camp management when judicial problems had to be fixed with regional Upper-Austrian authorities in Perg or Linz.

Kaltenbrunner's close interest in the concentration camps in his home region resulted in many visits to CC Mauthausen and CC Gusen.[206] He was an honorary guest on 19 July 1942 when he officially inaugurated the rifle range at St. Georgen in the presence of an honor guard from CC Mauthausen. During the rifle-range's construction at St. Georgen, a Polish professor assigned to its construction command was shot on 23 June 1940 as he tried to leave the construction site. Prisoners who left the site of an exterior command (either voluntarily or under compulsion of the guards who often forced prisoners to appear to flee) were shot by a line of guards as they ran away.[207] Incidents such as these taught the SS that their guards needed training with small caliber rifles. On his deathbed, Ziereis confessed, "In the year 1940, 320 Poles from Warsaw had to be killed. I had some of the prisoners shot several times because the untrained SS troops could not handle the small calibre weapons which were obligatory in the camps."[208]

Although Ziereis doesn't explain why the "prisoners had to be killed," from the start of the camp prisoners who couldn't work were seen as a liability to DEST-Werkleiter (plant manager) SS-Obersturmführer Paul Wolfram (who oversaw the work at the Gusen and Kastenhof quarries). Polish survivor Joseph Kowalski was a prisoner at Dachau in July 1940 when he first met Paul Wolfram, the engineer in charge of the DEST quarries after December 1939. Wolfram and Chmielewski came to personally choose stronger prisoners, having complained to Berlin that Dachau was sending them prisoners who were already sick. Wolfram reportedly checked out the prisoners' muscles himself, selecting a group that left Dachau for Gusen on 2 August 1940. Former prisoners also testified that Wolfram ordered prisoners too sick to work to receive beatings from which they died. In 1943, Wolfram sent 150 prisoners back to Gusen where they would be kept in an unfinished building known as the "Neubau" where they were given reduced rations until they died.[209]

---

[206] Marsálek, Mauthausen, [English], 188

[207] Klinger, Volkschulchronik, 144 ff and Marsálek, Gusen, 6.

[208] „Totenbettgeständnis des Kommandanten von Mauthausen". Letzeburger zu Mauthausen (Luxembourg: Amicale de Mauthausen, 1970), 58

[209] US vs. Wolfram, Vol. 45 (ETO Case No. 000-50-5-) U.S.A. v. Paul Wolfram, Box 50. It is very likely that the unfinished buildings of barracks 6,7 and 8 are meant here. In addition, Pierre Serge Choumoff also testifies that shootings were also carried out between these two buildings frequently.

Since the SS used prison labor to construct the administrative center and build roads in the municipality, the residents of St. Georgen, like the farmers who "leased" concentration camp labor, witnessed how the SS treated prisoners. Residents also learned quickly that whether or not they could leave food or water for the prisoners depended on the individual SS guard observing them. Only some SS guards allowed people to leave apples or bread for the prisoners.[210] While these stories of risking censure or even imprisonment to help prisoners might seem self-serving, the corroboration provided by a number of survivors lends them credibility.[211] Furthermore, after the early example of stonemason Johann Steinmüller, who had been fired for giving slave laborers water and then sent to Buchenwald and Dachau for publicly expressing pity for them, the risks of feeding prisoners were clear.[212]

On 18 January 1940, SS-Sturmbannführer Gerhard Maurer, an executive officer soon to leave DEST to work as chief of SS Hauptamt III A I (Verwaltung und Wirtschaft), a man who would be an important figure in the future of the tunnel projects at St. Georgen, negotiated the sale of DEST property at Gusen with his fellow Executive Officer Dr. Salpeter on behalf of DEST to HAHB.[213] This sale, and the fact that he claimed an air compressor to be delivered by DEMAG Duisburg to Granitwerke Mauthausen, which had been ordered on 21 February 1939, shows that Maurer had an early acquaintance with the local geography and SS facilities.[214]

In 1940 prisoners started work on the infrastructure for the administrative center and the housing units in St. Georgen. Streets and further enlargements of the housing developments were planned on a 4 hectare building site (4 hectares would be 40,000 square meters or about ten acres). Another important consideration when assessing the impact on the local economy of Maurer's and Salpeter's sale of property in Gusen and of this development in St. Georgen is the relatively small size of family farms in Upper Austria.

---

[210]   Klinger, Volksschulchronik, 144
[211]   Lax and Lax, Caraseu, 103
[212]   Pfarrbuch St. Georgen 1988, 43
[213]   Grundbuch Mauthausen, TZ 26/41
[214]   Schreiben SS-Stbf Maurer an DEMAG Duisburg vom 6. März 1940, Fa-600/3, Akz. 7669/88, Institut für Zeitgeschichte München

Beginning 13 June 1940, a commission attempted for several weeks to dig a well at the Apfelsteiner Farm in the neighbouring community of Luftenberg in order to provide the newly-constructed buildings with adequate water, but the well failed to yield as much as was needed.[215]

The housing estates of the SS in St. Georgen accommodated the high-ranking SS command staff of both Concentration Camps Mauthausen and Gusen. In March 1940 CC Gusen Commandant SS-Hauptsturmführer Karl Chmielewski moved to St. Georgen with his family. On 17 May 1941 SS-Obersturmbannführer Franz Ziereis also moved to St. Georgen with his wife and three children,[216] where he remained until 20 October 1942 when he moved to a house below Farmer Graf at Mauthausen, where another SS settlement was built.[217] Ziereis' Schutzhaftlagerführer I [Second in Command] at CC Mauthausen, SS-Hauptsturmführer Georg Bachmayer followed with his wife and children on 20 July.[218] Bachmayer would move his family back to Mauthausen on 28 September 1944.[219] Other new residents of St. Georgen were the following key-managers of DEST: SS-Hauptsturmführer Dir. Otto Walther (Werkgruppenleiter – senior manager, 8 April 1941), SS-Obersturmführer Ing. Alfred Grau (Kaufmännischer Leiter – commercial manager, 22 May 1941), SS-Unterscharführer Anton Kaufmann (Magazinverwalter – logistics manager, 20 April 1942), Rudolf Ronge (Leiter der Steinmetzbetriebe Gusen und Wienergraben – Head of the stone-masonrows at Gusen and Wienergraben quarry, 15 June 1941) and SS-Obersturmführer Paul Wolfram (Werkleiter – plant manager of the Gusen and Kastenhof quarries, 1941).[220]

Although DEST completed the first two administrative buildings in the spring of 1941, when the company headquarters relocated there, DEST had operated

---

[215] Klinger, Volksschulchronik, 143
[216] Meldeunterlagen [registration] für Franz Ziereis. Gemeindearchiv St. Georgen
[217] Klinger, Volksschulchronik, 145 ff.
[218] Meldeunterlagen für Georg Bachmayer. Gemeindearchiv St. Georgen
[219] Eventually Bachmayer, born on 12 May 1913 in Fridolfing, was in charge of the construction at Ebensee. After the war, on 8 May 1945, Bachmayer killed his family in Münzbach and then killed himself. Marsálek, Mauthausen, 200
[220] Meldeunterlagen. Gemeindearchiv St. Georgen

from St. Georgen prior to this date, giving the town as the place of signature on an October 1940 purchase contract with the community of Langenstein.[221] In the new DEST headquarters, Senior Manager Otto Walther[222] and Quarry Plant Manager Paul Wolfram[223] planned the construction of the most important center for granite quarrying in the Third Reich. Although DEST also operated quarries at Flossenbürg, Gross-Rosen, and Natzweiler, in a sworn affidavit Otto Walther (DEST Senior Manager for Granitwerke Mauthausen at St. Georgen after 1941) reported that the Gusen quarries were intended to be DEST's central quarries.[224]

This is underscored by the fact that officials at "Werkgruppenleitung (company group headquarters) St. Georgen" not only managed the local quarries "Gusen", "Kastenhof", "Pierbauer" and "Wienergraben," but also were responsible for managing other sites in Austria (Grossraming) and at Beneschau (near Prague) in Bohemia.[225] The importance of this new DEST facility at St. Georgen is furthermore underlined by the fact that Berlin organized the conference of all DEST company group leaders of late 1941 to be held in St. Georgen under the chairmanship of SS-Hauptsturmführer Karl Mummenthey.[226] It is also worth noting that Commandant Ziereis acquired a second income when he was hired by DEST in 1942 as "Betriebsdirektor" (plant director) of Werkgruppenleitung St. Georgen. This caused severe conflicts with the professional DEST managers at St. Georgen, as Otto Walther stated after the war.[227]

The housing development in St. Georgen expanded quickly as the SS and DEST needed more accommodations in 1941. The Steinsiedlung (it still has the same name today) and the housing estates behind the administrative

---

[221] Kaufvertrag abgeschlossem zwischen der Gemeinde Langenstein und der DEST vom 2.10.1940. Grundbuch Mauthausen, TZ 16/41.

[222] SS-Hauptsturmführer Dir. Otto Walther was born on 28 September 1905 in Strassburg. He moved from Kassel to St. Georgen on 8 April 1941. Marsálek, Gusen, 11 and Meldeunterlagen für Otto Walther. Gemeindearchiv St. Georgen.

[223] Marsálek, Gusen, 11

[224] Jaskot, 43; Affidavit Otto Walther, NARA microform publication M890/27/0047.

[225] DEST-Geschäftsbericht 1943, BArch NS 3/1168.

[226] Affidavit Erich Rupprecht, NARA microform publication M890/27/0650.

[227] Affidavit Otto Walther

center developed shortly thereafter. The general management of DEST organized and planned the project directly from Berlin without any consideration as to its feasibility. The needs of the local community were subordinated to the goal of unity within the SS community.

When the housing shortage continued, Rudolf P. asked Maria F. to move to the attic apartment in the old brewery. She was lucky to still have her own place, however. "It was nice. There was an exterior stairway to my apartment," Maria F. said. Three SS families also lived there.[228]

Along with CC Natzweiler, CC Gusen was an important DEST site for the deployment of apprentice programs among inmates. One training course with 38 inmates began on 18 February 1941. In October 1941, 535 inmates trained as stone masons[229] in the various DEST quarries at Gusen and Mauthausen. In addition, a specialized building for the training of hundreds of inmates was built at Gusen in April 1943 which was followed by Lehrlingshalle II (a second such building) in late 1943.[230] Up to 700 children and youngsters from the Soviet Union between 12 and 16 years were "employed" there in stone production.[231]

After June 1942 SS Tech. Sergeant Oskar Tandler was Blockführer in charge of the 13, 14 and 15-year-old Russians who were kept in Block 24. Survivor Pedro Gomez testified at Tandler's post-war trial that he observed Tandler beating them when they marched out of formation or when they refused to sing German songs on their way to and from work. While the youngsters were supposed to leave half an hour later than the other workers and return half an hour earlier, Gomez recalls they often returned from work with the others. These young men were forced to do very hard work crushing rock in the quarry. Although Tandler was supposed to ensure that they got extra food, Gomez accused him of stealing most of it. He also recalled hearing the young Russians singing as they left for work and as they returned. Tandler

---

[228] Interview, May 7 2001
[229] DEST-Monatsberichte, BArch NS 3/1346.
[230] Lehrlingswerkstättenhalle I was built in April 1943 and was followed by Lehrlingshalle II in late 1943. DEST-Geschäftsbericht 1943, BArch NS 3/1168, NS 3/1231 and NS 3/1239.
[231] Marsálek, Gusen, 22

was found guilty of this and other atrocities and sentenced to death, although this was eventually reduced to thirty years.[232]

Figure 9: Civilian apprentices of DEST at the Kitchen Barracks at St. Georgen, 1942
Source: AHDG; Collection Franz Walzer

Civilian boys from local communities also apprenticed alongside inmates – not willingly, however. They were assigned by the regional labor exchange to relieve the quarries' constant labor shortage. A former mayor of St. Georgen who apprenticed in the Wienergraben Quarry witnessed many atrocities. Forbidden to speak about what they had seen, nearly all of these civilian apprentices are still burdened by this brutal experience. In 1942,

---

[232] United States vs. Shuettauf, et al.Case No. 000-50-5-3 NARA Record Group 153 Entry 143 270/1/14-15/6-1 Box 12, Tandler testimony summarized by Jayne Klick, Nick Kendryna and Sundeep Srivastava. http://ecc.pima.edu/~gusen/Schuettauf/Index_to_Schuettauf_Summaries.htm

DEST built a hostel with a kitchen for these apprentices where the St. Georgen secondary school is today.[233]

With groundwork set for the industrial exploitation of the quarries and the detainees in St. Georgen, the so-called "Polenlager" (Camp for the Polish) became an industrial center for both the production of stone-construction material and for the extermination of particularly undesirable prisoners from other camps.

The 1 January 1941 decree from Berlin categorizing all concentration camps in the Reich read as follows:

CATEGORY I: "Hardly culpable and definitely reformable protective custody inmates, as well as exceptional cases and solitary confinement"
- Dachau Concentration Camp
- Sachsenhausen Concentration Camp
- Auschwitz main camp (not the extermination camp).

CATEGORY II: "Heavily culpable, but educable and reformable protective custody inmates"
- Buchenwald Concentration Camp
- Flossenbürg Concentration Camp
- Neuengamme Concentration Camp
- Auschwitz II Concentration Camp

CATEGORY III "Heavily culpable, incorrigible, and particularly those also previously convicted and antisocial; i.e. hardly reformable protective custody inmates."
- Mauthausen Concentration Camp[234]

Concentration Camp Mauthausen, and by extension Gusen, are the only camps assigned to "Category III" and, from this point on, received mostly "undesirable" prisoners. As Marsálek points out, this allowed Himmler

---

[233] DEST Geschäftsbericht 1942. BArch NS 3/1168/51.
[234] Le Chène, 36

and Heydrich to achieve their goal of "connecting forced labor with extermination."[235] Although some prisoners, such as Joe C. and Erwin Gostner, had been allowed to actually return home, after this decree being sent to either camp with the designation "Rückkehr unerwünscht" (return not desirable) meant certain death for all Jews and Soviet prisoners of war, as well as the majority of Poles, Czechs, Republican Spaniards, Yugoslavs, Belgians, the French, and Gypsies, as well as Austrian and German communists. This virtual death sentence was carried out by forced labor in the quarries or on the construction of the camp or the installations of DEST.[236] Despite innumerable deaths, a steady stream of new prisoners allowed the population of CC Gusen to increase to 6,500 during this period.[237] When the secret strategic armament projects developed, an "Entlassungssperre" (no further release) was also imposed, meaning that the Gestapo could no longer release inmates from the Mauthausen/Gusen concentration camps after August 1944 until the war's end – in order to maintain absolute secrecy.[238]

Even before 1941 local people noticed the numerous hearses taking dead bodies to Steyr or Linz for cremation. On 29 January 1941 the SS started its own crematorium in CC Gusen. In a letter of 25 June 1940 Hauptamt Haushalt und Bauten, Amt II wrote to the SS-Neubauleitung Mauthausen (SS New Construction Directorate for Concentration Camp Mauthausen) that a mobile crematorium originally intended to be used at Flossenbürg would be shipped to CC Gusen. Construction of the first stationary crematorium started after delivery of an incinerator to CC Gusen on 19 December 1940 for RM 10.635,40. It functioned poorly, was demolished in October 1941, and replaced. In January 1943 additional incinerators were delivered to CC Gusen but never set into operation. A final attempt to enlarge the Gusen

---

[235] Marsálek, Mauthausen [English], 33
[236] Marsálek, Mauthausen, 39 ff and Marsálek, Gusen, 12 ff.
[237] Marsálek, Gusen, 37
[238] Erlass des Chefs der Sicherheitspolizei und des SD – IV A 6 b Allg. Nr. 4344/44g of 3 August 1944. BArch, Z 11 1680 A.1, Stapoleit Düsseldorf.

crematorium was made in December 1944.[239] The cremation capacity reached 94 corpses a day.[240]

The National Socialists continued to try to sever the community's ties to the church by opening secular registry offices, unheard of in Austria before the Anschluss when the Nazis introduced them. Ironically, these secular registries were organized according to the Roman Catholic parishes, so deaths at CC Gusen were registered in St. Georgen until a separate registry was opened for the camp itself in 1941. At first only deaths were recorded, but on 6 October 1942, the SS registry noted the first marriage between a local woman and an SS man.[241]

The production of DEST increased exponentially due to both the labor of thousands of prisoners and the installation of one of the biggest stone crushers in Europe near the Meierhof north of CC Gusen, where it still stands today. The presence of this stone crusher is consistent with what Allen describes as DEST management's fascination with using state-of-the-art technology to achieve mass production. However, despite the availability of this stone crusher, SS guards continued to "discipline" prisoners, even to death, by forcing them to crush stones with sledge hammers as Joe C. had witnessed in 1940 during the construction of Gusen I. In his memoir *Caraseu*, CC Gusen II survivor Martin Lax, who arrived in 1944 with thousands of other Hungarian Jews transported from Auschwitz specifically to alleviate labor shortages on "large construction projects,"[242] describes the following scene in the tunnels on his second day at CC Gusen II:

> We were given a hammer that morning and set to work breaking up a pile of rocks. The rocks, each about a foot in diameter, were to be broken into two-inch fragments. It was another exercise in futility. Hundreds of prisoners, dead tired from our labours of the previous day, stood smashing big stones

[239] Briefverkehr der Bauleitung Mauthausen/Gusen betreffend Verbrennungsöfen für Gusen. BArch, NS 4/Ma/54.
[240] Keren, Daniel. „Cremation at Gusen: A Timesheet", http://www.holocaust-history.org/gusen-cremation-timesheet/index.shtml, 14 June 2004, 2
[241] Klinger, Volksschulchronik, 147.
[242] Ulrich, Herbert. "Labour and Extermination: Economic Interests and Primacy of Weltanschauung in National Socialism." Past and Present, No 138, (Feb. 1993) 144-145

into smaller ones, and smaller ones into smaller ones yet. Again it was busy work, done under the eyes of the SS who constantly harassed us, yelled at us to work faster, hit us if we stopped for a moment, and sometimes hit us for no reason at all. We worked without gloves, lifting our hammers and smashing them down on the rocks, and sometimes on our thumbs, over and over as our hands grew raw and bloody.

The tedious process continued the next day, and the next, and the next. For close to a week, the Nazis brought their new team of slaves into the tunnel and forced us to pound unendingly for no imaginable purpose, except to break us. We would get used to hard work, mindless work, they seemed to say, and we would learn not to ask questions but simply to obey. We learned to start when a German said start and to stop when a German said stop. We learned to be docile and disciplined, no matter how useless or difficult the work.[243]

Although Lax was unaware of the existence of the nearby stone crusher,[244] and so unaware of how truly "useless" his work was, this underscores the camp command structure's prioritization of discipline and "education" of prisoners over DEST's goals to mass produce gravel as a building material or to create underground factory space in the Bergkristall Tunnels.

From 1941 on, the SS occupation of St. Georgen advanced quickly. On 10 March the construction of a railway from the St. Georgen station to the quarries and CC Gusen was begun to solve transportation problems for the camps. Farmers, who had already lost much of their land to the housing development, were not told about the new railway until detainees began removing their topsoil.

Simultaneous with the railway construction, the SS began regulating the Gusen River downstream from the train overpass at the Griesäcker area (consisting of small vegetable gardens at the time). When regulation of a few hundred meters of the Gusen River was complete, prisoners built a concrete railway bridge in just two days, from 15 to 16 September 1941. Lighted by

---

[243] Lax, 87
[244] Martin Lax, Personal Interview, October 21, 2004

searchlights, the work continued during the night under the usual horrific conditions, which also increased the local resident's insecurity and fear.[245]

Around the end of 1941, inmates elevated the roadbed of the former main road No. B3, which is still in use today. In spring 1942, when the construction for the "Schleppbahn" (special railway normally used in mining) proceeded at this site, an underpass had to be constructed. In doing so, the SS discovered an important archaeological find near Koglberg Hill. Acting on orders from Berlin, the SS stopped the railway construction. The artefacts were collected by a quickly-formed excavation command and were exhibited until October 1944 in a museum barracks at CC Gusen I for the benefit of the SS stationed there.[246]

After the excavation was finished, the construction for the "Schleppbahn" continued. On 23 March 1943 the first freight train arrived at CC Gusen.[247] Between the railway station at St. Georgen and CC Gusen, the SS constructed an "Übernahmebahnhof" (a "hand over" or transfer station with multiple sidings) up to which the Reichsbahn brought trains meant for CC Gusen and its industrial installations. The railcars were transferred at this point to the camp locomotive which pulled them into the concentration camp. A witness recalls that half an hour before a train headed for CC Gusen arrived at St. Georgen, SS-troops were ready to receive it. After transferring command of the train, a Reichsbahn (railway) official had to escort the train to the station inside CC Gusen. There, after about two hours of unloading prisoners, he had to supervise the return of the rolling stock. Before he could return, however, prisoners had to clean the dirty wagons at the station inside Concentration Camp Gusen.[248]

---

[245] Klinger, Volksschulchronik, 145 ff

[246] To prevent the destruction of the „archaeological SS-collection Gusen" by allied bombings, high-ranking SS-leaders at Berlin ordered the dispersal of that collection to an underground facility at Pottenstein, Germany on 5 October 1944. Gerhard Trnka, „Das urnenzeitliche Gräberfeld von Gusen in Oberösterreich", Archaeologia Austriaca, Band 76 (Vienna: Franz Deutike Verlagsgesellschaft mbH, 1992), 50

[247] Klinger, Volksschulchronik, 146.

[248] Interview 861203. Transcript in the possession of the author.

Figure 10: "Schleppbahnbrücke" Railway Bridge, 1987
Source: Rudolf A. Haunschmied

The treatment of Soviet prisoners of war caused a hygienic catastrophe within the camp. Before the war against the Soviet Union, the labor shortage seemed to have been solved by the forced or slave labor in Germany of three million Polish and French POWs. In July 1941, Hitler was so sure of victory against the Russians and a resulting endless supply of slave labor for the Reich that he forbade the use of Soviet POW labor, making these prisoners entirely expendable to the commandants of camps to which they were transported. Nor did the Army High Command make provisions to feed Russian POWs. Of 3,350,000 Russian POWs 60% died, 1.4 million by early December. Göring also declared that Germany was under no "international" obligation to feed Russian POWs.[249] Nazi hatred of Russians resulted from the equation of Bol-

---

[249] Ulrich, 151

shevism with Judaism, resulting in an order to both the German army and the SS to eradicate the "Bolshevik-Jewish" threat.[250]

In the winter of 1941/42, survivor Victor Kielich witnessed the brutal treatment Soviet POWs endured. Dropped from the plasterers' command when winter cold slowed construction on the SS barracks, Victor was sent back to the Gusen Quarry Command. He was also transferred from Barracks 15 to Barracks 19 because Barracks 13 – 16 and 21 – 24 were vacated to "quarantine" the newly-arrived Russian prisoners of war. He reports:

> In Gusen the SS and the barracks-chiefs were only too ready to give the Bolsheviks the worst treatment they could devise. The Russians arrived half-naked with bits of rags hanging on their thin bodies, their bootless feet wrapped in rags or straw. For 'disinfections' the Russians were forced to shed their rags and, naked, were led to the open air showers where jets of cold water pounded their weak and tired bodies. On the way back the SS and barracks-chiefs beat them. The shower floor and the road back to the quarantine barracks were covered with so-called 'prisoners of war.'

> The camp's daily ration was halved for them. By the time barracks-chiefs, capos and the rest of the hierarchy took a triple share of food for themselves, the Russians were left with almost nothing. They just starved to death in the quarantine enclosure. The living threw the dead over the fence for the crematorium boys to collect.

> Camp Commandant Chmielewski and his accomplices would come to the gate of this dreadful place quite often. He would call out to the barracks-chiefs and ask, 'How many died today?'

> The barracks-chief would reply, "A hundred," or whatever the number was.

> Gesticulating with his famous whip, Chmielewski would shout, "Not enough. Tomorrow there must be more."

---

[250] Overy, Richard. *Russia's War* (New York: Penguin Books, 1997), 84

From behind the fence hundreds of living skeletons would beg, "Bread. Bread, please."[251]

Only 109 Soviet POWs would survive this "quarantine" until 1943, to then be integrated into CC Gusen. Typhoid became such a problem as a result of the extra burden on camp resources and hygiene that in October 1941 the quarries of Gusen came to a standstill because of a typhoid epidemic in CC Gusen.[252]

Restrictions actually meant to reduce infection were occasionally extended over the entire camp, as on 7 October 1940 when the Reichssicherheitshauptamt (RSHA) (Reich Security Main Office) announced to Staatspolizeileitstelle Düsseldorf that CC Gusen "is quarantined."[253] Even Schutzhaftlagerführer Chmielewski was infected in early 1942.[254] Increasingly the SS, many of whom lived on nearby farms, carried diseases from the concentration camp to local people. Eventually a restrictive quarantine was placed on the villages of Gusen, Langenstein and Frankenberg. Of the 32 stricken in these communities, seven died. The SS cases numbered about 200, twenty-five of them fatal. The number of inmates who died from epidemics inside the camp reached into the thousands. Between 1941 and 1942 approximately 6,665 inmates died of epidemic diseases at CC Gusen. The epidemics of summer and autumn of 1941 alone killed 60 to 100 SS guards and 600 to 700 inmates.[255]

---

251 Kielich and Mills, 132
252 DEST-Monatsbericht Oktober 1941, BArch, NS 3/1346
253 Fernschreiben vom 7. Oktober 1940 an alle Stapo(Leit)Stellen betreffend Infektionskrankheiten im Arbeitslager Gusen. BArch, Z 11 1680 A.1.
254 Sagel-Grande, 163
255 Sagel-Grande, 205

*Figure 11: Soviet Prisoners of War arriving in CC Gusen I
(the SS Kitchen can be seen in the background), October 1941
Source: Museu d'Història de Catalunya*

However, survivors report that the SS, anxious to have even fewer typhoid victims, gassed 164 POWs in Barracks 32 in the spring of 1942.[256]

These statistics reveal the desperation in CC Gusen. In order to get the extremely dangerous epidemic under control, the SS began to use a spring in Weih (another location in the neighbouring community of Luftenberg). Chmielewski put SS Tech. Seargent Oskar Tandler in charge of the detail "Well Construction Weih" and it had been partially complete in April 1941.[257] The SS also extended the construction of the fresh water utility of St. Georgen. After examination of local wells, the well in the kindergarten of St. Georgen

---

[256] Kogon, Langbein, Choumoff, 181; Kielich and Mills, 50
[257] United States vs. Shuettauf, et al. Case No. 000-50-5-3, NARA Record Group 153 Entry 143 270/1/14-15/6-1 Box 12, 401

was condemned.[258] The SS ordered medical exams and vaccinations on a large scale for the residence of St. Georgen. Along with the construction of the houses, the SS also installed a small sewage treatment plant at St. Georgen. In CC Gusen itself a sewer system was built.[259] Prior to a sewage treatment plant going on line at a later date, Jews, whose life expectancy in CC Gusen was very brief, were used to "clean the pit of faeces and clear away the dung in big containers" from the washrooms. Sometimes they had to do it naked, depending on the mood of the SS.[260]

Complicating the terrible lack of hygiene in the barracks and the lack of water, towels, or soap was the fact that the showers and latrines were used to store the dead on their way to the crematorium.[261]

The high death rate did nothing to help DEST's permanent labor shortage in the Gusen quarries, especially in early 1942 when plans to extend the stone production at Gusen flagged for the lack of 2,500 slave workers. Only 1,200 of 2,000 new slaves requisitioned by DEST arrived at Gusen in April 1942. So DEST requested that Berlin send 2,000 more Poles from CC Auschwitz to CC Gusen to make the expansion of the quarries at Gusen possible. Finally, 1,000 of the "needed" 2,000 CC Auschwitz inmates were sent in May 1942.[262]

In October of 1941, Hitler had reversed the ban on using Soviet labor for construction, but out of 3,500,000 Soviet POWs, only 166,881 reached German concentration camps by March of 1942.[263] Ulrich Herbert writes in "Labor and Extermination" that Hitler's decision to murder all the Jews was based on the belief that the labor shortage would be solved by using Soviet and Polish POWs. But the labor shortage became so dire Hitler actually ordered Jews

---

[258] Klinger, Volksschulchronik, 145.

[259] The sewers at camp Gusen were constructed by Messrs. Urban & Zwanziger, a company of Munich. Dirk Riedel, „Privatunternehmer im KZ: Aufstieg einer Firma im NS-Staat", Dachauer Hefte, Nr. 19 (Sonderdruck), without date.

[260] Marsálek, Gusen, 32.

[261] Stefancic, Dusan. KL Gusen I and II and the production of Messerschmitt aircraft Bf. 109 and 262, unpublished manuscript, 13

[262] DEST-Monatsbericht April 1942 and DEST-Monatsbericht Juni 1942. BArch, NS 3/1347.

[263] Allen, Business, 166

"imported" into the Reich from which they had recently been deported.[264] However, if DEST was suddenly convinced of the necessity of using Jewish labour as a stop-gap measure before eradicating them, the SS guards had been trained too well to understand their "duty" to murder them, and so the slaughter continued in the stone quarries of CC Gusen I.

DEST was not the only business struggling with a labor shortage. Austria as a whole experienced a shortage, but Steyr-Daimler-Puch AG Director and SS-Brigadeführer Georg Meindl came up with a unique solution. Appointed by Göring, Meindl used his contacts with top Nazis in Austria, especially Higher SS and Police Leader of the Donau District Dr. Ernst Kaltenbrunner, who had already shown so much creativity with Austrian laws and who would soon succeed Reinhard Heydrich as Chief of the Reich Security Main Office (RSHA). Kaltenbrunner helped Meindl convince CC Mauthausen Commandant Ziereis to transfer prisoners to a satellite camp near his airplane engine factory in Steyr in spring 1942. Prior to this innovation, prisoners were not allowed to work further than they could walk and return from in one day.[265] The idea caught on. While Mauthausen had 49 official subcamps, by the end of the war countless businessmen had made special arrangements with Ziereis and his superiors, as head of all concentration camp labor in Austria. Toward the end of the war, American GIs would stumble across these small camps.

In early May 1945 near Wels, then Corporal and Artillery Liaison Non-Com Lyle Storey and his jeep driver and wireman Private Robert Sorensen, liaison scouts with the 608th Field Artillery Battalion of the 71st Infantry Division, came across several hundred starving men housed in tarpaper barracks within a barbed wire enclosure with a pile of bodies just inside the gate. "It is hard to describe the reaction of the inmates as we drove into the camp. I motioned to one to close the gate behind us as I was afraid that they might all explode into the town and gorge themselves on any food, which their weakened condition could not tolerate. Incapable of emotion, they milled around the Jeep, eyeing us with silent disbelief. Some reached out to touch

---

[264] Ulrich, 173-177
[265] Marsálek, Mauthausen [English], 19; Allen, Business, 170

our arms, unable to comprehend that their ordeal was over. There was one boy, about twelve years old, sucking on a brown piece of fat which appeared to be honeycombed with now empty cells." Sorensen managed to find a box with several dozens of eggs for the prisoners before the GIs returned to what was still dangerous duty, "knowing the woods still held scattered remnants of various German units, some still organized, although certainly not protecting camps like this one."

"Along the road lay several inmates. Having raided the kitchens of the homes across the road, they apparently died as the food hit their stomachs. One inmate died with his face buried in a red berry pie. I felt guilty for having allowed them to leave the compound, but also felt as Sorenson did: 'I'm not about to become the jailer for these poor people'."[266]

Asked if coming across such a camp was a common experience, Storey said, "My God, everyone seemed to be finding them."[267]

Although Allied Intelligence began receiving reports about jet fighter production in Austria from POWs and informants as early as October 1943,[268] information about concentration camp labor at such factories in the Reich began appearing with more exactness as air reconnaissance and ground intelligence improved.[269] In November 1944 the Fifteenth Air Force relayed the coordinates of hundreds of "known Prisoner of War" camps in German held territory to targeteers to ensure POWs were not bombed.

---

[266]   Lyle Storey, unpublished memoirs
[267]   Personal Interview, 24 December 2002
[268]   Summary of POW interrogation by American Foreign Service to Air Intelligence, 18 December 1943 AFHRA
[269]   Mediterranean Allied Air Forces Intelligence Section Interpretation Report No U.11 Austria 1 January 1945; MAAF 25220 1944 1020 995.999, Air Force Historical Research Agency [AFHRA] 510-3665

Figure 12: *Aerial reconnaissance view of CC Gusen I & II, 15 March 1945*
Source: United States Air Force Historical Research Agency

The camp Lyle Storey and Robert Sorensen uncovered may not have existed when the 1944 list was compiled, but the camps at St. Georgen are described. Camp #124 is named "Steyregg[sic]/Gusen." The coordinates and description are clearly of Gusen I and II. "This camp consists of 40 large huts very closely spaced in a rectangular area 350 yards approx. and surrounded by wire with 6 watchtowers. Not included in the enclosure are some 20 more huts [Gusen II]. Immediately adjoining is a stone quarry."

The coordinates and description of camp #125 correspond with CC Mauthausen, but the camp is mistakenly called "Steyregg[sic]/Langenstein." [270] For targeteers, the errors in the camps' names were irrelevant. From a half a mile up, correct coordinates were more important to bombardiers wishing to avoid killing their comrades-in-arms. But this confusion over Mauthausen's name would have tragic consequences for inmates and the American ground forces in the spring of 1945. The errors on this list would be repeated on another issued in March 1945. The errors may have contributed to the failure to prepare for the large numbers of camps that awaited ground troops in Austria.[271]

By spring 1945, the exact nature of the production at Bergkristall was known to the Allies based on both ground information and aerial reconnaissance, but a January 22, 1945 Interpretation Report for Underground Activity at Linz/St. Georgen reveals another confusion* regarding the names and locations of the camps. The report "covers three large complexes of underground and surface activity seen and examined on sorties available of St. Georgen, Gusen and Langenstein (not Langenstein/Halberstadt)."[272]

[270]   Mediterranean Allied Air Forces Intelligence Section, APO 520, US Army A-2 Division, 17 November 1944, [AFHRA] NOTE: #106 is Oswiecim (A) and Oswiecim (B) 670-616-1 AFHRA

[271]   Location of Known and Possible Prisoner of War Installations in Germany and Occupied Countries as Known to PWX-GI-Division, SHAEF, 18 March 1945, [AFHRA] 670-616-1

*   This confusion with another important Allied target at Langenstein, Germany, may explain why to date the information available on CC Gusen through the Simon Wiesenthal Multimedia Learning Center http://motlc.learningcenter.wiesenthal.org/pages/t028/t02822.html reports only one camp at Gusen and locates it in Germany rather than Austria.

[272]   22 January 1945 Interpretation Report for Underground Activity at Linz/St. Georgen, AFHRA

POWs and informants had provided the Allies with information about "large underground aircraft works...for the manufacture of Messersmidt [sic] fighters." However, since the Army Air Corps needed nine thousand 250-pound bombs to destroy a 60 x 100 foot target in World War II, and only fifty percent of those bombs were expected to fall within a 3300 foot radius (one half a mile), bombing targets close to POW camps was considered too risky by the Allied Command.[273] Bomber crews suffered the heaviest losses in the Air Corps and were most likely to end up as POWs.[274]

---

[273] Mills, Dennis. Air Force Historian, Personal Interview, 23 September 2004.
[274] Ross, Stewart Halsey. Strategic Bombing in the United States in World War II. (London: McFarland, 2003), 9

The War Forced DEST to Change Its Production

Despite increasing requests from German armament industrialists to use concentration camp labor, by the end of 1941 only 4,000 SS slaves worked in private armament factories while 10,000 continued to work for DEST enterprises.[275] At CC Gusen I, the quarries continued to be the focus of production. That winter, when cold weather slowed construction on the SS barracks, Victor Kielich was transferred from the relative safety of the plasterers' command back to the stone quarries where SS brutality made the work "chaotic and dangerous," Kielich reports. "I had to be on constant guard against being drawn into the columns of working Mussulmen."[**] While the Spanish prisoners recently released from quarantine caught the worst treatment of the SS guards in the quarries, Poles who had survived for some time in CC Gusen I were now in a position to help others. Victor explains how he used personal connections to get a safer job:

> For days I thought and schemed about how to get a job in the sheds near the quarry with the stonemason command. While delivering lumps of square granite to them, I had noticed not only a civilian supervising the masons, but, most appealing that winter, a round stove burning in each shed.

> While still selling firewood to the SS guards, I had met a Pole named John, from near Czempin, who supervised a small four man joinery shop near the quarry which made goods for both the camp and the quarry. Since he did jobs for many capos, John was a very important person. I thought he might know someone who could get me a job in the mason command. The day after I talked to him, he found me at work in the quarry and took me to Capo Tiger's quarters[***] Fortunately, Tiger did not remember nearly knocking my

---

[275] Allen, Business, 171

[**] "Muselman" was a term given to prisoners who had lost all hope of surviving. Marsálek writes that the word reflect these associations these prisoners' haulting walk and disassociation with prisoners' images of Muslims at prayer. Mauthausen [English], 355

[***] According to Kielich, Tiger's civilian name was Gustav Krutzky. He was a German criminal and also block-elder for Block 19. He was one of the most feared men in CC Gusen because he unscrupulously cooperated with the SS in murdering inmates. His second nickname was „Hölle" (Hell).

front teeth out some months earlier for having needles and a scrap of cloth in my bed.

Chief-Capo Tiger supervised all the capos in charge of the many small commands, each with a different title and job, within the Gusen quarry's work force. He could dismiss any one of them without hesitation. Without much discussion, Capo Tiger led me to one of the six masons' sheds and introduced me to Hanz, a German mason capo who wore the red triangle of a political prisoner. Tiger told Capo Hanz that if I did not work out, he could send me back to the quarry. Fortunately I had enough experience to know how to hold a club hammer. Stonemason-Capo Hanz took me to a lump of stone on a trestle and asked me to start working. Without hesitating, I grabbed the club hammer and chisel, chipping away at the stone. Hanz knew I was no professional, but my willingness to work impressed him. Besides, Tiger himself had brought me to the shed; thinking me a special person, he was more than happy to help.[276]

As a member of the stonemasons command (for which he would work until liberation), Victor was able to escape the terrible weather and the constant brutality of the SS guards and capos. As he explains here, the stonemason capos had a vested interest in the health of their commands:

Every shed had a capo who was not necessarily experienced at stone work. Since they wanted to meet their stone production quota, they showed more tolerance toward prisoner stonemasons than regular workers in the quarry. One civilian Meister, Mr. Gruber, a very kind Austrian, controlled the six sheds. He selected the best tradesman in each to be his assistant (Anlerner) with whom he would discuss how that shed's stonemasons were to make the stones. The assistant helped those less skilled at reading measurements and showed them how to start the stone. The capo's function was to deal with visiting SS and to ensure we processed a certain volume of stone.

---

[276]   Kielich and Mills, 43

Although by 1942 some in the Third Reich had grave misgivings about the war, according to Williamson Murray, *Strategy for Defeat: The Lufwaffe 1933 – 1945,* Rommel's success in North Africa left many Nazi military leaders enthusiastic through the spring and summer of 1942. That winter, however, Hitler's decisions caused both the Wehrmacht and the Luftwaffe to fight a war of attrition which proved catastrophic to both, especially in the battle for Stalingrad. Sixty-percent losses of fighters and bombers between November 1942 and May 1943 checked the confidence of many,[277] but the underground construction to protect armament manufacturing that resulted from these raids and continued up to the last moments of the war reveals how the "true believers" in the SS assumed final victory.

Himmler remained convinced, however, that Germany would win the war with Russia and resettle the East with German communities built by DEST. As a result, Oswald Pohl continued to consolidate control over concentration camp labor. On 3 March 1942 the Inspectorate of Concentration Camps became Office Group D-IKL under Oswald Pohl, now Chief of the SS Business Administrative Office (Wirtschaftsverwaltungshauptamt [WVHA]). Two weeks later armaments officials met with IKL officials and agreed that any armament factories wanting to use slave labor would have to relocate to concentration camps, where the original firm would supervise production. Interestingly, CC Mauthausen/Gusen was not on the list of concentration camps made available to armament firms at this meeting.[278] This omission perhaps explains why the reorganizations the SS underwent in early 1942 did not directly affect St. Georgen residents until mid-1943, although other reforms that Pohl undertook would affect CC Gusen prisoners. Marsálek notes that on 16 March 1942, perhaps at the same meeting, Speer's new Department for Armaments met for the first time. Otto Saur, reported a directive from Hitler to devote concentration camp labor to armament production, but then SS General Richard Glücks reported that CC Mauthausen had only 600 workers suitable for armament production despite there being at the time 5,500 prisoners in CC Mauthausen and 6,000 in CC Gusen I.[279] This

---

[277] Murray, 147-163
[278] Allen, Business, 170-177, Marsálek, Mauthausen, 20 ff
[279] Marsálek, 19, 126

low number of "suitable" prisoners offered suggests that Glücks either didn't know the actual number of prisoners at these camps or wanted to cooperate with Himmler's plans to focus labor on stone production.

Himmler's plans were not allowed to proceed without interference, however. In May 1942, Armaments Minister Speer ordered DEST to halt its large brick factory at Prambachkirchen (40 km west of Linz). The factory was designed to produce 30 million bricks per year and was already equipped with most modern machinery.[280] Kaltenbrunner had taken a particular interest in brick production at Prambachkirchen as well as establishing a timber industry in Austria. When Reinhard Heydrich died in June 1942, Himmler began to consider Kaltenbrunner for head of the RSHA. Himmler told Pohl of this decision in December. Kaltenbrunner authorized arrests, both individual and mass, and decided lengths of sentence. He was also responsible for transporting prisoners to camps. His disregard for the fate of Slovenes, Czechs and Slavs, not to mention Jews, was notorious.[281]

By 1942 some residents of St. Georgen had grown accustomed to the presence of their new neighbours, men who daily wielded life-and-death power over thousands of prisoners. In private life these same neighbors could be quite cordial to those whom they presumed possessed the desired genetic make-up and ideological outlook. Some St. Georgens received invitations to evening programs planned for SS and DEST personnel by the "Kraft durch Freude" (Strength Through Joy) organization. The St. Georgen gym was converted to a cinema or recreation center for such occasions, and St. Georgen's main square was used for formal gatherings of the SS.

Maria F.'s background did not qualify her for these evenings out. She became familiar with SS families under different circumstances; she took in their laundry and cleaned their homes to supplement her husband's army pay and her job at the brick factory. But with her mother thirty kilometers away in Gutau, with no one to help her with the baby or the three year old, she was exhausted. One day her landlord, Rudolf P., overheard her complaining. His

---

[280] DEST-Monatsbericht Mai 1942, BArch NS 3/1347, Marsálek, 20
[281] Black, 112 ff

response reflected his view of her place and the place of her children in the new world the National Socialists were building in St. Georgen: "You were born just to work."[282]

Figure 13: St. Georgen market place was decorated for official SS-events, c. 1940 Source: AHDG; Collection Franz Walzer

Other families continued to experience the Nazi presence and influence more ominously. On Christmas day, 1942, Heinrich B., the railway station worker who had reported the Nazi stationmaster eight years before for shooting the cross off the wall of the St. Georgen station, returned after four years in Dachau and Flossenbürg.[283] His punishment, and that of his family, was not over. He was ridiculed for being a "KZ-ler," a concentration-camp prisoner,

---

[282] Personal Interview, Maria F., 21 September 2000
[283] Heinrich B., Bericht. Die Nationalsozialistische Tätigkeit in Österreich in der Zeit 1933/34 bis 1938. In the possesion of the author.

111

and his family would long be reminded of his "shame" for standing up for his faith.[284]

In the summer of 1942 a harbor was planned for the junction of the Danube and Gusen Rivers. The Stöhr Company from Hamburg cleared trees from the forested riverbanks and added new barracks to CC Gusen for the "Kommando Hafenbau" (Harbor Construction Command).[285] Interest in restructuring local rivers began in the 1940s. At that time, when CC Gusen guards had asked prisoners gathered on Roll Call Square if any of them were masons, Joe C. had volunteered. He was taken to the Gusen River to build a channel using natural stone. Joe had never done any masonry, but his experience with volunteering for other jobs had taught him such work was a source of extra food, so he gambled he would be able to use a trowel convincingly enough to fool the SS guard. Fortunately, he reports, the guards overseeing the work command near the river had no experience with masonry either. Joe and his fellow prisoners made a show of placing stones carefully and then tapping them with their trowels as they had seen masons do in their hometowns before the war. Because this job was done for the SS rather than local civilians, however, he received little extra food to relieve the dysentery from which he suffered after several months in the camp, worsened by the addition of grass and garbage prisoners foraged along the riverbanks. Nor did working for DEST insure better treatment: on this work command Joe received the beating, described earlier, for "slacking." Overcome with dysentery, he had stopped work to find a place to relieve himself.[286]

The guard might very well have killed him with impunity regardless of the effect it would have had on the project. This incident also shows the lack of qualified oversight provided to work details by the Neubauleitung (New Construction Directorate for Camp Gusen). While the guard knew nothing about masonry and so could not evaluate the quality of Joe's work, he understood, and fulfilled, his duty to torture the prisoner.

---

[284] 7 May 2004. Interview in possession of author.
[285] Klinger, Volksschulchronik, 145
[286] Personal Interview, 7 May 2004

Disturbed by what such scenes of abuse were doing to construction projects (not prisoners), in 1942 Oswald Pohl again initiated reforms meant to improve production. In June 1942, SS-Obersturmbannführer Gerhard Maurer now headed the new Office Group D II, Labor Action.[287] As mentioned earlier, Maurer was the former Executive Manager of DEST who had sold part of the DEST property for CC Gusen I in Gusen to HAHB. In his new capacity, he would continue his acquaintance with St. Georgen, touring the local concentration camps on 7 July 1942 with the commandant of CC Struthof.[288]

Another indication that Maurer and Mummenthey were invested in the success of the DEST enterprises at St. Georgen is the DEST personel file of Josef Latzel, a graduate of the "Silesian State College for Stone Processing." A highly trained quarry specialist, Latzel first contacted Stonemasonry Foreman Rudolf Ronge about work at the "Granite Works Mauthausen at St. Georgen." (Ronge left in 1943 for the new St. Georgen DEST quarries in Bohemia). Both Maurer and Mummenthey used their influence to pressure the district labor exchange office in Silesia to release Latzel to move to "Mauthausen". DEST actually managed to exchange Latzel for two former employees of the Silesian firm G. Frank und Brüder after first securing their release from the Wehrmacht. Latzel's employment with DEST did not protect him from being drafted, however, into the German Navy. In order to keep their employee, the WVHA recruited him as a private in the SS.[289]

Maurer made use of the Labor Action Leader (Arbeitseinsatzführer) that Burböck had introduced into each camp, a position that remained ineffective, however, because it was still subordinate to the camp commandant. The decisions about the allocation of labor and the survival of prisoners continued to be at the whim and ideological understanding of the camps' administrators.[290]

---

[287]   Allen, Business, 179

[288]   Bernadac, Christian. „Rapport d´activité No. 2", Deportation 1933/1945, Vol. 3 (Paris: France-Empire, 1993), 840

[289]   NARA RG 549 Entry 290 59/5/4 JAG War Crimes Cases Tried

[290]   Allen, Business, 179 ff

Maurer's contribution to the effort to modernize SS business practices was to provide "standardized, statistical surveillance as a means of centralized control" to track labor and coordinate its use through preprinted standardized forms. Unlike Burböck's office, which never knew where prisoners were working or how many prisoners there were, Maurer's office made it possible to communicate this information between labor sites. However, fervent Nazi that he was, Maurer collected data almost exclusively about the physical condition of prisoners. Where Burböck's reforms made selections specifically for murder in "Operation 14 f 13" possible, Maurer's innovations allowed eugenics to figure even further in the daily operation of the camps. Prisoners unfit for work were not only murdered as a matter of duty to keep the state from having to support "useless eaters," they were now murdered to improve production by improving the "human material" doing the labor. Thus, the medical staff of concentration camps became increasingly involved in selections for both immediate extermination and extermination by labor.[291]

In *IBM and the Holocaust,* Martin Black states that "The SS Economics Administration, which had total operational control of all camps, could supply exactly the skilled workers required and transfer people from camp to camp, and factory to factory, by setting the dials of their Hollerith systems that had stored the details of all inmate cards."[292] While this possibility may have been intended as a result of using Hollerith machines (as Black claims) or card files (as Allen writes) to record and sort data on inmates, the reality for CC Gusen survivors indicates that while increasing attention was paid to a prisoner's suitability for or previous work experience in a job, genocide and murder remained the top priority for camp administrators, who continued to have the final say over how labor was to be allocated and how prisoners were to be selected for it. Black's claim that the system, however murderous, was well run and that exact and accurate records were kept on all prisoners, and that these records were used when selecting prisoners for certain work,[293] does not appear to be true at Gusen I through 1943, according to survivors' experiences. While records were used more consistently later (after the

---

[291]   Ibid., 179-190
[292]   Black, Martin. IBM and the Holocaust, (New York: Crown, 2001), 61
[293]   Ibid., 85

Bergkristall construction began), in 1943 contacts with important prisoners seemed to be more valuable. Of course, the ability to recognize an opportunity at a time when one still possessed the strength to act seems to always be present in survivors' testimonies, but as CC Gusen I developed and certain long surviving prisoners became part of the administrative functioning of the detention camp, personal contacts remained key to survival.

In 1940, in the earliest stage of CC Gusen I's development when no group of prisoners had any influence (other than the capos who tended to be German habitual criminals),[294] Joe C. secured work away from the dreaded quarry through personal initiative alone – volunteering whenever the SS asked for skilled workers. A year later, Victor Kielich used personal contacts to join the stonemasons command, where he worked until the liberation. In 1943 Gusen I survivor Pierre Serge Choumoff also relied on this combination of personal initiative and contacts to avoid the quarries. A member of the French Underground, Choumoff was arrested in 1942. At Ft. Romainville outside Paris, the Gestapo compiled an alphabetical list of prisoners to be shot in a reprisal against insurgent activities. The misspelling of Choumoff's name with an "S" rather than a "C" spared him, however (a story that accurately conveys the importance of luck, or providence, as some would have it, in determining who survived). Deported as a Night and Fog[*] prisoner to Mauthausen in 1943 and then to Gusen I, Choumoff reports that years after being in the system he was able to volunteer as experienced in maintaining hydraulic drills, much as Joe C. and Victor Kielich had volunteered as experienced craftsmen. Mr. Choumoff had never used experience using a drill, but the ruse earned him better working conditions in the Steyr factory barracks: he ran the shop which sharpened the drill bits for tunnel construction, thus allowing him to avoid the quarries. Eventually he worked in the electricians' command, a job he got on the recommendation of another inmate.[295] If Mr.

---

[294]   Marsálek, Mauthausen [English], 52
[*]   The Nacht und Nebel (Night and Fog) decree in September 1941 ordered that suspicious persons who were not shot immediately under Action K (K being an abbreviation for Kugel, or bullet) could be deported to camps without notification to their families. Deborah Dwork, ed. Voices and Views: A History of the Holocaust, 124. Marsálek, Mauthausen [English], 354
[295]   Personal Interview, 7 May 1998

Choumoff had a card in Maurer's system, it was either not consulted or these skills were added to it long after his arrest and deportation.

In 2005, Mr. Choumoff explained that the Hollerith cards and the personnel cards were kept in two different offices and not consulted together. That cards were used for several different purposes and kept in various locations at Gusen is clear from post-war investigations and trials. At Gusen, as revealed in the Dachau War Crimes testimony of Waffen-SS Sergeant Wilhelm Grill, the prisoner post office also possessed cards on all prisoners. With exceptions for the most reviled prisoners like Jews and Night-and-Fog prisoners, families could send food packages to their loved ones parcel post. Survivor Stefancic reports that by his arrival at Gusen in September 1944 mail could only be written in the German language and sent to and from Germany.[296] Parcels were another matter.

According to Grill's testimony, by 1943 the Reichsbahn could not handle the volume of packages, 700 to 800 a day, so Gusen I was given its own mail car. Every morning, including Sunday, the car arrived directly at the camp from the station at St. Georgen. Another interesting detail revealed at the trial is that, according to Grill, "From the moment the mail car was opened until the time the last parcel was disposed of, always a civilian employee of the German Post Office, of the Austrian post office at St. Georgen was present."[297] The parcels were first taken to the SS mailroom outside the camp and checked with the parcel post receipts. Here the parcels were "sorted," which, as those testifying against Grill report, meant that the best food items were pilfered by the SS for their own use. Parcels were then loaded on a large vehicle and brought through the gates of the Jourhaus to the parcel mailroom, a single room in Block 2 reserved for the "censoring" of prisoner mail and packages. The parcels were unloaded and "all parcel post cards went through the filing system of the camp office." The camp post office had cards on all inmates who were permitted to write and receive mail. Grill also received daily reports on prisoners who had died or were transferred "to outside details."

---

[296] Stefancic, 12
[297] Shuettauf et. al., 328, 376 Summarized for the Gusen Memorial Digital Archive Project by Pima Community College student Rocklyn Winchester

Unfortunately, these cards were not secured after liberation. Another group of cards were found, however, by the Review of Activities Report written in June 1945 for the Legal Division of the US Army. The team arrived at Mauthausen on 17 May 1945. Despite having been told by Lt. Col. Seibel of the 11th Armored Division that most SS records had been burned, the men discovered "Haeftlinge-Personel-Karte" [sic] in an SS Barracks which they believed were for "all camps and work camps within the Mauthausen group of camps."[298] It's doubtful, however, that these were complete, however, as Exhibit P in the report states that the number of prisoners released from Mauthausen at liberation was 12,634 and from Gusen 3,765. Apparently no cards were found for Gusen II.[299] As these numbers are tens of thousands short of the actual population of the camps at the end of the war, we can readily assume the cards were not complete. Whether these were Hollerith cards is not clear from the description.

Russian Gusen I survivor Fjodor Solodovnik's story is illustrative of one way Hollerith cards were used in 1944. Deported for slave labor as a young teenager, he escaped from a farm near Dresden, Germany in August 1942. After being recaptured, Solodovnik was sent to CC Gross-Rosen and then to CC Gusen I via Mauthausen in January 1943, where he worked in the quarries. By March his weight was reduced to 44 kilograms. Fortunately, he became acqainted with another Russian prisoner, Peter Popek, a Lagerläufer (a prisoner running within the camp to deliver messages) who managed to get him transferred to the Steyr factory where he worked on a milling machine. In spring 1944, Peter managed to change the occupation on his friend's Hollerith card to read "electrician" rather than "student." Mr. Solodovnik was transferred to the electricians' command where he worked with Mr. Choumoff until the liberation.[300]

[298] NARA AG 254 Detention and Internment Camps USGCC Record Group 260 39.40.17.02
[299] Ibid.
[300] Biographical notes of Fjodor Solodovnik in possession of author.

Figure 14: *Barracks of the Construction Directorate of Waffen-SS*
and Police at Gusen, c. 1942
Source: Museu d´Història de Catalunya

For these survivors, personal contacts within the camp meant more than their real professional experience. Black proves that exact information was kept on some prisoners, and while there was the possibility to record each prisoner's profession on the "Inmate Cards" kept at D II's Central Inmate File,[301] the experience of many prisoners at this time in Gusen I does not reflect that this system was always used to match labor and laborer. Later, however, when the work commands were being formed at Bergkristall, much more attention seems to be given to identifying and exploiting skilled prisoners.

---

[301] Black, Martin, 361

Concurrently with Maurer's attempts at reform, Dr.-Ing. Hans Kammler reorganized the Neubauleitung (New Construction Directorates). Not only were they responsible to him rather than the camps' commandant, but, as mentioned earlier, he also attempted to install SS men whose SS rank was equal or superior to the Death's Head SS camp command staff. Above the Construction Directors placed within each camp, he created Central Construction Directorates, (Zentralbauleitungen or ZBLs). The ZBLs would assign projects to the New Construction Directorates who then appointed staff for specific sites (Baustellen) and then under them directors for specific jobs. This plan allowed supervision of job sites by technically-qualified personnel. Furthermore, at the ZBL level, there was a great deal of flexibility and inter-changeability. Managers could go from site to site, wherever needed and observe the use of labor, time, and materials. Previously, the separate New Construction Directorates within each camp were not administratively linked to one another and were accountable only to the commandant.[302]

For prisoners, jobs within valued commands continued to be safer than work commands requiring unskilled labor. While the ZBLs would apparently take some advantage of the information provided about prisoners' skills, eugenics continued to play an important role in determining prisoners' chances of survival. Karl Littner, the welder from CC Gross-Rosen's experience arriving in the winter transport from Buchenwald attests to the vulnerability of even skilled prisoners among the most hated groups. Unlike many other top Nazis, Kammler didn't care whose labor he exploited, but until a Jew or Russian or other hated prisoner secured a job in a skilled command, he was still at the mercy of the guards whose murderous agenda remained unchanged.

Increasingly, accommodations were made at CC Gusen I for arms manufacturers. A new workshop hall was erected for a repair shop of Feldzeugkommando XVII Wien (the Army Arsenal Authorities of Vienna) in the area north of the "Industriehof" (an assembly of several barracks belonging to the administration of CC Mauthausen/Gusen housing the warehouse for prisoners'

---

[302] Allen, Business, 148-155

belongings and workshops of the camp administrators like joiners, tailors, etc.). The command "Rüstung Wien" had 234 prisoners after 23 February 1943 when a corresponding contract was signed between DEST and Feldzeugkommando XVII Wien.[303] Artillery carriages and fighting vehicles were delivered to CC Gusen by the hundreds from throughout the Reich, arriving from the direction of Linz and Güstrow at the railway station in St. Georgen on 23 February 1943. In the beginning of March 1943 more gun carriages arrived by train from Neu-Ulm, Posen, Güstrow and Warsaw.[304]

Some no-longer-needed stonemason halls were converted into a carbine factory for Steyr-Daimler-Puch AG who first leased them in spring 1942,[305] although the official agreement was signed between DEST and Steyr-Daimler-Puch AG for the Gusen facilities on 30 April 1943. By March 1943, the essential machines for armament production at CC Gusen had been delivered and installed. By the end of 1943, 1,308 prisoners were employed on 9,000 square meters in production halls for Steyr-Daimler-Puch AG at Gusen. Most of the 18 halls leased to Steyr-Daimler-Puch AG were erected in 1943 exclusively for Steyr-Daimler-Puch by DEST for RM 166.300. Additionally Steyr-Daimler-Puch paid RM 49.475 rent each year and RM 12.080 for administrative costs beginning on 1 February 1943 and 1 July 1943 respectively.[306]

CC Gusen's prisoners would produce countless barrels and components for submachine guns, assault rifles, carbines, and components for the aircraft engine Daimler-Benz 605 in halls code named "Georgenmühle I, II, III and IV." In the first half-year of 1943, Steyr-Daimler-Puch AG produced at its different plants – CC Gusen being one of them – 372 aircraft engines (type DB 605), which were mainly used in the fighter plane Messerschmitt (Me)

---

[303] DEST-Geschäftsbericht 1943, BArch NS 3/1168/48 and 54. This command specialized in the repair and overhaul of artillery carriages. Klinger, Volksschulchronik, 147.
[304] Wagenkontrollbücher des Bahnhofes St. Georgen für die Güterabfertigung. Deutsche Reichsbahn, unpublished. Now in the possession of the Austrian Federal Railways.
[305] Affidavit Otto Walther.
[306] DEST-Geschäftsbericht 1943. BArch NS 3/1168/56.

109, as well as the K98 carbine, the MG 42 machine gun and the MP 44 automatic assault rifle.[307]

The SS and DEST may have planned bomb-proof production facilities for these "Georgen-Mühle" work commands as early as spring 1942. According to an interoffice memo, there was already an "air force command St. Georgen/ Gusen at the concentration camp of Mauthausen/Gusen" on 23 August 1942. The (Sankt) Georgenmühle I was reportedly the first production command transferred into the partly finished tunnel construction at Kellerbau. Work command "Georgenmühle I" was later renamed "Georgenmühle II."[308] These shifts in code names have confounded researchers for years, but understanding them is essential to the history of the Gusen camps.

As Victor Kielich reports, the change in production also caused a shift in prisoner working conditions and relations:

> When machinery of all kinds was ready to install in the completed new barracks, tradesmen were immediately recruited in the camp to man the new factories. At this time, a huge new hall was also erected in Gusen Quarry to accommodate stonemasons who had been working in the wooden barracks. We were grouped in the new building as we had been in the wooden barracks: first, Spaniards; second and third group, mixed nationalities; fourth, our group under Capo Hanz; fifth, Capo Prusinowski's group, and finally Capo Halupka's group. Working in the huge open hall in the middle of the quarry, we had difficulty organizing extra food. Ignac's bread [he worked in the bakery] had more obstacles to navigate on the way into the camp. A short time later my contact with Ignac ended. Still, we had a new chief-capo, a good man, directing all capos in the stonemasons' commando. Mr. Gruber appointed me an assistant (Anlerner) responsible for thirty men, which entitled

---

[307] Schausberger, Norbert. Rüstung in Österreich 1938 – 1945, Publikationen des Österreichischen Instituts für Zeitgeschichte und des Instituts für Zeitgeschichte der Universität Wien, Vol. 8 (Vienna: Verlag Brüder Hollinek, 1970), 120 and 147 and Marsálek, Gusen, 8 and Rief, Silvia. „Wir schmieden das Schwert: Arbeits- und Alltagserfahrungen eines Rüstungsarbeiters im Zweiten Weltkrieg, Steyr-Daimler-Puch AG, Werk Letten und Konzentrationslager Gusen" (Diplomarbeit, Universität Wien, 1996).

[308] Letzeburger, 350.

me to an extra bowl of soup at midday, somewhat compensating me for the loss of Ignac's bread.[309]

Figure 15: *The former DEST canteen building at St. Georgen.*
It was adapted for school purposes in 1950 and pulled down in 2002, 1989
Source: Rudolf A. Haunschmied

Along with the detainees' labor transferred from stone production, constructing weapons required many highly-qualified civilians who lived in barracks and makeshift structures thrown up in the vicinity of St. Georgen and Gusen. In April 1943 the first of such wooden barracks was set up near the main administration center at St. Georgen as a canteen to feed about 600 employees of DEST. In spite of having the street number 164 in St. Georgen, it was situated where the music school was in the 1980s. On 4 November

---

1944 that barracks burned down and was replaced by a brick building, which existed until 2002.[310]

To this day, older people recall the canteen's "chief cook" Walther Thiemann (born on 19 July 1901 in Hamburg) who was ordered to set fire to the barracks by the SS to cover all traces of misappropriation of the food. Thiemann was then imprisoned in an attempt to cover up the conspiracy by SS-Hauptsturm-führer (R) Fritz Seidler, Schutzhaftlagerführer I of CC Gusen after May 1943. Presumably Seidler killed him during an interrogation. The "official" cause of his death is stated as suicide committed in the prisoner's cell on 16 November 1944.[311]

By March 1943 a new railway line to the intended port basin stretched through the village of Gusen. The harbor construction project which was started in summer 1942 was halted by Reich Minister of Armament and War Production Speer personally. Albert Speer remembered this harbor project in his trial at the Nuremberg International Military Tribunal on 19 June 1946 but subsumed his actual visit to Gusen once more with "Mauthausen".[312] Speer, Professor Porsche, Gauleiter Eigruber and the general manager of Reichswerke Hermann Göring visited the "SS production facilities at Mauthausen" (which were in Gusen) and other important strategic plants in Upper Austria and Styria from 30 March until Friday, 2 April 1943. After finishing his tour, Speer flew directly to Obersalzberg, only to leave for Linz at midnight on Saturday, 3 April 1943 with Hitler, where Speer and Hitler made "Besichtigungen" (visits).[313]

There is no record of what Hitler and Speer discussed, but if they discussed St. Georgen, it would not have been Hitler's only discussion about the area.

---

[310] Erlaubnisurkunde des Landrates des Kreises Perg Zahl: II/G/243-1942 vom 14.4.1943 betreffend den Betrieb einer Werksküchenkantine durch DEST, Gemeindarchiv St. Georgen and Chronik des k.K. Gendarmeriepostens Sankt Georgen an der Gusen.
[311] Chronik des k.K. Gendarmeriepostens Sankt Georgen an der Gusen, 4 November 1944.
[312] Albert Speer, Interrogation. Trial of the Major War Criminals before the Nuremberg International Military Tribunal, 19 June 1946
[313] Chronik der Dienststellen des Reichsministers Speer 1943. BArch, R3/1777/69-71. Klinger, Volkschulchronik, 146

According to his boyhood friend, August Kubizek, Hitler stayed near St. Georgen and Gusen for several days around 1904 while a student at "Realschule" at Linz. Hitler was researching the murder of 300 people during the Thirty Years' War on the Frankenberg Mountain. The victims, murdered on order of the Emperor, were members of a Protestant sect led by Martin Aichinger, a local farmer from nearby Luftenberg. The few survivors of the battle, Aichinger and his 4-year-old son among them, were executed in front of some 30,000 spectators on the main square of Linz on 20 June 1636.[314]

If Hitler's interest had broadened beyond those of his school years, then Speer had Hitler's support when, on 5 April 1943, he accused Himmler of inexpedient use of the prisoner labor. In April Speer announced that, to succeed, the war economy required all detainees be incorporated into armament manufacture, thus rendering the highest efficiency at the lowest cost. Despite the changes in production at Mauthausen and Gusen, Speer was apparently not satisfied. About one month later, he again challenged Himmler regarding his use of labor. Consequently, DEST was ordered to lower granite production in the Gusen and Wienergraben quarries.[315]

Even so, stone production continued on a more limited basis at CC Gusen in 1943, where DEST exploited 2,800 slave workers in the quarries while only 1,200 were assigned to the Wienergraben Quarry, once more illustrating how much more active were the Gusen quarries.[316]

Eventually, however, prisoner labor was made available to the growing armament production in the camps. By June 1943, DEST had already partially halted granite production in the quarries at Concentration Camps Flossenbürg[317] and Mauthausen as well as Gusen and started producing components and whole fuselages for the Me 109 fighter plane.[318] In June 1943, DEST had four large

---

[314] August Kubizek, Adolf Hitler mein Jugendfreund. Graz, Leopold Stocker Verlag, 2002, 35
[315] Marsálek, Mauthausen, 23
[316] Affidavit Otto Walther
[317] Already by 5 February 1943 at CC Flossenbürg, DEST used 200 prisoners from their stone-production for Messerschmitt aircraft production. In March 1944 the number of inmates employed in the aircraft production rose to 2.200. DEST-Geschäftsbericht 1943. BArch, NS 3/1168/12.
[318] Marsálek, Mauthausen, 94.

production halls dedicated to Messerschmitt at CC Gusen[319] where 26 Me 109 aircraft fuselages and pairs of wings were produced per day later on in 1944. Detainees riveted them on building cradle assembly lines with air hammers. Fixtures were not attached to the Me 109 fuselages, but they were painted in CC Gusen.[320] One Gusen inmate, Franciszek Julian Znamirowski who signed his art with "F.Z.," painted a folio of pictures for his foreman with the paint used on Me 109. One painting shows Znamirowski's manager, a Messerschmitt engineer, smoking a pipe and gazing wistfully out of a barracks window.[321]

Figure 16: Foreman of Messerschmitt Command at Gusen.
Painting by Francisek Julian Znamirowksi, 1944
Source: Reinhard Hanausch

---

[319]   Lageplan der Steinbrüche Gusen, Kastenhof und Pierbauer, 15 June 1943.
[320]   Interview 881120. Transcript in the possession of the author.
[321]   Painting in possession of Reinhard Hanausch.

From the summer of 1943 on CC Gusen and St. Georgen would experience rapid change after Speer and Kammler, and perhaps Hitler as well, began discussing Upper Austria as a preferred site for underground installations.[322]

---

[322]   Neufeld, Michael. The Rocket and the Reich (New York: Freepress, 1995), 200

The Nazis' Loss of Air Superiority Accelerated the Allies' Military Success

For decades, historians, relying on the USSBS Air Craft Industry Report [ACIR], have generally assumed attempts to disperse the aircraft industry followed the time line and pattern that leading Nazis reported in post-war interrogations. According to the ACIR, the official order to disperse was given in 1944, which resulted in a "scattering" of the aircraft industry into small factories. The ACIR discusses dispersal to underground mines (where slave labor is not reported to have been used to create factory space) and to "forest factories." The Messerschmitt Company itself provided the USSBS with a comparison of their underground plant at Kematen (45,000 sq ft) and a forest factory at Gauting (60,000 sq ft). The report shows the forest factory better in all ways and, USSBS concludes, "The success of forest factories is demonstrated by the fact that the exact location of none of them was discovered." By this measure the Kellerbau Tunnel complex (built in Langenstein near the Meierhof and north of Gusen I in 1943) and the Bergkristall Tunnels (built in St. Georgen beginning in 1944) are clearly superior, as they do not appear in the report at all.[323]

However, five months before construction on the first Kellerbau tunnel began, a DEST map dated 15 June 1943 shows the layout of the complex in the hills northeast of CC Gusen I, indicating that the area of St. Georgen and Gusen had been considered early on for an underground armament dispersal site of the aircraft industry.[324] In a post-war interview, Speer reported that underground dispersal was first seriously considered in 1943 but too few manufacturers were willing to relocate underground.[325] Prof. Dr.-Ing. Messerschmitt, however, complained that he had wanted to place his factories underground in 1935 but received no support from the government (because of the expense) or from the Luftwaffe (whom he characterized as

---

[323] United States Strategic Bombing Survey: Aircraft Division Industry Report, 24-31. While St. Georgen an der Gusen is identified on an USSBS map of Messerschmitt GmbH as the location of a subcontractor, no mention of either tunnels or production is made in the report.
[324] Lageplan der Steinbrüche Gusen, Kastenhof und Pierbauer, 15 June 1943
[325] 15 May 1945 Interview No. 11 USSBS AFHRA

"overconfident").[326] Apparently, Summer 1942 changed their minds. The oldest available draft layout of the Bergkristall underground plant dates back to August 1942.[327] Not inconsquently, at this time nearby Linz adopted the cities first air raid precautions[328] and Prof. Messerschmitt made his first request for concentration camp inmates to be used on the assembly of one of his aircraft, the Me-323 planes at Leipheim.[329]

Much has been written about the effects of the British Bomber Command's raids on German cities in 1943, particularly the raids on Hamburg in July which killed 30 – 40,000 civilians, shaking many Germans' confidence in the Luftwaffe's ability to protect them. The Luftwaffe itself, already shaken by the huge loss of aircraft suffered by mid-1943, was further alarmed by the 17 August 1943 American "strategic bombing" of Messerschmitt GmbH Regensburg's air armament center.[330] One hour into the next day, the British bombed the German rocket development center at Peenemünde.[331] Although underground dispersal of government projects like the A4 rocket (later renamed the V2)* became a priority for Hitler, armament and aircraft companies were told it was their responsibility to locate dispersal sites.[332]

On 22 August 1943 Himmler, with Hitler's full approval, put Hans Kammler (still chief of Office C-Construction in the WVHA) in charge of "Sonderstab Kammler" (a "Special Staff" or special operations command) to ensure the serial production of the A4 rocket. Although the Sonderstab functioned within Speer's ministry, Kammler structured it as he had the SS Building Inspectorate

---

[326] 11 – 12 May 1945 Interview No. 6 USSBBS 137.315-6 AFHRA

[327] Draft layout of Bergkristall "Magistrat Linz AB. 3" (in the possession of the author). This draft layout is accompanied by a file card of "Luftwaffenkommando St. Georgen/Gusen" dated with 23 August 1942.

[328] LS-Führerprogramm. Deckungsgräben – Korrespondenz A-Z. B0029 n. Archive of the City of Linz.

[329] Peter Schmoll, Die Messerschmitt-Werke im Zweiten Weltkrieg. Mittelbayerische Druck- & Verlags-Gesellschaft. Regensburg 1998, 98.

[330] Murray, 171 ff and Vilsmeyer, Gabriele. Der Flugplatz Obertraubling (Obertraubling, 1976) and Letter of the City of Neutraubling of 23 December 1988 to the author.

[331] Neufeld, 197

 *   Aggregat 4 (Aggregate 4) rocket would later be renamed the Vergeltungswaffe (V)2 (Retaliation Weapon No. 2)

[332] United States Strategic Bombing Survey Aircraft Industry Report, 83

within Office C in the WVHA. The two remained separate, however. Like the Central Construction Inspectorates' (ZBLs) authority over the New Construction Directorates in each camp, the Special Force Kammler, headquartered in Construction Bureau Kammler in Berlin, oversaw SS-Sonderinspektionen (SS Special Inspectorates) throughout the entire Reich. These in turn had authority over local SS-Führungsstäbe (Leadership Staffs).

Thus, "SS-Sonderinspektion IV" at Vienna was responsible for SS-Führungsstab Zement (Ebensee-Zement), B8 (St. Georgen-Bergkristall) and B9 (Melk-Quarz). Like the ZBLs, the Sonderinspektion allowed flexibility and inter-changeability of managers, allowing Kammler to appoint a competent technician to direct specific aspects at multiple construction sites.[333] Although Kammler was formally RFSS Himmler's subordinate, he enjoyed the interest and support of Hitler, who personally asked him to build air raid shelters just 15 kilometers west of St. Georgen for the City of Linz. Along with his projects at St. Georgen, Melk and Ebensee, on behalf of WVHA – Amtsgruppe C, Kammler worked on the air raid shelters with Hitler's personal architect Generalbaurat Prof. Hermann Giesler and Zentralbauleitung der Waffen-SS und Polizei Linz (Central Construction Directorate for the Waffen-SS and Police Linz). To achieve this goal, 300 well-qualified prisoners were sent by Pohl and Kammler to Linz from Mauthausen and Gusen where they formed Aussenlager Linz II.[334] Sonderstab Kammler could expect cooperation from experts of the Wehrmacht and the Luftwaffe. Additionally, he had already received Himmler's permission to hire private engineers when the SS could not offer a qualified engineer or technician. Furthermore, since both the New Construction Directorates within concentration camps and the local Leadership Staffs were directly responsible to him alone, he was able to illicit cooperation at an unprecedented level from all those involved in construction projects using slave labor. He had civil engineers within the camp system and technical expertise at the construction sites. The one group who would never fully cooperate with Kammler's system would be the SS camp command staff and most career SS guards who continued to find opportunities to murder

---

[333] Allen, Business, 147
[334] Schreiben Pohls an RFSS vom 7.2.1944 und von Pohl unterzeichneter Bericht Kammlers vom 18.2.1944, BArch, Microfilm No. 3344

prisoners regardless of their value to production. A distinction should be made here between career SS guards and the Volkssturm˙ and Luftwaffe units which supplemented the guard units as the younger SS were drafted to the front. While some prisoners report these guards were less fanatical or cruel,[335] there is nevertheless evidence that other former Luftwaffe members committed crimes at the SS-projects of St. Georgen and Gusen. Three former Luftwaffe members were sentenced at the Dachau Mauthausen trials for crimes committed at St. Georgen or Gusen.[336]

Kammler is best known for having directed slave labor in the construction of the tunnels at Concentration Camp Dora-Mittelbau, a subcamp of Buchenwald, where the A4 rocket program was moved after the bombing of Peenemünde. Kammler's name is also associated with another subcamp of Mauthausen, Ebensee, whose slaves constructed tunnels for the A4 (and A9/A10) test-and-development site under the direction of "SS-Führungsstab 'Zement'," the Leadership Staff for Ebensee at the Upper Danube. Although Marsálek refers to this program as "B9," it was not, in fact, numbered but is only referred to by its code name "Zement." As one of the first projects, presumably it would have been numbered "B 1."[337] Neufeld writes in *The Rocket and the Reich*, that on 26 August 1943 Speer and Kammler chose Austria as the location for this underground test-and-development facility. Code named "Zement," it was constructed by concentration camp labor from CC Ebensee, which opened on 18 November 1943.[338] Dr. Paul le Caer, a French survivor of CC Schlier-Redl-Zipf (another subcamp of Mauthausen opened 11 October 1943), has written about Kammler and SS-Führungsstab B9's [sic] use of slave labor from Schlier-Redl-Zipf to construct an underground liquid oxygen factory, code named "Schlier," to produce fuel for the A4.[339]

˙   Defense force made up of men too old for the Wehrmacht after 1944. Richard Grunberger, The Twelve Year Reich, (New York: Da Capo Press, 1995), 39

335 Kielich and Mills, 77

336 Dachau Mauthausen Trials, Reviews and Recommendations, http://www.hhs.utoledo.edu/dachau/mautr&r.html, 6 June 2006). Case 000-50-5-11 (US vs Andreas Battermann) and Case 000-50-5-30 (US vs Bernhard Fernikorn)

337 Marsálek, Mauthausen, 25-30, and Manfred Bornemann in Geheimprojekt Mittelbau (Bonn, Bernhard & Gräfe Verlag, 1994) lists Ebensee and considers the designation of "B1", 87

338 Neufeld, 204-213 and Marsálek, Mauthausen, 73-76

339 Le Caer, Paul. Schlier, 43-45 (Paris: Amicale Francaise de Mauthausen, 1984), 8

Map 2: *Map of CC Gusen I & II with Kellerbau Tunnels. September 1944*
Source: Collection Rudolf A. Haunschmied

Less familiar to historians is the relationship between the Sonderstab Kammler and St. Georgen and der Gusen, where tunnels were also constructed by slave labor from "subcamps" of Mauthausen (Gusen I and, later, Gusen II) to safeguard construction of the Messerschmitt (Me) 262, the first operational jet fighter, another of Hitler's "wonder weapons." One reason for confusion regarding the history of these projects is a misunderstanding about the development of the concentration camps involved. Unlike other satellite camps of Mauthausen, CC Gusen had been administratively independent from Mauthausen in many aspects and was only "annexed" to CC Mauthausen on 12 February 1944, as Evelyn Le Chène noted in her 1971 history, *Mauthausen – The History of a Death Camp*. Prior to this, as has been shown, CC Gusen had a separate system of numbering inmates, of registering deaths and of sending mail.[340] In 1942 CC Gusen also had its own "Bauleitung" (Construction Directorate). It was presumably the strategic restructuring of CC Mauthausen/Gusen that led to the administrative annexation of CC Gusen into CC Mauthausen in February 1944. But this melding of the two camps systems has resulted in the perception that CC Gusen was similar to other "satellite" camps, when in fact it developed as an equal but larger twin in the bifurcated system created in 1938. This has misled countless historians into dismissing the Gusen camp histories, preventing the real history of CC Mauthausen/Gusen and its relationship to the history of the DEST headquarters at St. Georgen from being written. The history of large scale Me 262 production at St. Georgen by DEST has been lost as well.

On 27 June 1943 shortly after the Sonderstab was established, Hitler demanded that aircraft manufacturers mass produce the newest models of sophisticated airplanes. After the bombing of Regensburg the next month, an event that surely breathed life into Prof. Messerschmitt's dream of underground factories, DEST's collaboration with Messerschmitt GmbH Regensburg would transform the SS' most significant manufacturer of granite to an important production partner in the manufacture of Me 262s for which Kammler and his SS-Führungsstab Gusen (also named Führungsstab B8)

---

[340] Le Chène, Evelyn. Mauthausen – The History of a Death Camp (Ealing: Corgi Book, 1973), 83 and 190

would direct the tunnel construction.[341] On 5 June 1944 Göring congratulated Messerschmitt GmbH Regensburg for fulfilling the planned production for the previous month by 26 May 1944. Since Göring also mentioned in a corresponding teleprint that the DEST enterprises at "Bürg" (Flossenbürg) and "Hausen" (Mauthausen) – the latter site de facto was DEST at CC Gusen – were already contributing 35% to the productivity of Messerschmitt GmbH Regensburg (which made this success possible), and it only took a few days before Pohl personally reported the success of "his" DEST enterprises directly to Himmler.[342]

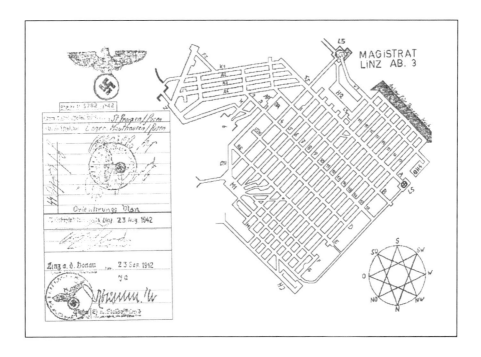

Map 3: *Early design draft of "Bergkristall", c. September 1942*
Source: Collection Rudolf A. Haunschmied

---

[341] Hanausch, Reinhard. Sklavenarbeit für den Düsenjäger. KZ-Produktion und Zwangsarbeit bei den Regensburger Messerschmitt-Werken 1939 – 45 (unplublished).

[342] Fernschreiben Görings vom 5. Juni 1944 an Führung, Gefolgschaft und Werksbeauftragten des Werkes Messerschmitt Regensburg und Schreiben Pohls vom 14. Juni 1944 an RFSS Himmler. BArch, NS 19/3571 (NO-4242)

Armed with these twin administrative structures allowing him centralized authority and a clear command structure down to the most discreet work detail, Kammler approached the construction of the Bergkristall Tunnels at St. Georgen. He recruited to his organization the special abilities of Dipl.-Ing. (graduated engineer) Karl Fiebinger, who worked on a significant number of the tunnel projects assigned to Kammler's Sonderstab. Fiebinger was an assistant of Prof. Sallinger at the T.H. Wien (Vienna College for Advanced Technology) until 1938, working as a skilled structural engineer and expert in steel-reinforced concrete, Fiebinger also ran an office for industrial construction employing about 30 highly-qualified civil engineers who specialised in transport and sewage. Fiebinger made a name for himself (although all too quickly forgotten) planning and constructing the infrastructure for underground dispersal plants to order for Sonderstab Kammler. At the end of the war, Fiebinger brought his expertise to America, where he constructed underground launch pads for intercontinental nuclear ballistic missiles. In the 1960s and 1970s Fiebinger participated in lucrative building projects in Mexico, which were partly financed by Austrian foreign aid credits.[343]

But in autumn 1943, still just a contractor of the SS, Fiebinger first focused his considerable talents on building project "Zement" in Ebensee and Redl-Zipf and "B8" in St. Georgen. There is no evidence to date that Fiebinger also worked on the Kellerbau tunnels at Gusen. Documents only show that he was the main contractor for Bergkristall at St. Georgen. Most presumably, the construction of the Kellerbau tunnels was started on the sole initiative of DEST and probably by Kammler before he had full support for his ideas outside of the SS organization. The construction is similar to what the current exhibit in the Deutsches Museum in Munich refers to as the "Austrian Method" of tunnel construction, using bricks to reinforce the excavation. While the exhibit does not discuss the extensive tunnels built by German firms like DEST during the Third Reich, there are marked similarities between the "German Method" of construction and Bergkristall tunnels, with the exception of the two-tiered excavation method, which Martin Lax

---

[343] Freund, Florian and Bertrand Perz, Das KZ in der Serbenhalle: Zur Kriegsindustrie in Wiener Neustadt. Industrie, Zwangsarbeit und Konzentrationslager in Österreich. Vol. 1. (Vienna: Verlag für Gesellschaftskritik, 1987), 43

reports was not used at St. Georgen.[344] The Kellerbau tunnels, which were never completed, were reinforced with different material such as granite, bricks, and concrete – materials DEST would have had on hand without requiring any support from higher commands in Berlin for this project. It is also very likely that DEST carried out the first preliminary planning for the project at St. Georgen, but at a certain point it must have been handed over to the professionals of Mssrs. Fiebinger.

Figure 17: Granite reinforcement of a Kellerbau III Tunnel, 2001
Source: Reinhard Kaspar

---

[344] Personal Interview, 21 October 2004

It is also evident that sufficient material resources and funds were only made available for the strategic underground aircraft plant at St. Georgen, since Bergkristall shows a few hundred meters of additional raw (unconcreted) tunnels that might have been built for the tank production plant that is shown on a very early draft layout prepared by "Magistrat Linz, AB. 3" (an engineering office of the City of Linz)[345] presumably before Fiebinger took over the project. The problem of acquiring funds and building material also appears to be the reason that the Kellerbau project could not be finished. Another interesting detail in this regard is that Tunnel No. 4 of Kellerbau III appears to have housed a branch of "Waffentechnische Lehranstalt der Waffen-SS (WTL) Graz" (an SS college of armament technology from Graz)[346] at the end of the war which might have carried out aerodynamic experiments according to reports on the WVHA and its enterprises written shortly after the war.[347] Although this report attributes the aerodymanics experiments to the Technische Hochschule Wien on the orders of Oswald Pohl, it appears very likely that WTL Graz actually conducted them as an SS organization in close relation to the Research and Development Unit of Technische Hochschule Graz. Thus, the SS appears to have occupied at least one tunnel for its own projects since Kammler was assigned Reichsbevollmächtigter für das Strahljäger-Notprogramm (Plenitpotiary of the Reich for Securing the Jetfighter Emergency Production Program) by Hitler on 27 March 1945 and thus surpassing Field Marshall Göring. From this date on, Kammler was also responsible for the further technical development of the Me-262 program.[348]

Survivors in general knew about the activities of Messerschmitt and Steyr-Daimler-Puch but nothing about WTL Graz (which indicates it must have been under a higher degree of secrecy). Along with the strategic armament projects of the SS at Gusen it is worth noticing that Himmler was de facto the chief of armament when he was assigned "Befehlshaber des Ersatzheeres

---

[345] Draft layout of Bergkristall „Magistrat Linz AB. 3" (in the possession of the author). This draft layout is accompanied by a file card dated with 23 August 1942.

[346] Lageplan Gusen I u. II. NARA RG 549 Box 334

[347] Das SS-Wirtschaftsverwaltungshauptamt und die unter seiner Dienstaufsicht stehenden wirtschaftlichen Unternehmungen, 138 (NO-1573). Archiv des Institutes für Zeitgeschichte München.

[348] Hans-Günter Richardi, SS-Geiseln in der Alpenfestung – Die Verschleppung prominenter KZ-Häftlinge aus Deutschland nach Südtirol. Bozen, Edition Raetia, 2005, 152-154

(BdE)" (commander-in-chief for the reserve army) by Hitler after the attempted Putsch of the Wehrmacht on 20 July 1944. This becomes evident in the memoirs of Alfred Grau, the commercial manager of DEST at St. Georgen. He writes that Flieger-Generalstabsingenieur Rulof Lucht, the manager in charge of Messerschmitt GmbH Regensburg and thus Bergkristall told the leading DEST staff at St. Georgen (his SS partner organization) in February 1945 that Hitler was in urgent need of jetplanes to succeed in his strategic strike against the Soviets code named "Weichselstoss" (counterattack on the Wysla River in todays Poland). Hitler hoped to defeat the Soviet armies in the area of the Wysla River through massive employment of the new Me 262 jetplanes, the new "Ramm-Jäger" (the attack fighter planes used in Kamikaze style) and the available troops. The hope was to get a basis for negotiating a cease-fire and a peace treaty with the West. Lucht usually commuted by plane to Wels and St. Georgen. On this specific visit, Lucht came directly from Hitler and ordered 24-hour full production to maximize the air material output at St. Georgen and Gusen.[349]

Stanislaw Dobosiewicz gives November 1943 for the beginning of the construction of the "Kellerbau" tunnels at CC Gusen, which means that they predate the tunnels at "Zement" as Ebensee was just being established at this time.[350] Victor Kielich, who shared Barracks 3 with Dobosiewicz that year recalls:

> By the end of 1943 the war was not going too well for the Germans, so the SS reshuffled the barracks to make room for more prisoners coming from camps in Eastern Europe to work in the tunnels. The pace of killing prisoners in the quarry slowed somewhat only because they were needed to build the tunnels where they died by the thousands. Drilling the hard rock in the tunnels, prisoners worked practically on top of each other, making the tunnels the most dangerous place to work. Our barrack got a number of stonemasons

---

[349] Alfred Grau. „Der Zusammenbruch 1945 wie wir ihn erlebt haben, 1975". St. Georgener Heimatblätter, Folge 55 (St. Georgen a.d. Gusen, September 2007), 15-25

[350] Dobosiewicz, Stanislaw. Mauthausen/Gusen – Oboz Zaglady (Warszawa: Wydawnictwo Ministertwa Orony Narodowej, 1977), 50

from other barracks, among them Russians from the disbanded Russian camp and a few Spaniards.

The Wagenkontrollbücher, the record of shipments to and from the station at St. Georgen, note several interesting shipments at this time. After 17 September 1943, DEST received an inordinately large amount of cement. At nearly the same time the Central Building Inspector for Concentration Camp Gusen also got a large number of bricks for "Sonderbauvorhaben RFSS" (special construction project of Reich Leader SS) as correspondence between the City of Linz and DEST of St. Georgen reveals.[351] In November several freight cars with field train wagons from Arnheim were addressed to the *"Reichsführer in Gusen."* Then, on 29 November 1943, the first freight car with components for Messerschmitt planes was transported from Regensburg to Gusen. Subsequent deliveries of Messerschmitt components were modest but regular. On 30 November 1943 more freight cars with machine parts arrived from Flossenbürg. In December 1943 the first "Flügelwagen" (devices for the production of wings) arrived in Gusen from Regensburg.[352]

The first rather modest Kellerbau project consisted of only five tunnels built into the hill next to the Meierhof and behind the stone crusher in Langenstein to the north of CC Gusen. Each five-meter-wide tunnel was approximately 250 meters in length.[353] Judging by the different styles of tunnel construction, those involved had little experience with brickwork for tunnels dug in sand. The two tunnels furthest east were better developed. After the fifth tunnel, excavation came to a halt. To this day, no one knows exactly when or why this pilot project was abandoned. It is likely that, sometime in winter 1943/44, the excavation command came across the natural spring which still floods

---

[351] Schreiben Direktor Walther an den Oberbürgermeister von Linz of 3 May 1944. B0029n, Mappe Stollenbauten – Korrespondenz A-L. Archive of the City of Linz.

[352] Wagenkontrollbücher. After 30 September 1943 many railway loads carrying parts of barracks were also shipped from CC Gusen to Redl-Zipf which underscores the fact that CC Gusen also played a key role for several „real" satellites of Mauthausen-Gusen like Redl-Zipf.

[353] E. Fritsch, „KZ-Stollen – ein zeitgeschichtliches Denkmal," Mitteilungen des Landesvereins für Höhlenkunde in Oberösterreich, 1988/1, 31 ff A 1987 survey of the remaining tunnels reveals an overall length of 1,400 meters and a total area of 5,000 m2 installed. Currently (autumn 2004) these tunnels are to be refilled by its new onwer – the Bundesimmobiliengesellschaft (BIG) – for safety reasons.

the majority of the tunnel ruins today. Owing to this flooding, the SS would install a pump in Gusen in spring 1944. In the beginning of 1944 the construction of a water reservoir was started above the tunnels on the premises of the Wasner Farm. [354] CC Gusen II probably should have been supplied with fresh water from this reservoir, as the water in the camp would never be potable.[355] Many Jews were massacred along with the construction of the corresponding pipeline to the camp.[356] These tunnels housed underground installations of Messerschmitt and Steyr-Daimler-Puch AG which eventually became known as "Kellerbau III."[357] Additionally, a second but much smaller system of two tunnels (later known as "Kellerbau I" and "Kellerbau II") was built using a more advanced concrete technology more in keeping with the "German Method" displayed in the Deutsches Museum. Further research will perhaps determine if this shift in construction method also signals a change in designers and engineering staff.

After extensive stone production stopped in Gusen, SS Plant Manager Paul Wolfram oversaw armament production for Steyr-Daimler-Puch AG and for Messerschmitt code named "Ba II" ("Ba II" stands for Betriebsabteilung II [production section No. 2] of DEST St. Georgen).

By January 1944, DEST already produced 25 fuselages per day at "Mauthausen"[358] for the standard Me 109 fighter planes by order of Messerschmitt GmbH Regensburg. Messerschmitt GmbH Regensburg operated an offical branch plant at Gusen called "Messerschmitt GmbH, Zweigbetrieb: St. Georgen a.d.G. bei Firma: Deutsche Erd- u. Steinwerke." On 1 February 1944 five halls with 9,000 square meters production area were in use.[359]

---

[354]   Klinger, Volksschulchronik, 184.
[355]   Malgaroli, Felice. (survivor IT 115577 of Gusen II), Diario, (unpublished manuscript). In the possession of the author.
[356]   Ivan Skrjanec, „Erinnerungsbericht – Der Abgang nach Gusen II". (France Filipic, Slowenen in Mauthausen. Mauthausen-Studien, Band 3. Bundesministerium für Inneres. Vienna, 2004), 245
[357]   Stefancic, Dusan suvivor Gusen II; Marsálek, Gusen, 11
[358]   Aufstellung der von Häftlingen geleisteten Arbeitsstunden für die Luftfahrtindustrie, 21 February 1944. NARA, microform publication M890/9/0707 (1584-PS). However, survivors Dusan Stefancic and Jerzy Wandel dispute this number. They recall producing 26 fuselages and 26 pairs of wings per day at this time.
[359]   Lageplan RLM GL/C-B 2/I Nr. 16012/43, 1 February 1944. In the possession of the author. Again, Dusan Stefancic contests these numbers. According to his memory, only four of these halls were

During the first half of 1943, as the German economy again experienced a labor shortage, working and living conditions improved in many camps, but the SS solution for improving production was always to increase the number of workers rather than to improve living conditions.[360] While a canteen and brothel were opened in CC Gusen I in 1942 and certain skilled prisoners such as stonemasons were paid a very minimal wage to encourage production, only the most valued prisoners were part of this incentive program. Kielich recalls,

> Prisoners in stonemason commandos received some kind of payment for their work, depending on the stonemason's productivity, which had to reach a 30 RM minimum. The prisoner received a credit of 5%, or 1.5 RM, in the canteen, for which he could buy fifteen cigarettes per month. Some stonemasons barely earned the minimum but others produced from 50 to 100 RM or more per month. Each capo and assistant's credit was also figured on the total production. For some this could come to 10 marks per month. However, German political prisoners, criminals and homosexuals were often given no such privileges.[361]

Kielich recalls buying "preserved fruit from Yugoslavia in barrels unfortunately infested with dead fruit bugs and small white caterpillars." However, survivor of Gusen I and II Dusan Stefancic reports, "There was no canteen." By 1944 one could only buy cigarettes which, Stefancic insists, should not be seen as an indication of good living conditions.[362]

The death rate in most camps (with the important exception of the death camp at Auschwitz) dropped below 3% in 1943. Two other exceptions were Project Dora, where all but 2,882 of 17,000 prisoners would die by March of 1944,[363] and CC Mauthausen/Gusen, where the death rate reached 17.2% for December 1942.[364] In 1943 there were 5,116 deaths in CC Gusen, where the

---

complete, and the production area was closer to 7,000 square meters at this time.
[360] Ulrich, 185
[361] Kielich and Mills, 54
[362] Personal Interview, 7 May 2004
[363] Ulrich, 178-232
[364] Allen, Business, 188

average number of prisoners was 8,000.[365] Pohl explained the high mortality rate at CC Mauthausen/Gusen to Himmler in a letter, "It is certain to assume that Mauthausen received the worst human material."[366] Conditions in the camp or on the job site were not seen as contributing factors to the deaths, only the genetic make-up of the prison population.[367]

Figure 18: The brothel of CC Gusen I today, May 1995
Source: Rudolf A. Haunschmied

But conditions were, indeed, horrible. For some, there was not even the hope of securing a place on a skilled work command. Of the 160,000 prisoners registered in camps controlled by the WVHA in 1943, 15% worked in camp maintenance (probably the best jobs because the SS Construction Directo-

---

[365] Marsálek, Mauthausen [English], 126, 144
[366] Allen, Business, 185
[367] Ibid., 183

rates were invested in the outcome of the work and therefore invested in the prisoner), 22% were classified as "arbeitsunfähig"(unfit for work) and 63% were working on construction projects, various SS enterprises and in private firms.[368] Kielich recalls,

> As the German war-machine needed more men to fight the Russians, the German army drafted the younger SS officers as well as civilian Meisters from the Steyr factory and the quarries, causing shortages of skilled workers. Older Germans came to replace the draftees and carry on with the duties in the camp and in the quarries, as well as at the Steyr factories in the ever expanding tunnel system. A search was mounted amongst the prisoners for mechanics, blacksmiths and all kinds of other professions to operate the Steyr machines. Prisoners with no experience volunteered in droves for jobs that promised food and better working conditions. Only reasonably healthy prisoners could work at Steyr, where they had a better chance to survive. Thus, improvements made for the Steyr workers did not bring improvements for the thousands of ghost men and Russian Muselman who filled the ranks in the quarry and did the hard and dirty work.[369]

The Gestapo and SS continued to arrest large numbers of civilians without cause to work on construction sites, in factories or on farms. Often these were young adults, like Fjodor Solodovnik. The horror of life at CC Gusen, where guards and capos were expected to beat prisoners to death and where the dead lay covered with fleas and lice until the "crematorium boys" came for them, must have been a terrible shock to the very young, arriving, as they did, directly from their families' arms. One Slovenian youth, Dusan Stefancic was arrested at the age of sixteen, recalls thinking as he waited with other detainees on a train platform, "This is the first time I've stayed up all night."[370] The novelty would soon wear off.

From early 1944, the smaller tunnel system, Kellerbau I and II, housed Messerschmitt installations. As tunnel space became available at Bergkristall,

---

[368] Ulrich, 186
[369] Kielich and Mills, 56
[370] Personal Interview 7 May 2004. In possession of the author.

Messerschmitt successively moved its operation to St. Georgen. The Kellerbau Tunnels were then handed over to Steyr-Daimler-Puch AG according to Dusan Stefancic, who worked in the "salt bath" where aluminium was heat treated before being shaped in the huge presses of the underground plants.[371] The "Salzbad" was also chosen by the Oberkapo to torture prisoners. The unfortunate boys who worked in this area not only had to witness the sadistic tortures but had to remove the nearly dead victims and clean up the room afterwards. Despite this, the boys considered themselves lucky to have water to wash with and to be supervised by a civilian engineer from the Regensburg Messerschmitt works who was kinder than either the Obercapo or his superior the SS Kommandoführer.[372]

While most civilians, either skilled Austrians or Germans from the Messerschmitt factories, were "generally fairly tolerant," survivor Stefancic reports that others intentionally caused problems for slave laborers, even going so far as to denounce them. Few, if any, gave prisoners a piece of bread or a cigarette.[373] Working conditions in the cold of winter were made worse by malfunctioning equipment and the constant noise. Punishment for losing a drill bit, or having one stolen, a common practice, was 25 blows with a rubber hose or an electrical cable.[374]

The Gusen site's increasing importance is shown by the fact that Steyr-Daimler-Puch AG sent hundreds of railcars full with specialized machinery in fall 1944 from its premises at Radom and Warsaw to Austria, when the Soviet advance forced the Nazis to withdraw from occupied Poland. A significant part of this machinery was installed at Gusen – a part of them undergound.[375]

---

[371] Personal Interview 8 May 2000
[372] Stefancic, 8
[373] Ibid., 9
[374] Ibid., 10
[375] Perz, Bertrand. Projekt Quarz, 181 ff

Figure 19: A typical scene inside the barracks. Inmates living side by side with their dead comrades, 6 May 1945 [This photograph by Ornitz is said to have been taken at Mauthausen but the dirt in the barracks and the scene itself make it representative for the situation in Gusen or the Sanitary Camp at Mauthausen]
Source: NARA

Steyr continued to install specialized machinery in the Kellerbau Tunnels but had no operations in the Bergkristall Tunnels.[376] Plant Manager Wolfram also made the move from the Kellerbau Tunnels to oversee slave laborers in the "Bergkristall" Tunnels at St. Georgen, code named Ba III.[377] Wolfram remained a civilian, and a very proper civilian, for a long time before

---

[376] At the end of the year 1944 there was production for Steyr-Daimler-Puch AG in tunnel No. 1 of Kellerbau, Marsálek, Gusen, 9. Since the winter of 1944 metal-sheet parts for MP 40 and MP 44 submachine guns were produced in a tunnel of Gusen according to Marsálek. Marsálek, Mauthausen, 95.
[377] Marsálek, Gusen, 11 and Stellenbesetzungsplan St. Georgen der DEST (in the possession of the author).

appearing in an SS uniform in 1944.[378] For his abuse of prisoners in both the Kellerbau and Bergkristall Tunnels, he would be sentenced to life imprisonment by a US military court in 1947.[379]

---

[378] Interview 881120. This interviewee also states that in 1945 the Americans took him to an undisclosed place.

[379] Mauthausen Trials, US vs. Paul Wolfram, Case 000-50-5-49, RG 338 (new RG 496), Box 423 and 424, Records of the U.S. Army Commands, 1942 – Records of Headquarters, US Army Europe (USAREUR), War Crimes Branch, War Crimes Case Files („Cases Tried"), 1945-1959, NARA.

Subcamp St. Georgen an der Gusen

On 2 January 1944, 272 detainees were officially brought from the main camp of Mauthausen to the "subcamp Gusen Bergkristall-Bau" (Bergkristall Construction), a name that signals the purpose of the camp which came to be known as CC Gusen II. On this day an architect, three builders, two miners and many other "skilled workers" were detained as prisoners. The 272 detainees were reportedly "Spaniards, Russians, Poles, Yugoslavs, Greeks, French and in some cases also Italians and Czechs."[380] With the start of constructing Bergkristall under the direction of "Ingenieurbüro Dipl.-Ing. Karl Fiebinger" and under the command of the "SS-Führungsstab Gusen," skilled workers would become increasingly important. In coordinating the use of unskilled labor, Allen explains that Kammler established an office within each camps' Construction Directorate, known as Betriebsdienstleiter (Special Operations Director) to work with Maurer's office. The Betriebsdienstleiter was in charge of locating skilled prisoners.[381] Records kept by the Gestapo or recorded on arrival at concentration camps were more likely to be consulted, but even this did not guarantee anyone placement in a valued command, especially at this early stage of construction when unskilled labor was most in demand.

From the start of construction in early 1944, DEST, as SS building contractor, was directly involved in "Bergkristall-Bau." Until the end of February 1944, preparations were made for the civilian-workers camp to house skilled workers who would oversee the tunnel construction and the installation of machinery, and who would manage production in the finished factories. Many orders for barracks were sent directly to "Ing. Kammler" at the railway station in St. Georgen, according to the Wagenkontrollbücher. Water and energy supplies were secured. Arrangements were made for a cement mixer

---

[380] Transportliste of 2 January 1944, Archiv Museum Mauthausen (AMM) at the Austrian Federal Ministry of the Interior, Vienna, AMM B13/I. Herein after cited as AMM.
[381] Allen, Business, 226

and a mixing area was built. Rails and fences were ordered and in March 1944 about 600 detainees began to draw and lay the rail track system.[382]

Figure 20: The huge concrete mixer at St. Georgen, 1945
Source: AHDG; Collection Franz Walzer

To optimize the tunnel structure, Reichsamt für Bodenforschung (Reich Agency for Geology) carried out an experimental explosion some four kilometers north of St. Georgen in sand cellars near the village of Niederthal where SS-Standartenführer Peterseil and other illegal Nazis had their clandestine meetings in the period before the Anschluss. Along with these tests a 2,000 kg high impulse explosive charge (a "Luftmine" in German) was detonated on 23 April 1944 to simulate the loads that would impact Bergkristall in the case of high impulse bombings. Local witnesses of this explosion recall

---

[382] Esche II Work Plan, 4 April 1944, (Figure 9c), J.I.O.A. Final Report No. 1, Part 1, Section III, Appendix A. Washington, DC, Joint Intelligence Objectives Agency, September 1945. NARA, RG 319, Army Staff, „P"-File, Location: 7/23/42/5, Box T169.

a shock wave and the type of mushroom shaped cloud which they later saw in news coverage of nuclear detonations in the Pacific Theater.[383]

Figure 21: *Remnant of the Bergkristall Sewage Treatment Plant which*
was pulled down in 2007, January 2000
Source: Rudolf A. Haunschmied

In St. Georgen, 1,250 prisoners worked on the excavations of the Bergkristall pilot tunnels. The first trial drills were given to detainees in February and March. From April 1944 onwards 500 more prisoners began the concrete work on the first part of the tunnel. Additional prisoners laid streets which

---

[383] Gindelstrasser, 54 ff

are still used today, the Bahnhofstrasse and the Brunnenweg. In May 1944 the sewage treatment plant was finished for Bergkristall.[384]

With the advent of CC Gusen II, the village of St. Georgen itself was transformed into a subcamp of Concentration Camp Mauthausen/Gusen where no distinction would be made between human beings and machinery. The prisoners' suffering was no longer confined to the quarries and concentration camp barracks but was now part of St. Georgen's daily existence. Mrs. Johanna B. lived in a small house behind the St. Georgen market place where the bakery's cars are now kept. Although the guards forbade people to look at prisoners up close, she could watch from a distance as big columns of people were driven into the tunnels. "They were building the streets, too, with big machines. We were not allowed to give them food, but the children would roll apples under the machinery. The guards would look the other way if children did something adults were forbidden to do."[385]

According to the 4 April 1944 Esche II Work Plan, the end of the "construction works" (probably the first stage of construction) was scheduled for 1 December 1944 and according to internal correspondence of Messerschmitt, the end of construction-works for the full system was planned to be 25% by 15 November 1944 and 100% by 1 April 1945.[386] As a report of 2 February 1945 shows, 165,000 cubic meters of a total 240,000 cubic meters were excavated by 21 January 1945. This means an excavation progress of 69% was achieved by this date. According to the report, all concreting was planned to be finished at the end of March 1945. The report also states that the construction site of Bergkristall was under quarantine due to epidemic typhus on this day and that concreting capacity was higher than mining capacity at the site. Furthermore the companies "Grün-Bilfinger" and "Kunz & Co." had begun the mining in March 1944, but in June 1944 all mining work was taken over by "Grossdeutsche Schachtbau- und Tiefbohr GmbH". By November 1944 this company "employed" 25 technical staff, 215 miners, 9 unskilled workers

---

[384] Esche II Work Plan
[385] Personal Interview, Johanna B., 18 September 2000. Translated by Martha Gammer.
[386] Übersicht über die wesentlichen Verlagerungen Regensburg. Zentralplanung Serie, Blatt 3 von 4. Smithsonian National Air and Space Museum, Captured German/Japanese Air Technical Documents, ADRC/T-2, Microfilm R 2497

and 1855 concentration camps inmates working in mining underground.[387] An earlier report of 27 January 1945 gives 792 additional inmates working for Grossdeutsche Schachtbau- und Tiefbohr GmbH above ground.[388]

Altogether about 3,500 prisoners were used in "Bergkristall-Bau" in 1944. Modification announcements between June 1944 and the middle of August 1944 show a constant number of prisoners of about 4,000 at Gusen II. The July excavations of the very first tunnels were accomplished with considerable pressure as there was little experience concerning construction of such tunnels. Notably, during this time several carpenters from the Mühlviertel area died in so-called "workplace accidents." Such workplace accidents occurred all too often,[389] Several civilian workers' deaths were registered in the death books of the St. Georgen Parish and the St. Georgen Registry Office. Frequently the death certificate of Austrian civillians was signed by Dr. Vetter who was acting at that time as the "Lagerarzt KLM/Gusen als Amtsarzt i.V.", the camp doctor of the Gusen part of the Mauthausen/Gusen complex with the authority to substitute the public health officer of the District of Perg.[390]

Until the cessation of construction work in May 1945, about 6,600 prisoners were continuously employed in the work-command "Bergkristall Bau."[391] By comparison, the combined populations of Langenstein and St. Georgen were less than three thousand in 1951, the first year after the war for which statistics are available.[392] If one recalls that the guard to prisoner ratio was one to fifteen at this point, one has some idea of how these small towns were swallowed into the Third Reich's frenzy to burrow their sins below ground.

---

[387] Bericht „Überprüfung des Bauvorhabens Bergkristall am 21. Januar 1945" vom 2. Februar 1945. Kommission zur Überprüfung des Einsatzes von Bergleuten bei U-Verlagerungen (gebildet durch: Zentralstelle für bergbauliche Sonderaufgaben, OT – Amtsgruppe Bauwirtschaft und Reichsvereinigung Kohle). In the possession of the author.

[388] Bericht „Überprüfung des Einsatzes von Bergleuten beim Bauvorhaben Bergkristall" vom 27. Januar 1945. Zentralstelle für bergbauliche Sonderaufgaben, OT – Amtsgruppe Bauwirtschaft und Reichsvereinigung Kohle (in the possession of the author).

[389] Testimonies of different survivors.

[390] Death certificates, Standesamt (registry office) St. Georgen.

[391] Esche II Work Plan, 4 April 1944, (Figure 9c)

[392] Engelbert Singer, Analyse der Pfarrgemeinde St. Georgen/Gusen (St. Georgen a.d. Gusen: Pfarre St. Georgen a.d. Gusen, 1983)

According to a Joint Intelligence Objective Agency Final Report dated September 1945, of six underground factories, "the most noteworthy are the Messerschmitt Plant at St. Georgen, Austria, and the Misburgh Oil Refinery at Minden, Germany. The Messerschmitt plant is one of the most complete and modern underground factories in Germany. Its production progress was especially rapid. This large factory, with a floor area of 12 acres, was almost completed in 13 months and had produced 987 jet-propelled planes."[393]

The rapid development of Bergkristall may be seen as an effect of the February 1944 raids on German fighter assembly plants known as "Big Week," during which fighter planes escorted bombers to their targets for the first time.[394] Both the destruction and this new utilization of fighter planes encouraged the Nazi leadership to speed up the underground dispersal of especially sensitive airplane assembly plants. It is unclear if the SS-Führungsstab Gusen started the work on "Bergkristall" in spring 1944 under the authority of DEST and the SS, or if work began by arrangement of the leading authorities in Berlin.

Either way, one of Kammler's organizations, or a concerted effort by both, directed the work done by slaves from CC Gusen I and II. But the separation of Kammler's Construction Directorates and the Sonderstab (and later Jägerstab) from the concentration camp administration is made clear by Ziereis' deathbed confession. When asked about Bergkristall, Ziereis directed his interogators to ask the commander of the SS-Führungstab (SS-Obersturmführer Werner Eckermann) because he was not involved in the details.[395] Kammler's ability to create managerial organizations with clear lines of responsibility ultimately accounts for Bergkristall's rapid development.

---

[393] The six factories were the Misburgh Oil Refinery at Minden, Germany, the Messerschmitt Plant at St. Georgen, Austria, the Hermann Goering Werke at Langenstein, Germany (Thuringia), the Project „Dogger" at Happburg, Germany, the Eugen Grill Werke at Hallein, Austria and the M-A-N Fabrik at Mainz-Weisenau, Germany. J.I.O.A. Final Report No. 1, Part 1, Section III, Appendix A.
[394] Ross, 72
[395] Letzeburger, 62

Flexibility and organization became increasingly important as Kammler was himself given more responsibility and power over jet production and underground dispersal. While Kammler's Sonderstab was created by an initiative of Speer and Himmler, when the strategic goals were changed from the V2 assault rockets to defensive fighter aircraft in early 1944, Göring entered the group around Kammler and formally invoked the "Jägerstab" with a state-decree on 4 March 1944. In this decree, Göring (in full agreement with Himmler) confirmed Dr.-Ing. Kammler as the chief for the underground installations to ensure the production of fighter aircraft on a large scale.[396] This further committed Kammler to the success of Bergkristall.

Kammler's Office C in WVHA and/or the Sonderstab-turned-Jägerstab, already had contracts with engineers possessing the particular expertise needed to handle an underground construction project, such as Karl Fiebinger. Although Allen discusses the similarity in structure between the Building Directorates and the Jägerstab,[397] the relationship between the two requires more research. What Allen makes clear is that Kammler's organizations had the flexibility to assign engineers to a variety of projects at the same time, perhaps even under different commands (SS, DEST, or Sonderstab). Because the Jägerstab was modelled after the Central Building Directorates, understanding the latter's structure is valuable. As Allen explains, the ZBLs

"… worked as managerial clearinghouses with a flexible corps of trained engineers. Like Russian dolls that contain smaller and smaller concentric units within their shells, the ZBLs parsed out specific projects to Construction Directorates. In turn, Construction Directorates broke down into construction sites *(Baustellen)* for the supervision of individual buildings and, finally, into individual construction works *(Bauwerke)*, to oversee discrete technical jobs (e.g. bricklaying, excavation, cement pouring, or carpentry). Previously the engineers at Flossenbürg had worked differently from those at Buchenwald, Sachsenhausen, or Auschwitz. From now on, they executed their tasks in the same way, using the same forms, subject to the same audits. Now any engineer could move from directorate to directorate and find colleagues who

---

[396] Marsálek, Mauthausen [English], 24, Allen, Business, 232
[397] Allen, Business, 236-237

were used to working the same way within the same system. Their activities – and thus their experiences within the Office II – became normalized and subject to interchangeability."[398]

This structure, and Kammler's previous knowledge of the terrain around St. Georgen, explains how (once the decision was made to exploit the former beer cellars) engineers like Fiebinger could descend on the town with supplies and equipment and efficiently begin a massive work project using slave labor in what seemed to residents like a matter of days. For instance, Kammler had the authority to command the delivery of machinery from other projects. The larger building machinery used at Bergkristall was transferred to St. Georgen after 9 March 1944 from the unfinished construction of the hydraulic power plant at Ybbs-Persenbeug (at the Danube River in Lower Austria) which was halted in 1943.[399]

The Reich Air Ministry had still not decided in early 1944 what type of aircraft to produce at St. Georgen. Hitler, as is widely known, wanted the Me 262 built as a "jet bomber," despite protests from nearly all quarters. A rivalry had developed between Armament Minister Albert Speer and Air Minister Hermann Göring. According to Speer, Hitler finally put his foot down and empowered Kammler to have sole jurisdiction over the production of all modern airplanes.[400] On 1 April 1944 Kammler was appointed leader of the newly established Jägerstab (fighter aircraft staff),[401] a date which complicates Speer's story because construction of Bergkristall was well underway prior to Kammler's takeover and Speer's subsequent memory failure regarding the tunnel system. This is underscored by the fact that Adolf Hitler personally showed interest in the underground dispersal of a Steyr-Daimler-Puch ball bearing plant to tunnels built at Linz in the same geological formation as the tunnels in St. Georgen and Gusen. Hitler himself doubted that this sandstone would withstand bomb attacks. Therefore on 15 April 1944 he personally

---

[398] Ibid., 148

[399] Wagenkontrollbücher and Kurt Frischler, Lebendiger Strom: Die Donaulandschaft – heute (Vienna and Munich, Jugend und Volk, 1983), 51 ff.

[400] Speer, Albert. Erinnerungen (Berlin: Propyläen Verlag, 1969), 456.

[401] Vorschlag für die Verleihung des Ritterkreuzes zum Kriegsverdienstkreuz mit Schwertern an Dr. Ing. Hans Kammler, 20 August 1944, BArch, SSO-Film 151-A, 204 ff.

sent Franz Dorsch, his new chief of Amt Bau in the Armament Ministry, and deputy of Speer to Linz to inspect the underground dispersal of that Steyr plant. Already in Linz, Dorsch made a visit to "Kammler's project for Messerschmitt near CC Gusen" and reported back to Hitler on the same day that the Linz tunnels could be considered safe as long as they were sufficiently reinforced.[402] The experiments carried out on the Bergkristall and the Linz tunnels at Niederthal near Lungitz may have helped Dorsch to reassure Hitler. A few weeks later, Speer himself visited the underground installation "B8" at Gusen (St. Georgen) and "Zement" at Ebensee on 6 July 1944, returning to Hitler the same day. Reporting on this visit to Himmler's personal staff, Kammler thought that Speer should have been satisfied with what he saw on both construction sites. A few days later, on 10 July 1944 Hitler and Speer decided to use parts of the tunnel capacity at Ebensee for the production of gearboxes for tanks.[403] With this decision, Kammlers' project at Ebensee lost a great deal of its strategic importance because it was no longer dedicated to Wernher v. Braun's Peenemünde research group.

Kammler also brought his old contacts to his new responsibilities, including the head of Office Group D II, Labor Action, Gerhard Maurer. Maurer had already contemplated issues of labor and construction at CC Gusen on his visit there in July 1942 with the commandant of Struthof, so he was familiar with St. Georgen and its surroundings. On 8 June 1944, now an SS-Standartenführer, he asked a meeting of the Jägerstab for a list of locations where concentration camp inmates could be exploited to ensure Me 262 production. He wanted a basis for advising the SS Hauptamt (Main Office) in its decision. At this meeting, he made his preference known for the use of as much "concentrated" labor as possible because it lessened the need for guards and because the population around concentration camps was too helpful to fleeing inmates or inmates attempting sabotage.[404]

---

[402] Perz, Projekt Quarz, 186

[403] Freund, Florian. Arbeitslager Zement – Das konzentrationslager Ebensee und die Raketenrüstung. Industrie, Zwangsarbeit und Konzentrationslager in Österreich. Vol. 2. (Vienna: Verlag für Gesellschaftskritik, 1989), 76 ff

[404] Jägerstab-Schnellbericht vom 8. Juni 1944, BArch R3/1756

After Kammler became the chief of the "Jägerstab" (fighter aircraft staff charged with increasing fighter plane production in 1944), the most important parts of the German aircraft industry were dispersed to large underground factories like St. Georgen. The "Jägerstab" (Fighter Aircraft Staff) was renamed "Rüstungsstab" (Armament Staff) on 1 August 1944 and was to be the headquarters of the RMfBuM (the Reich Ministry for Armament and Ammunitions) in order to increase the production of fighter planes for the "defense of the Reich" to a maximum by the end of the war. The Rüstungsstab became a coordination center between industry and the German Air Force and was led by Kammler. On 8 August 1944 Kammler was also appointed "Special Representative of Reichsmarschall Göring for Smashing the Allied Terror in the German Air Space."[405]

The large number of armament plants being dispersed that fall resulted in the creation of many more sub camps of Mauthausen/Gusen besides Ebensee and Redl-Zipf. All prisoners living in these new camps and their material logistics were managed from Concentration Camps Mauthausen and Gusen. Most of the detainees brought to Concentration Camp Mauthausen to work in these armament projects were first brought to Mauthausen for "quarantine." After that they were selected and – if able to work – many were brought to CC Gusen I. The older camp could thus be called the "transit camp" for forced laborers. On call, these laborers had to replace dead prisoners in subcamps like Gusen II, Hinterbrühl, Ebensee, Melk, etc. As these camps (with the exception of Melk and Ebensee) did not have crematoriums, dead bodies were also brought back to Gusen I. On one day in February 1945, for example, truckloads with five to six hundred corpses were brought from an unknown place to the incinerators of Gusen.[406]

---

[405] Marsálek, Mauthausen, 30
[406] Marsálek, Gusen, 40.

Underground Installation B8 – "Bergkristall"

In spring 1944 a few hundred meters west of CC Gusen I, detainees started setting up temporary barracks where prisoners were treated like animals. This subcamp, known as Concentration Camp Gusen II (CC Gusen II), epitomized horror and terror and meant certain death for thousands of prisoners. On 9 March 1944 the SS and the Luftwaffe put the first detainees in CC Gusen II and declared it officially "in operation."[407] In just four months time, the number of prisoners brought to the Concentration Camps Gusen doubled to 16,000.[408] Of these, 6,020 worked in war production and 3,210 underground. By 1 September 1944 there were 19,409 inmates. Of these 11,480 worked in war production. A peak was reached on 1 January 1945 with 24,161 inmates. Of these 18,500 worked in war production. On 28 April 1945 there were 20,312 inmates. Of these 8,985 at Gusen II and 268 at Lungitz (Gusen III) were used similarly.[409]

St. Georgen's residents had to submit to the building project and were not allowed to ask questions since the underground installation was "Geheime Kommandosache" (a top secret project). Even at the DEST headquarter at St. Georgen only senior manager Otto Walther and commercial manager Alfred Grau had an overall security clearance and more insight to the top secret underground plant.[410] Overnight the area just 100 meters southwest of the St. Georgen parish church was restricted and controlled by SS and Luftwaffe guards. The area was prohibited to anyone without a special permit and a green ribbon signifying he or she was a DEST employee or a person authorized by DEST to trespass. A fence soon enclosed the area where many detainees began the excavation. Eyewitnesses simply say, "They were suddenly there."[411]

---

[407] Aufstellung der ausserhalb des Hauptlagers errichteten „Arbeitslager" (Nebenlager). BArch, NS 4/Ma/57/32.

[408] Veränderungsmeldung (daily report on change of numbers of inmates) KLM/G für den 2. März 1944. (7,550 inmates). Veränderungsmeldung KLM/G für den 30. Juni 1944 (16,207 inmates).

[409] Veränderungsmeldung K.L.MAUTHAUSEN/UK. GUSEN vom 28. April 1945. AMM B/12/14

[410] Grau, 16

[411] Summarization of independent impressions of the older population of St. Georgen and its surrounding, which were generally the same.

On 8 March 1944 at 11 p.m. the last freight car of sand for Mögle (the local firm that owned the Mariengrube Sandpit) left St. Georgen railway station.[412] That month the SS confiscated the Mariengrube Sandpit as well as the sand cellar near the brewery without compensating the owners. The main entrance to "Bergkristall" would be built in the KL Sandpit, to which the SS-Neubauleitung KZ-Lager Mauthausen (New Construction Directorate for CC Mauthausen) had attained exclusive rights in August 1939.[413]

Figure 22: *The barracks of the Luftwaffe guard companies directly north of CC Gusen II were burned down by US troops along with the camp, 11 May 1945*
Source: Major Charles R. Sandler

---

[412] Messrs. Mögle was in the possession of this huge sandpit since 1933. Grundbuch Mauthausen, TZ 535 / 33. Inmates of Gusen II started to dig tunnels from this sandpit too.
[413] Treaty between the Reichsführer SS and owner of 4 August 1939. In the possession of the author.

Two large barracks were erected for the Luftwaffe just a few meters north of CC Gusen II to house the 26th and 27th guard company of KLM/Gusen[414]. Due to a lack of SS guards, given this sudden influx of prisoners, the SS units at St. Georgen and Gusen were supplemented on 14 July 1944 with two Luftwaffe guard companies with a battalion staff. The SS had such difficulties with the Luftwaffe men, however, their incorporation into the SS troops was requested to make them subject to SS discipline.[415] Another 1,779 Luftwaffe men were incorporated into the SS guards of "Mauthausen" on 31 August 1944.[416]

Figure 23: A Gusen II victim lying in the sands at St. Georgen, c. 1944
Source: Museu d´Història de Catalunya

---

[414] Sketch „Gusen II with Airraid Shelter". NARA RG 549 Box 346.
[415] Aktenvermerk für SS-Gruppenführer Fegelein of 14 July 1944. BArch, Film 713.
[416] Verfügung des Luftwaffenwehramtes im Oberkommando der Luftwaffe of 31 August 1944. BArch, NS 4Hi/21/345.

Although the excavations began at three different places (the two sandpits and the cellar of the brewery), the nucleus was the Mariengrube Sandpit, perhaps because prisoners working there were well hidden. Five tunnels were completed in the summer of 1944. The finishing of aircraft parts with special machine tools probably began in these five tunnels. Preserved plans show Tunnels No. 4, 5, 6, 7, 8 and 9 as the first finished, coherent tunnel complex. Looking at other tunnel grids, built later, one can recognise a clear similarity between tunnels Nos. 4 – 9 and the Kellerbau III tunnels in Gusen, built earlier. This part alone was designed using a system similar to the earlier tunnels.[417]

Figure 24: Small adits at Mariengrube Sand Pit into Bergkristall, c. 1945
Source: Museu d'Història de Catalunya

---

[417]   Haunschmied, 99

To camouflage them from the air, the full-sized tunnels had no outlets directly to the surface, only small adits through which prisoners entered the underground plant.

Parallel to these five tunnels, three more tunnels were built at the KL Sandpit which the SS had been using since summer 1939. Later on, these three tunnels were also used by the local civilian population as air-raid shelters. During air raids, even the primary school was evacuated regularly into these tunnels where an entire generation of school children witnessed the inmates' suffering.[418]

Mrs. Johanna B. and her three small children were among those sent into the tunnels during alarms. Her youngest was a newborn, she recalls. The prisoners were kept near the entrance and would wait for the women with children. "We would take biscuits and drop them and they would know it. This was forbidden. The prisoners were only kept at the entrance, but the townspeople were told to go much further into the caves. The prisoners were allowed to help women over the railroad tracks with their children, but this was an exception. They could not come near us, but the guards looked the other way and allowed this."[419]

Connected to the underground plant, the KL Sandpit tunnels also held the administrative center of the underground complex and were used as a "main entrance" for non-prisoners. The tunnel entrances were protected by massive slabs of steel reinforced concrete. The most extensive concrete reinforcement at Bergkristall was in the area parallel to the old beer cellar and near the former brewery where Maria F. lived. The reinforcements protected the entry for a new underground railroad.[420] Reinforced concrete also protected a second underground railway in another tunnel. This railway could not be used right away because of the conveyer belts that ran along its route

---

[418] Klepp, Monika and Reinhold Eckerstorfer, 200 Jahre Öffentliche Volksschule St. Georgen a. d. Gusen (St. Georgen/Gusen: Volksschule St. Georgen an der Gusen, 1996), 57

[419] Personal Interview, Johanna B., 18 September 2000. Translation by Martha Gammer.

[420] First railway switches were delivered to Fiebinger and to the management of CC Gusen starting 7 May 1944. On 11 May 1944 up to 18 m long railway tracks followed for Fiebinger. Wagenkontroll-bücher.

transporting sand from inside the hill.[421] These concrete reinforcements, finished at the end of July 1944, were immediately camouflaged to avoid detection,[422] although Allied intelligence reports document that the SS construction sites at St. Georgen and Gusen were regularly monitored by aerial reconnaissance flights from 11 November 1943.[423]

Figure 25: Concrete reinforcements that protected the railway entrances into Bergkristall (note the US investigators and the Me 262 fuselage on the right), May 1945
Source: Major Charles R. Sandler

---

[421] Fiebinger got the first conveyor system for sand on 9 April 1944 from Bochum, Germany. Wagenkontrollbücher.

[422] Camouflage mats were delivered to the SS-Führungsstab on 13 June 1944, 22 July 1944 and at the beginning of August. Wagenkontrollbücher.

[423] Interpretation Report No. U.18, Underground activity at Linz/St. Georgen, 22 January 1945. Airforce Historical Research Agency (AFHRA), intelligence reports of the Mediteranean Allied Air Forces' Files (Intelligence Section – Target Analysis, reel 207, microfilm roll 25194).

By summer 1944 the tunnels begun in three different places in May 1944 merged into a large underground production plant. In July, the first mining locomotives entered the tunnels. These were followed by larger locomotives needed to pull loads of armaments out of the hill. A rail line was completed in the last days of May 1944 leading from the SS "Übernahmebahnhof" (transfer station) in St. Georgen alongside the Gusen River, which had been regulated by the SS in 1941,[424] to the unused underpass of the rail line from Linz to Ceske Budejovice. At this point the berm of the railway had been disrupted by the brook of the Wimmingermühle Mill which had flowed there for a time. In order to avoid changing the berm's height to allow trains to pass under, a bridge with a flatter underframe was built allowing for more clearance.[425] This accommodation also allowed the larger Type 52 locomotives to drive into the track tunnel by passing over another bridge which was quickly built across the Gusen River, and which is still in use today as "Gusen-Steg" (now a small bridge for pedestrians).

Thousands of cubic meters of sand, brought to the tunnel portals on conveyer belts, were at first deposited just 100 meters outside the tunnels but directly adjacent to the public railway from Linz to Ceske Budejovice. To hide the truth from passing trains, the SS put up a billboard on this sand hill proclaiming, "Deutsche Wohn- und Siedlungsbauten für Bombengeschädigte" (mining of sand for a German housing agency that is going to replace accommodations for people bombed out of their homes).

In May 1944, when there was no more room to dump sand near the tunnels, prisoners transferred the sand off the conveyer belts at the tunnel portals onto hand held lorries. Prisoners then pushed these lorries about one kilometer, only to transfer the sand onto another conveyer belt at the fields near the sewage treatment plant which had just been completed by the "Liebenau"

---

[424] This regulation was done in conjunction with building the railway connection between St. Georgen and camp Gusen. Klinger, Volksschulchronik, 145. In August 1941 some 150 prisoners worked in the corresponding command „Gusen-Regulierung" at St. Georgen. Dobosiewicz, 105

[425] Documents about the cession of the bridge and reports of contemporary witnesses. Gemeindearchiv St. Georgen.

command exclusively for Bergkristall.[426] Here a thirty-meter-high "sand-mountain" eventually formed and was named "Arbeitskommando Kippe" (Dumpers' Command).

Figure 26: *The "Mountain of Sand" of "Kommando Kippe" in the years after the war, c. 1955*
Source: AHDG; Collection Franz Walzer

A sewage treatment plant was necessary for the 10,000 slaves expected to work in the underground plant because untreated sewage from so many people would have overwhelmed the small Gusen River, thereby giving clear evidence of the existence of this huge underground plant to Allied aerial reconnaissance.

---

[426] Angelo Ratti (survivor Gusen II 57616), and Rigamonti Franco (survivor Gusen II 57617), Memorie di Mauthausen – Gusen I e Gusen II (Milano, unpublished, in the possesion of the author) and Bernard Aldebert, Gusen II – Chemin de Croix en 50 Stations, ed. transl. Elisabeth Hölzl (Weitra: Bibliothek der Provinz, 1997), 95 and 207. Furthermore, technical drawing No. 322/L/31 of the sewage treatment plant, designed 18 March 1944 by Ing. Büro Dipl. Ing. Karl Fiebinger are part of J.I.O.A. Final Report No. 1, Part 1, Section III, Appendix A

The detainees' daily shift change and the huge accumulation of sand were the only clues the people of St. Georgen had as to the building project's implications. It was kept strictly top secret, and there were many counterintelligence officials. Hundreds of guards also kept the local population away from any details. Martin Lax recalls seeing a Wehrmacht man (on leave at his home near the tunnels) approach a passing column of prisoners only to be pushed back with a gun by the SS. In 1974, Lax returned to St. Georgen with his son Michael, and met the man by chance. Lax and his son knocked at the door of a farmhouse as they were looking for the home of a young woman who had dropped food to Lax from a second story window when he was a prisoner. The Wehrmacht veteran answered the door. He recalled being pushed away from the column by the SS and told Lax, "We saw the prisoners, but we didn't know what was being done to them."[427]

From her window on the top floor of the former brewery, Maria F. had a much clearer view of the prisoners entering the rail tunnel. She recalls,

> Each shift leaving the tunnel carried two or three dead people on their shoulders as they left and there were more on the wagons. There was a big pool built of concrete at the house of Rudolf P., left from the former brewery. I walked there one day and someone from the schwäbisch guards ... these SS were better and they liked my little sons...and one said, look here. The capos have thrown the corpses here. I wanted to move away from there because the capos had drowned the prisoners there. Thrown the corpses in there. I can see this in my heart up to now.

She had to be careful when talking to the SS living in the other apartments about what she saw, however. Concerned about a transport of young Jewish boys in concentration camp uniforms she saw trying to sleep on bags of cement outside the tunnels, she asked an SS man, "Why are these children in prison?" He answered, "If you see a snake in the forest, you don't just kill it. You kill the young, too, or they will grow up and poison you."[428]

---

[427] Lax and Lax, 103, Personal Interview 21 October 2004
[428] Maria F. Personal Interview 20 September 2000

In St. Georgen a large number of barracks and makeshift houses were built near the St. Georgen railway station at Wimming and in the Weingraben Valley (not to be confused with Wienergraben) for the skilled workers and experts who arrived in droves. While waiting for these accommodations, hundreds were quartered in private homes in St. Georgen and its surroundings. Even the parsonage was forced to billet "armament workers" in the church council's room.[429] In April 1944, the DEST canteen at St. Georgen was enlarged to feed them. Most of these civilians, indispensable for construction and management, were conscripted as well. Since the location was top secret, they were forbidden to communicate where they worked and lived to their relatives. Under strict observation of the counterintelligence officials, they were only allowed to tell their relatives that they were working "at Linz" and could only receive mail via post office box 599/1 at Linz.[430]

In March 1944, the High Command of the Luftwaffe and the Armament Ministry in Berlin approved 20,000 square meters of underground factory space at St. Georgen (one third of what was reportedly possible) for the "first wave" of dispersal under the code name "Esche I" (R-Nr. XVII 44 Z b 1 Esche I).[431] Still undecided about what type of advanced fighter aircraft to build at Bergkristall, the Luftwaffe High Command approved the Esche I plan to transfer part of the serial production of fuselages (Zellen) there[432].

---

[429] Chronik der Pfarre St. Georgen (chronicle of the St. Georgen parish), Tom. I, p. 217.

[430] Interview 971229. Transcript in the possession of the author.

[431] Schreiben des Chefs des Rüstungslieferamtes an den Chef des Amtes Bau im RMfRK, 3 March 1944 and 13 March 1944. BArch R3101/31.173/266 and 272.

[432] Schreiben des Jägerstabes – Abt. Planung vom 13. April 1944 betreffend „Deckung des Bedarfes an bombensicheren Räumen (unterirdisch und Bunkerbau) – Zellen". BArch R 3101/31.173/186

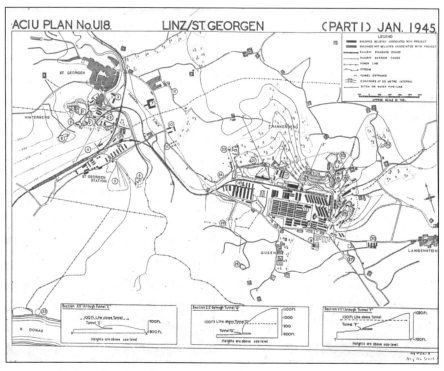

Map 4: Allied Combined Intelligence Unit
Plans showing the St. Georgen-Gusen-
Mauthausen Complex. January 1945
Source: AFHRA

1   Mariengrube sand pit (the prisoners' entrance into "Bergkristall")
2   KL sand pit (the civilians' entrance into "Bergkristall")
3   Sanitary infrastructure for civilian "Bergkristall" workers (e.g. showers)
4   St. Georgen railway station with barracks of SS-Leadership staff B8 (Gusen)
5   Sand mountain of "Kommando Kippe" at "Liebenau"
6   Sewage treatment plant of "Bergkristall"
7   DEST hostel for apprentices
8   Ventilation tower "S1"
9   Watchtowers (Postenkette)
10 Garages for DEST vehicles
11 DEST "Steinsiedlung" settlement
12 Air raid shelter for DEST employees with DEST administrative center
13 KL Gusen I concentration camp
14 missing
15 "Jourhaus" KL Gusen I (main entrance)
16 Infrastructure for "Gusen" quarry
17 Messerschmitt aircraft assembly buildings
18 Sewage treatment plant of KL Gusen I with production halls for Steyr-Daimler-Puch
19 KL Gusen II concentration camp
20 "Oberbruch" quarry
21 "Kastenhof" quarry
22 Workshops of SS-Verwaltungsführung Mauthausen/Gusen [location nicknamed "Westerplatte"]
23 Water reservoir for KL Gusen II
24 Area of barracks for "Luftwaffe" soldiers (26th and 27th guard company)
25 "Pierbauer" quarry

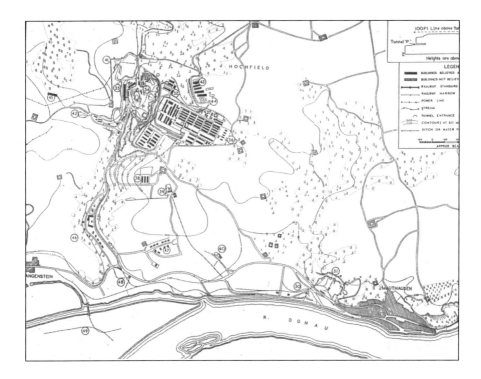

26 "Gusen" quarry
27 unknown
28 unknown
29 unknown
30 "Hafenbau" barracks (erected 1942 to
    accommodate personnel for harbor
    construction between the villages of Gusen
    and Langenstein).
31 "Kellerbau" tunnels
32 Workshops and living quarters
33 KL Mauthausen concentration camp
34 "Wienergraben" quarry
35 Messerschmitt production halls
36 Camp extension No. 3 (extermination)
37 Execution site with camp workshops
38 unknown
39 unknown
40 unknown
41 unknown
42 unknown

43 Tent camp near KL Mauthausen concen-
    tration camp
44 unknown
45 unknown
46 DEST "Fahrersiedlung" (drivers' settlement)
    at Wienergraben valley
47 SS settlement
48 Pump station
49 Bridge and railway lines constructed in
    1942 along with harbor project
50 unknown
51 "Bettelberg" quarry (operated by Mssrs.
    Poschacher)
52 missing
53 Gravel pit at the northern banks of the
    Danube river (connected by railway to the
    huge concrete mixer at the "Bergkristall"
    construction side)

In April St. Georgen was approved as the site for the serial production of jet fighters. On 14 April 1944, two weeks after being appointed to head the Jägerstab, Dr.-Ing. Kammler reported that 50,000 square meters of underground factory space could be achieved in St. Georgen.[433] That month another 10,000 square meters was approved for completion by September 1944 and a further 20,000 square meters were approved for completion by October 1944. Prof. Messerschmitt must have been frustrated by the delays in choosing Bergkristall for production of his Me 262, but Hitler refused to even allow its development as a fighter until 20 September 1944.[434] Permission to assemble the jet at Bergkristall didn't come until October. Code named Esche II, this plan was accompanied by approval for yet another extension of the tunnel system to accommodate Me 262 production. When Hitler's order to maximize production of Me 262 jet fighters by any means possible came in November,[435] the pace of tunnel construction stepped up even more.

Marsálek reports Me 262 production was projected to be 1,250 aircraft per month by April 1945 (just five months after Bergkristall was approved for an assembly plant), a larger production goal than was set for the Concentration Camp Dora-Mittelwerke, where 1,000 Me 262 were scheduled to be produced every month along with the A4 rockets (V2).[436] Nothing was spared to meet this goal and it was very nearly reached. According to an Air Division Report for the U.S. Forces in Austria dated 10 June 1946, this "underground installation" in the Russian zone, "St. Georgen ME 262 Assembly Plant," was "quite active in war production," based on "the large amount of aircraft parts that were found on the site."[437] The post-war J.I.O.A. Final Report estimates about 987 turbojets that were produced in St. Georgen a. d. Gusen.[438]

---

[433] Planungsdokument „Bedarf und Bestand unterirdischer Bauvorhaben", 14 April 1944. BArch R3101/31.173/188.

[434] Speer, 416 ff.

[435] Sammelbericht des Rüstungsstabes an das RLM, 22 November 1944, 7-22.11.(57). BArch, R3/1757/93.

[436] Marsálek, Mauthausen, 94 and 107.

[437] Air Division Headquarters United States Forces in Austria, Intelligence Section, APO 777, US Army, 20 June 1946 506.619B AFHRA

[438] J.I.O.A. Final Report No.1: p.1.

According to an internal paper of Messerschmitt AG Augsburg dated 26 January 1945, Bergkristall (with 21,430 square meters productive and more than 23,000 square meters of additional capacity yet to be completed) was the biggest plant being operated in the top secret Messerschmitt production network at that time.[439]

One indicator of the pace of tunnel construction at St. Georgen is the record of cement shipments arriving at the train station. Small quantities of cement from Upper Austria had been arriving during the first wave of underground dispersal, but deliveries doubled between June and July 1944. As more tunnel space was approved, the change in intensity of construction can be verified through the corresponding change in the volume of cement shipments to St. Georgen. After August 1944 when the first tunnels were completed, shipments of cement decreased.[440] October 1944 saw the minimum consumption. However, after Hitler's decision to produce the Me 262 that month, cement shipments to St. Georgen increased radically, arriving on longer and longer trains. Train length reached up to 55 cars on 9 November 1944. The increase of cement arriving in St. Georgen between September (140 total cars) and November (403 total cars) makes obvious the sudden priority given the tunnel extension. However, construction of the main part of the underground plant at St. Georgen (the jet plane assembly line area) was not started until very late in December 1944.[441]

At this time, Steyr-Daimler-Puch AG continued to use special machinery in a few of the Kellerbau Tunnels at CC Gusen I[442] to produce components for

---

[439] Messerschmitt-Betriebe – Fertigungsübersicht Werk Regensburg. Messerschmitt A.G. Augsburg, Zentralplanung Serie, Blatt 2 von 2. Smithsonian National Air and Space Museum, Captured German/Japanese Air Technical Documents, ADRC/T-2, Microfilm R 2497. Related other plants in the production survey of Regensburg plant were (square meters productive in paranthesis as of 26 January 1945): „Babel" (7,600), „Burghausen" (1,900), „Ente" (5,182), „Gauting" (1,500), „Johannisthal" (1,000), „Staufen" (1,900), „Zell" (2,250) and „Elbus" (4,600). Those of Augsburg plant: „Stammwerk" (2,300), „Miebach" (5,200), „Günzburg" (2,300), „Bergen" (2,845), „Genz" (900), „Brummingen" (5,600), „Kittelberg" (9,000), „Stolzenberg" (2,300), „Spiessingen" (3,600), „Misgeldingen" (1,000), „Kiesweg I" (700), „Kiesweg II" (700) and „Kiesweg III" (700).

[440] Haunschmied, 99

[441] Progress Chart – St. Georgen. (Figure 8 (c), J.I.O.A. Final Report No. 1, Part 1, Section III, Appendix A.

[442] At the end of the year 1944 there was production for Steyr-Daimler-Puch AG in tunnel No. 1 of Kellerbau according to Marsálek. Marsálek, Gusen, 9. Interestingly, Eugene Thome wrote that his

the most modern MP 44 assault rifle.[443] DEST's production of so called "spare parts"[444] (the code name railway officials used to register goods shipped by train) also increased at this time. On 9 October 1944 the first shipment of "spare parts" produced in Bergkristall was recorded in the Wagenkontrollbücher.[445] On 21 October 1944 the provisional ventilation was shut down because the regular air shaft, "S1," was opened near the Karlinger family's house for the first time. As completed tunnels were immediately equipped with machinery,[446] total production increased apace with the construction of underground factory space. The components' production of the DEST would increase by about 150 % after October 1944.[447] Production prospects for the Me 262 were finally looking good to Prof. Dr.-Ing. Messerschmitt. A captured October 1944 German document from Oberammergau* intended for Brigade Commander von Schultz-Tratzigg in Berlin in which Dipl.-Ing. Ludwig Bölkow purports to re-

---

work command operated already in the production of parts for the MP 40 in one of the Kellerbau tunnels, when the allied invasion took place (in June 1944). Letzeburger, 343 ff.

[443] Since the winter of 1944 metal-sheet parts for MP 40 and MP 44 submachine guns were produced in a tunnel of Gusen according to Marsálek. Marsálek, Mauthausen, 95.

[444] In fact this term designated both parts for aircraft and parts for small rifles. Wagenkontrollbücher.

[445] Statistical evaluation of the Wagenkontrollbücher. Haunschmied, 99.

[446] Übersicht „Zentralfertigung Me 262" der Messerschmitt-Zentralplanung Serie (26.1.1945). Smithsonian National Air and Space Museum, Captured German/Japanese Air Technical Documents, ADRC/T-2, Microfilm R 2497

[447] Haunschmied, 99

* In October 1943 the project managers and design engineers of Messerschmitt AG Augsburg were moved from Augsburg to Oberammergau. To camouflage this new Messerschmitt headquarter the unit was renamed „Oberbayerische Forschungsanstalt". From Oberammergau (O´gau) this unit coordinated the different Messerschmitt plants and dispersal sites. In addition, new advanced anti-aircraft missiles and jet planes like the Messerschmitt P 1101 were developed there (the latter design was adapted by Bell Laboratories for its Bell X-5 after the war). In February 1945 Dr.-Ing. Kammler and his staff took over control over Obb. Forschungsanstalt. On 11 April 1945 Wernher v. Braun and his staff of 400 rocket experts arrived at Oberammergau under the guard of 100 SS men. Dr.-Ing. Kammler himself was responsible for their move to the south and was present at Oberammergau for a short time, as well. Obb. Forschungsanstalt Oberammergau was liberated by US troops on 28 April 1945. Kammler left Oberammergau earlier and was seen in early May at Ebensee. From there he drove to Enns (a town just 8 km south-east of Bergkristall) shortly before American troops arrived. Richard Heigl. "Die Messerschmitt AG in Oberammergau (1943 – 1945) – Auslagerung, Projekte, Fremdarbeitereinsatz", Mohr-Löwe-Raute – Beiträge zur Geschichte des Landkreises Garmisch-Partenkirchen – Band 3 (Garmisch-Partenkirchen: Verein für Geschichte, Kunst- und Kulturgeschichte im Landkreis Garmisch-Partenkirchen e.V., 1995), 233 ff and Rädlinger, Christine. Zwischen Tradition und Fortschritt – Oberammergau 1869 – 2000 (Oberammergau: Gemeinde Oberammergau, 2002), 198 ff. and Markus Schmitzberger. Was die US Army in der Alpenfestung wirklich suchte – Eine Theorie zum Decknamen der Anlage "Quarz" in Roggendorf bei Melk (Schleusingen: Amun-Verlag, 2001), 171 ff

veal facts "symptomatic of the Luftwaffe and its command," reports that Prof. Messerschmitt was very confident that the Me 262 would be rapidly produced. He revealed this in a meeting with "Director Lusser of the Fieseler factories, the creator of the V-1, possessor of the Knight's Cross to the War Service Cross with Swords [sic]." Lusser is reported to have said, "If I had known what Prof. Messerschmitt told me, that in a comparatively short time the Me 262 will cost only 1800 hours, I would never have submitted my proposals to the Amt (Administration). I feel like being burdened [sic] regarding my then made proposals [sic]."[448] This discussion provides some insight into how even top engineers had to compete for these projects.

The relationship of the Bergkristall facility to Messerschmitt was complicated, and has also contributed to the obscurity of this history. Messrs. Messerschmitt was subdivided into two "Fertigungskreise (FKS)" (production circles), one being Messerschmitt AG Augsburg and the other being Messerschmitt GmbH Regensburg. Formally, with Messerschmitt facility code "93", Bergkristall was part of "FKS Regensburg" but it was not controlled by the Messerschmitt Company in Regensburg. Similar to Kammler's ZBL's, which explains why they worked so well together, the Messerschmitt plants were controlled by several specialized staffs located at the Oberbayerische Forschungsanstalt at Oberammergau (Obb. F.A. or OFA O'gau), Germany. For instance, there was a "Führungsstab Kontrollwesen" (coordinating aspects of quality control across all Messerschmitt plants of that time), a "Führungsstab Arbeitseinsatz" (work operations), a "Führungsstab Energieversorgung" (energy supply), a "Führungsstab Montageinspektorat im Betriebsausschuss" (inspectorate for aircraft assembly within an across-factory-board), a "Stab Schweisstechnische Betreuung" (welding technology), and so on. Direktor Linder at Regensburg was only involved when Messerschmitt GmbH Regensburg had to give resources to Bergkristall, but he had no authority in regard to the operation and the aims of this production site at St. Georgen.[449]

---

[448] „Translation of German Document, Oberammergau," Dipl. Eng. Ludwig Bolkow to von Schultz-Tratzigg, Inclosure 1 [sic], 25 October 1944 AFHRA 512.6259

[449] Correspondence sent form Berkristall to Obb. Forschungsanstalt Oberammergau in March and April 1945. Smithsonian National Air and Space Museum, Captured German/Japanese Air Technical Documents, ADRC/T-2, Microfilm R 3996

Another important detail is that one Hungarian plant of Wiener Neustädter Flugzeugwerke (WNF) at Györ that produced around 500 fighter planes per year was transfered to Bergkristall at the end of 1944.[450] According to a letter of the Rüstungsstab to the Air Ministry provisions were to be made to compensate Hungary with 60 (jet) planes each month for accepting the transfer of WNF/Györ to Bergkristall.[451]

By 30 November 1944, the whole network was enlarged to 21,000 square meters and the new extension begun. The first fuselages were shipped from Bergkristall in December 1944 under the code name "Ba III" (Betriebs-abteilung III [production section No 3]) of DEST St. Georgen.[452] These code names, intended to maintain secrecy during the war, have made research-ing Bergkristall difficult for decades. The managers of Obb. F.A. O'gau and Messerschmitt systematically used the code-name "Bergkristall" in most of the correspondence to avoid identifying a location. In about two hundred documents, the term "St. Georgen" is only used in one or two cases. To confound the matter, several different addresses were used for the produc-tion facility at St. Georgen: DEST, Linz/Donau 2, SS-Führungsstab Linz BA III or simply SS-Führungsstab Linz. Clearly, researchers without detailed knowledge of the geography and infrastructure of the St. Georgen-Gusen-Mauthausen area would find it difficult to combine terms like "Linz" with the huge top secret plant at nearby St. Georgen (15 km east).[453]

One other important detail is that this huge key plant in the Messerschmitt network was operated and administered more or less by DEST itself.[454] As a

---

[450] Freund, Florian. Arbeitslager Zement, 108 ff and Bertrand Perz, Projekt Quarz, 180 ff.

[451] Bericht des Rüstungsstabes über die Besprechung mit Exc. Hollebronth am 20.12.1944 an RLM-Hauptausschuss Flugzeuge (Oberstingenieur Alpers). BArch R3/1757/27.

[452] Recall that "Ba II" was the code name for the earlier Messerschmitt production in the production halls in CC Gusen, the old "Polenlager" which became the industrial park.

[453] Correspondence sent from Berkristall to Obb. Forschungsanstalt Oberammergau in March and April 1945.

[454] Das SS-Wirtschaftsverwaltungshauptamt und die unter seiner Dienstaufsicht stehenden wirt-schaftlichen Unternehmungen, 132 ff (NO-1573). At first, DEST only contracted to produce parts for aircraft, but when it demonstrated its capabilities to Messerschmitt and the Air Ministry, it was awared a contract to assemble entire airplanes. To achieve this, Messrs. Messerschmitt agreed to finance the start-up and provide key personnel. DEST agreed to supply all its premises, personnel and necessary (new) buildings. Messerschmitt was responsible to pay a sum as a deposit and to pay

consequence, Messerschmitt's fighter production became totally dependent on the SS. In fact, with Bergkristall the SS controlled Me 262 production in 1945 because most of the fuselages (the heart of each jet) were pre-assembled there. The labeling of DEST as a "small" contractor within the production network might be one reason why this most modern of underground plants never appeared in the US Strategic Bombing Survey in its full significance. Certainly, the post-war interrogations of Speer and Göring do not correct this mistake. It remains unclear if this constellation was done to mislead Allied intelligence or whether it is the first act of the total absorption of Messrs. Messerschmitt by Pohl's WVHA.

Unbelievable sacrifices were extracted from the prisoners in order to complete a new assembly plant for the Me 262 in the new extension. About 97 heavy flat cars of the type "ss, xx, gltrs ..." left Bergkristall after January 1945, revealing a peak production of about 400 fully assembled Me 262 fuselages per month, assuming one flat car could carry about 4 such fuselages. A 4 April 1945 Obb. Forschungsanstalt Oberammergau report confirms this, giving a daily production capacity of 15 complete fuselages, providing an average number of 450 fuselages per month. So, the maximal number of finished fuselages at St. Georgen was around 1,560 "operational" fuselages.

The report also finds increased production was inhibited by problems with both men and machines. A lack of tooling, the limited size of hydraulic presses which could be used in the tunnels, and interruptions in the power supply causing black-outs for one to two hours daily were problems which engineers could have solved. But problems with labor still confounded Messerschmitt, which was apparently having trouble, as the report states, finding "personnel for plant management" and "German professional workers." The implication here is that better "human material," i.e. Aryan, could have increased production. By this time, all of the German economy, as well as the Wehrmacht, was having

---

leasing rates to DEST further on. It was furthermore negotiated that DEST will buy back the buildings that were errected for Messerschmitt after the war. The underground plant itself (Bergkristall) was errected and financed by „Amtsgruppe C Sonderstab Kammler" on behalf of Reichsministerium für Rüstung und Kriegsproduktion. Messerschmitt and DEST were to pay rents to the Reich, but the Reich collapsed before any such payments were made. DEST's sole responsibility was to ensure the production in the tunnels.

trouble finding Germans to employ. But the use of business jargon to describe problems with labor in a concentration camp underscores how routine brutality had become for Messerschmitt management. The armament industries insisted on control over production when using SS slaves, but the report reveals that even in this most successful project, slavery and extermination of the workforce inhibited production. The report cites a problem with "fluctuation in concentration camp inmates." This most assuredly refers to the high death rate, as Gusen II survivors Karl Littner and Dusan Stefancic say assignments to production jobs were more or less permanent. Once trained, one worked at a job until one died.[455] The death rate undoubtedly also caused the "lack of qualified personnel to produce a sufficient number of fixtures." The report ludicrously cites a lack of "quality assurance personnel." This highlights two problems. The first is that the SS guards and capos' methods of assuring quality – brutality and murder – had not changed and could never be conducive to production. The second problem was the assumption that "Aryan" managers would be as invested in Nazi ideology as were the SS and Messerschmitt. An incident which Karl Littner recalls in Tunnel 7 at Bergkristall illustrates this point:

> One day shortly before the shift's end, the [Austrian] foreman came out of his office to inspect the quality of the work we produced. He bent over my box of welded parts, took out a bunch, and exchanged them with parts from the next welder. When the foreman finished with his work, I asked him why he was doing this? "I like to mix up the work," he answered, "and even out the production to make at least 50% acceptable. This may prevent some of you from being hanged or accused of sabotage when the work quality is less than 50%."[456]

Clearly, not all managers placed production goals above human life. The report also cites problems with "improper transport of fixtures by concentration camp inmates and improper configuration of hulls and canopies which were supplied from outside." Since much of this "outside" work was also done by concentration camp inmates, the problems apparently existed throughout the system.

---

[455] Personal Interviews, 7 May 2004
[456] Littner, npag

Despite these challenges, Messerschmitt and Kammler were investing a great deal of confidence in the future of Bergkristall. For better coordination between the serial production there and the aircraft research and development engineers at Obb. F.A. O'gau, an "Aussenstelle der Oberbayerischen Forschungsanstalt Oberammergau" (a branch office) was installed at Bergkristall on 10 March 1945.[457] Different pieces of design-related correspondence also give clear evidence that Prof. Messerschmitt and Direktor Gerhard Degenkolb (the authorized representative of Speer for the promotion of the production of the jet-planes and the A4 rockets earlier) received messages out of Bergkristall and thus must have been directly involved in the design-change and production program at Bergkristall. One document of 11 March 1945 also states that Dir. Degenkolb had recently visited Bergkristall.[458]

Along with this "research and development branch" (Aussenstelle) at St. Georgen, the Waffentechnische Lehranstalt (WTL) of the Waffen-SS Graz in Tunnel No. 4 of Kellerbau III appears to have importance. Captain Samuel G. Wilson of the 34th Bomb Squadron reports seeing "complete testing laboratories" in Bergkristall in June 1945.[459]

The Luftwaffe and the Armaments Ministry were scrambling to get smaller underground projects similar to Esche I (the aircraft component production begun in the first extension of the beer cellars) merely approved even as Pohl and Kammler moved ahead to complete Esche II (the serial production of the advanced fighter planes) with 10,000 slaves.[460] Their plans would be fully realized by the end of the war in the 50,000 square meters of underground factory space at Bergkristall. Only a few hundred square meters in the north-eastern corner of the tunnel-complex remained uncompleted. Also parts of the jet plane assembly line that was to be supplied by Messerschmitt GmbH Regens-

---

[457] Niederschrift der am 11.3.1945 in Bergkristall (= St. Georgen) abgehaltenen Besprechung betreffend 609-Fertigung. Smithsonian National Air and Space Museum, Captured German/Japanese Air Technical Documents, ADRC/T-2, Microfilm R 3996

[458] Ibid.

[459] Wilson, Captain Samuel G. Disarming the Luftwaffe, unpublished (in the possesion of the author). The author thanks Mr.Ronald S. Macklin for providing this report.

[460] Aufstellung der von Häftlingen geleisteten Arbeitsstunden für die Luftfahrtindustrie, 21 February 1944. NARA, microform publication M890/9/0707-0709 (1584-PS).

burg were never completely finished. By the time the plant came fully on line, the war had ended.[461] According to Prof. Messerschmitt, if the underground dispersal had been allowed to continue at this pace for just six more months, damage by Allied bombing would have been completely overcome.[462] Other key production companies for Me 262 parts like Flugzeug- und Metallbauwerke Wels GmbH were moved underground to St. Georgen, as well.[463] While the latter company was responsible for the production of the highly-sophisticated leading edges used for the Me 262, it also produced entire wings.[464]

About 6,000 square meters of storage space was bomb-proofed in B8 Bergkristall for thousands of components which arrived in St. Georgen needed to fully equip the Me 262 fuselages. On 16 December 1944 another subcamp of the Mauthausen/Gusen complex, CC Gusen III, was opened in Lungitz, about three kilometers north, to help transport incoming aircraft hulls. The old brick production plant there had been used to warehouse aircraft parts since 1943. The storage capacity was around 80 railway wagons. The first thirty inmates to work at Lungitz commuted daily from their barracks at CC Gusen.[465] About 300 CC Gusen III detainees eventually worked in the bakery and logistics for the underground Messerschmitt plant at St. Georgen. They delivered airplane fuel tanks and prefabricated aluminium metal to DEST's joint ventures at St. Georgen, Gusen and Mauthausen-Wienergraben. According to eyewitnesses in Lungitz, a tunnel was planned through Frankenberg Mountain to link the bakery and aircraft parts warehouse at CC Gusen III with the Kellerbau tunnel system above Gusen I. The tunnel entrance at Lungitz was pegged out by the end of the war, but excavation had barely begun.

---

[461] Presumably the building project B8 was planned earlier as for instance was Building Project Zement (production intercontinental ballistic missiles). According to an interoffice memo there was already an „air force command St. Georgen/Gusen at the concentration camp of Mauthausen/Gusen" on 23 August 1942.

[462] 11 – 12 May 1945 Interview No. 6 USSBBS 137.315-6 AFHRA

[463] Planungsunterlagen zu den Verlagerungsbetrieben der Messerschmitt-Fertigungskreise. Smithsonian National Air and Space Museum, Captured German/Japanese Air Technical Documents, ADRC/T-2, Microfilm R 2497

[464] Kriegstagebuch Rüstungskommando Linz, NARA microform publication T77/744.

[465] Reichl, Leo. „Das KZ-Lager Gusen III – Beginn und Aufbau einer Grossbäckerei in Lungitz und Abbruch dieser Anlagen" Oberösterreichische Heimatblätter, 54. Jahrgang, Heft 3/4 (2000), 158

Stone production slowed further at the Wienergraben Quarry as Mauthausen inmates went to work on the production of aircraft components in the Wienergraben stonemason halls which were converted for the DEST joint venture with Messerschmitt.[466] Messerschmitt paid DEST 4,– RM per day for a non expert's work in Gusen II and 6,– RM for an expert's. DEST itself paid only 1,50 RM for an expert and, for the non-expert's, only 0,50 RM to the Reich. [467] By June 1944, DEST supplied 35% of the airplane production of Messerschmitt GmbH Regensburg through its production facilities at St. Georgen, Gusen, Mauthausen and Flossenbürg.[468] Even as the territory of the Third Reich shrank toward the war's end, the presence of the administrative center of DEST, the huge number of concentration camp inmates at Mauthausen/ Gusen and the unrelenting underground plant construction made St. Georgen one of the most important centers for the air armament industry.[469]

By early spring 1945 the production of fuselages for the Me 262 jet was running at considerable capacity.[470] Simultaneous with this serial production, the extension of the underground complex progressed rapidly. Consequently, it was possible to take preliminary steps toward building another production plant southwest of the jet-plane assembly area. By war's end the area of the tunnels far exceeded the original plan of 50,000 square meters. According to older fragmentarily plans, an extension for a tank production factory was intended before the circumstances of the war demanded an increase in airplane production in that area instead. However, one can see plans for another "doubling" of the tunnel area at St. Georgen. Speer spoke of 100,000 square meters

---

[466] Marsálek, Mauthausen, 94
[467] Marsálek, Gusen, 24.
[468] Schreiben Pohls an Himmler betreffend eines diesbezüglichen Fernschreibens von Reichsmarschall Göring, 14 June 1944. BArch, NS 19/3571 (NO-4242).
[469] J.I.O.A. Final Report No.1, 1.
[470] The following main components of the Me 262 jet-plane were produced by DEST at Bergkristall: Anschlussbeschlag links und rechts (110-007/008), Deckel oben (110-009), Rumpf (F 105), Spante (100-001/005/004, 100-007/035), Schottskade (110-003/004), Rumpfmittelteil (F 110), Rumpfteile (100-030/031-002, 100-004/006), Rumpfhinterteil (F 104), Behälter und Befestigung (904-091, 904-092), Steuerungsteile für Rumpf (917-002), Flettnerantrieb (401-005). Furthermore: Rumpfbau, Wannenbau, Kabine, Heckleitwerk, Rumpfspitze, Tankdeckel. Main production divisions had been: Mechanische Bearbeitung, Spenglerei, Schlosserei, Presserei. Fertigungs- und Lieferantenübersicht 8-262 of 20 March 1945, Messerschmitt AG Augsburg, Zentralplanung Serie (ZPS/Re). Richard Eger. „Re: Me 262 Production at St. Georgen underground plant". E-mail to the author. 23 June 2004.

of tunnel area for the planned major underground complexes of the Reich. This was, perhaps, a reference to the final goal for the planned extensions of the tunnels in St. Georgen. According to a secret project drawing of Bergkristall of 5 April 1944, an extension of the tunnel grid for additional 21,000 square meters was already planned to the northwest.[471]

The production itself was carried out by thousands of prisoners, their number steadily increasing as the tunnels were completed. On an assembly line several kilometers long, prisoners assembled prefabricated metal parts transported to St. Georgen from throughout the Third Reich. Thousands of components for leading edges and fuselages for the Me 262 jet fighters were stored in the tunnels. Once completed, they were loaded onto trains and taken hundreds of kilometers from St. Georgen to the hidden "forest factories" which the Messerschmitt Company was more than willing to discuss with the USSBS after the war. There, the completed fuselages, leading edges, wings, jet-engines, etc. were finally assembled into completed airplanes. In many cases, the fighter planes were given their operational test at airbases near these forest factories. This production network was kept highly secret. Even the test pilots did not know from where the aircraft came. This is another reason why the underground plant at St. Georgen remains unknown to many "experts" and thus is not included in any history of the war or in aviation history in general. Components made in Bergkristall were sent to the following locations (only key locations are given here): Berlin, Bodenwöhr, Brandenburg, Ceske Budejovice, Burgau, Cham, Flossenbürg, Günzburg, Hagelstadt, Kahla, Kubohütte, Leipheim, Obernzell, Obertraubling, Regensburg, Schwäbisch Hall, Vilsek, and Wels.[472]

While many scholars, including the authors, are clearly indebted to Hans Marsálek's scholarship on the history of Mauthausen, his reference to the tunnels at Gusen II as "unfinished" and his statement that only a "few" companies had transferred production are unintentionally misleading and may have discouraged researchers from pursuing information about CC Gusen I and II.[473]

---

[471] Lageplan „Esche" prepared by „Ing.Büro Dipl Ing Karl Fiebinger", Drawing No. 322/L22, 5 April 1944. Project drawing in the possession of the author.
[472] Wagenkontrollbücher.
[473] Marsálek, Mauthausen, 26

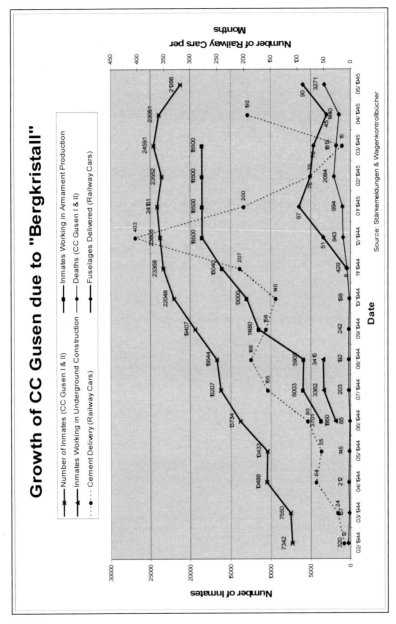

Diagram 2: Growth of CC Gusen due to Bergkristall. 1988
Prepared by Rudolf A. Haunschmied

As has been shown, a reliance by US military scholars on USSBS has been equally misleading. David McIsaac criticizes the USSBS directors for the aura of "'the Eastern Establishment banking-and-commercial complex' (a forerunner to the so called military industrial complex) that hung over [their] meetings." He doubted that they ever gave a thought, or knew how to approach, questions of labor.[474] The USSBS's Aircraft Industry Report (long mistaken as the final word on the number and location of aircraft factories in the Third Reich as well as on the working conditions within them) states that, among the "incentives" to increase production in aircraft factories, time-and-a-quarter was paid for hours worked over 48 a week. Those who worked over 72 hours reportedly received "an increase in meat from one-half to one and one-half pounds a week, plus such luxuries as cognac, cigarettes and chocolate."[475] Although there is a column in Exhibit IV "Make-up of Working Force: German Aircraft Companies" for October 1944, showing "Per Cent: Political Prisoners, Prisoners of War and Jews" in each plant, including "reported sub-contractors" (those operating at CC Gusen I at the time not shown) there is no analysis of the different "incentives" these workers might have received. For that, we must turn to the survivors.

---

[474] McIsaac, David. Strategic Bombing in World War II: the Story of the United States Strategic Bombing Survey (New York: Garland, 1976), 159

[475] United States Strategic Bombing Survey Aircraft Industry Report, 83

Life and Death in St. Georgen and Concentration Camp Gusen II

Acquiring a large number of detainees never presented a problem for the project's mastermind, Dr.-Ing. Kammler. His confidence in Himmler's ability to deliver prisoners was matched by the ability of the Gestapo and the SS to imprison ever more innocent people. From the end of 1943 on, Himmler and Göring had secretly prepared to deport people from all occupied areas of Europe to use as human loot, forced labor for the German air armaments industry. By the beginning of 1943 the chief of the SD (Security Service of the German Police) assured Oswald Pohl that prisoners would be delivered to the concentration camps by way of increasing arrests in the simplified policy. In a teleprint of 15 February 1944 Göring "pleaded" with Himmler to support him in calling on prisoners for the "industrial seizure" of new airplanes.[476] Many detainees who worked in St. Georgen and Gusen in the special production programs were imprisoned by the local SD and sent to CC Gusen for trifles or because their vocational profile fit. On 21 February 1944, Pohl arranged for 10,000 detainees to be assigned to the assembly plant "Esche II." This huge number was the same for the factory "Anhydrit" at CC Buchenwald, for which another 10,000 prisoners were intended to work for Junkers.[477]

But the grab for human loot did not end there. According to a report of the Fighter Aircraft Staff of 3 March 1944, it was planned to deport 100,000 Italians to safeguard the production in the Air Armament Industry in the Third Reich.[478] Hundreds were used in "Bergkristall-Fertigung" (Bergkristall aircraft assembly and manufacturing command).[479] Angelo Ratti was 17 years

---

[476] Allen, Business, 234 refers to this as PS-1585(I), Hermann Göring to Heinrich Himmler, 15 Feb. 1944 "Aufstellung der 7. Staffel/Fliegergruppe zB V.7"; Perz, Projekt Quarz, 145-48

[477] Aufstellung der von Häftlingen geleisteten Arbeitsstunden für die Luftfahrtindustrie, 21 February 1944. NARA, microform publication M890/9/0709 (1584-PS).

[478] Jägerstab-Schnellbericht, 3 March 1944. BArch R3/1756/310

[479] Survivor testimonies from Sesto San Giovanni, Italy, which is twinned with Langenstein, Austria. The BREDA aircraft works were in Sesto, and so the workers of this plant were sent to Bergkristall after being rounded-up by the Gestapo and SD in the Milano area.

old when he was deported with other Italians in March 1944 to Mauthausen/ Gusen. After a few weeks in quarantine at CC Mauthausen and work in the Wienergraben Quarry, he was sent to CC Gusen II where he worked in Kommando "Stollenbau" (tunnel construction command) and helped to dig Tunnel No. 3 of Bergkristall in the "KL" sandpit. This was only one of the work commands Ratti reports at St. Georgen. There were Kommando "Pötschgrube" (the command that dug the tunnels at the former brewery), Kommando "Möglegrube" (the command that dug the tunnels at the Marien-grube Sandpit), Kommando "Beton" (the concreting work command), Kommando "Ausbau" (the work command that finished the tunnels), Kommando "Lagerplatz" (the work command where the construction wood was stored), Kommando "Bahnhof" (the work command that managed the incomming railway car loads), the Kommando "Transportkolonne" (the work command that had to move the building materials), the Kommando "Elektriker" (the work command that had to do the electrical installations), the Kommando "Geometer" (the surveyor work command), and many more. Since Ratti was very young and remained healthy, he soon got a job in a smithy where he was responsible for distributing the sharpened chisels to the different work commands. This job helped him to survive. He also saw Jewish boys from the ages of 10 to 15 years working at Bergkristall, but their fate is uncertain.[480]

In April 1944, Hitler ordered Himmler to bring 100,000 Jews into arma-ment manufacture in the Reich, after having ordered them all removed 18 months earlier. As Ulrich points out, Hitler, Himmler and Speer became "ideologically flexible" about exterminating Jews and other hated groups when the war economy required them to be. The ultimate goal of genocide was only modified, never changed. "Individual skilled workers were looked after, while enormous numbers of easily replaceable prisoners were sacrificed to the need for speed on the construction projects rushed through in the final months of the war." [481] However, the experience of survivors of Gusen II shows the camp guards, under whose authority prisoners were first placed during "quarantines" and who patrolled the tunnels, could not be dissuaded

---

[480] Angelo Ratti (survivor Gusen II 57616), and Rigamonti Franco (survivor Gusen II 57617), Memorie di Mauthausen – Gusen I e Gusen II (Milano, unpublished). In the possesion of the author.

[481] Ulrich, 189-194

from pursuing their extermination of the "inferior" races whose moral and genetic weaknesses they believed they could detect through physical screening (comprised of ritualistic torture-by-labor).

Deportations of Hungarian Jews began in April 1944. In fact Adolf Eichmann massed his "Sonder-Einsatzkommando für Judenfragen in Ungarn" in early March 1944 at Mauthausen/Gusen as a subordinate of SS-Standartenführer Dr. Geschke of the corresponding SD-Einsatzgruppe for Hungary.[482] By July 458,000 were sent to Auschwitz. 108,000 were selected for labor and the rest were murdered immediately. Martin Lax's experience on his journey from his native Hungary to the Bergkristall construction site demonstrates the emphasis put on selecting "human material" whose value was only, as Ulrich says, "what physical strength [one] could provide for a few weeks."[483] At Auschwitz, when Martin Lax's family arrived, the selection either for the gas chamber or for construction work was made by a "group of SS officials and men in white coats."[484] These doctors sent Lax's parents, Mozes and Mariam, and his eleven-year-old sister Gizella to the left, to be gassed and burned. Lax, directed to the right, was selected for slave labor. In an interview, Mr. Lax said he believes the camp administration at Auschwitz was so overwhelmed with the number of people arriving at once, those who went immediately to the gas chamber were never registered in the camp. As Jews unfit for labor, their "human material" value did not warrant even this much attention.

Those who were selected for work were asked questions about where they came from and about their professions and skills, but they were not given numbers at Auschwitz before being sent to labor camps. Records show Rudolf Höss, Commandant of Auschwitz understood "Me Betr. Bergkristall" was a work command of CC Mauthausen for which selections at Auschwitz

---

[482] Statement of Dieter Wisliceny, at the Nuremberg International Military Tribunal, 3. January 1946

[483] Ibid., 190-192

[484] Lax and Lax, 67. Mr. Lax also lost his sisters Suri and Frida, who died in other camps, and his brother Shloime, who died in a prisoner of war camp in Russia.

supplied labor.[485] Lax's registration card followed him to CC Mauthausen, where he was given a wire wristband with a number. Regardless of recorded skills, those selected for labor and sent to CC Gusen II were seen by the guards as uniformly qualified to be murdered unless they could prove otherwise. None of Kammler or Maurer's reforms could change this. On the first work day at Bergkristall the prisoners were forced to carry huge stones and run up and down a hill, much as Joe C. experienced four years earlier when building CC Gusen I, much as thousands of prisoners from all over Europe had experienced in DEST stone quarries from the company's beginnings in 1938:

> For eight hours, we were forced to go up and down a hill in pairs, each pair carrying a rock. The rocks were big and heavy; each weighed about four hundred pounds or more. They were hell to carry, and as the day wore on, they got heavier and heavier. SS men were scattered all along the hillside, from top to bottom. Those at the top and bottom of the hill threatened us with guns and snarling dogs. Those on the hillside held sticks shaped like rough baseball bats and faced each other in two rows … "Run, Jews. Run!" they screamed, and we ran, each pair struggling with its burden between the rows of stick-wielding SS men … [Prisoners] who dropped their rock were beaten mercilessly until they managed to pick it up and begin running again … Most of the men were unused to heavy labor, and slowly they gave out. They slowed down, they strained to hold the rock up, and gradually they began to drop it more and more often until eventually they were unable to lift it. The SS beat them every time they dropped the rock and whenever they ran too slowly. When they were finally unable to lift the rock at all, the SS beat them until they fell unconscious and then gave them a shove, rolling their senseless bodies down the hill, where they were dragged away.[486]

Clearly, the goal of the SS guards (immediate murder by traditional, ritualized means developed in the quarries at CC Mauthausen/Gusen), still conflicted

---

[485] Erklärung der Markierungen, die ich auf der Landkarte mit dem Titel Concentration Camps vorgenommen habe. Anlage I zu Document No. NI-034. Records of the United States Nuremberg War Criminal Trials, United States vs. Oswald Pohl et al. (Case IV), January 13, 1947-August 11, 1948, NARA microform publication M890/13/0153 (NI-034).

[486] Lax and Lax., 83-84

with the efforts of DEST to provide laborers *to be murdered* constructing tunnels or assembling planes. Those who survived this selection, a brutal mockery of a physical exam, were thought to be good "human material." The working conditions within the tunnels would be no better.

Concentration Camp Gusen II, already known for terror, earned an even worse reputation for treating prisoners like so much war material. In winter 1944 several railway cars loaded with new arrivals were left standing in the DEST transfer station because the SS had no immediate use for them. As Eugene Thome (inmate No. 47489 of CC Gusen I) explains in *Letzeburger zu Mauthausen*, "They were left in the cold on the sidetrack without any food or water for a week. When they opened the box cars, only frozen corpses fell outside – fuel for the crematorium." [487]

In *Nazi Mass Murder,* Pierre Serge Choumoff reports a second phase of Operation 14 f 13 at Hartheim Castle from April to December 1944 that was restricted to inmates from Mauthausen and Gusen. Correspondingly, as Allen explains, emphasis was put on eugenics to improve production during this period; the selections were made by the camp doctors. After 3,228 inmates were killed, prisoners dismantled the gas chamber at Hartheim.[488] However, survivors of Gusen II also report a continuation of "wild euthanasia," selections made by the camp doctor (or even Gusen II's Head Capo Van Loosen in a white coat masquerading as a doctor), ending in lethal heart injections or in deadly beatings.[489]

Martin Lax does not recall seeing heart injections administered although he also points out that no one prisoner can speak for all. There were more than eight thousand prisoners at Gusen II at liberation,[490] and so it was quite possible for prisoners to have different experiences within the same camp. However, he reports, at the end of every shift prisoners judged to be too sick or weak were taken to the "hospital" where Lax himself was taken after a

[487] Letzeburger, 325.
[488] Kogon, et al. 49-50
[489] Orski, Marek. Gusen 2004 – the Past and the Present. (Gdansk: Wydawnictwo Gdanskie, 2004), 33, 41 and Kielich and Mills, 70,
[490] SHAEF G-5/2711/7.2. NARA 331/290/7/10/3

workplace accident in a tunnel crushed his leg. However, his description of the "hospital" routine more closely fits the practice of "wild euthanasia" than that of medical treatment. Rations were cut for the invalids and they were left to die. Even here, a capo and a "tall intern" selected the most seriously ill to be taken to a room known as the "Bahnhof" (so called because prisoners referred to it as the "train station to paradise"). "Once in the Bahnhof, they were ignored and forgotten. They were given no food at all, only one bucket of water and another bucket in which they defacated and urinated. They were condemned men, and those well enough to think knew it and begged to be released, to no avail," Lax writes.[491]

At first, prisoners from Gusen II marched from the "subcamp St. Georgen"[492] (which was actually at Gusen) several kilometers to St. Georgen along the rails of the Schleppbahn, their route flanked by a fence. Later, some would be driven into boxcars and taken to the tunnels under extreme duress. Karl Littner recalls the dangers he encountered on this ride,

> We waited for the day shift to unload before we took the train to work a twelve-hour night shift. Just for fun, the capos and the SS created unnecessary chaos, shouting, clubbing, and confusing the bewildered Jews. Scared and confused, we started running, trying to outrun the dogs. Many would try to reach the front wagon, leaving the farther wagons empty. One night I decided to change the routine and run toward the empty wagons in the back. Running and looking back I saw a vicious dog follow on my heel, his jaws trying to grab my behind. With the little strength borne of the self-preservation left in me I reached the wagon without being bitten, grabbed the lamp bracket to slow myself down and swung myself into the boxcar. Before I could get a solid foothold to stabilize my landing, someone grabbed my throat in both his hands and started to strangle me. My heaving breath nearly stopped. As he suffocated me the murderer said in Polish, "*Udusze Cie Skorwysynie*"(I will suffocate you, you sonofabich). Realizing who the killer was, I felt resigned

---

[491]   Lax and Lax, 117, Personal Interview, October 21, 2004
[492]   This expression is used by the author to underline the specific situation of CC Gusen II. While the inmates were „accomodated" at Gusen, their actual destiny was to work and to die for the huge underground plant at nearby St. Georgen.

and miserable, ready to end my dreary existence, once and for all. Near death anyway, I managed to say, "Udus"(Suffocate). Surprised to hear Polish, he released me, saying. "You are lucky you answered in Polish. I thought you were a Hungarian Jew, the one I missed."

"I thought I had killed them all," he added.[493]

Although Lax does not recall the level of ethnic strife ("We were too busy to argue," he said),[494] Littner's experience is not uncommon. Kielich reports similar scenes in the Russian Camp at Gusen I.[495] In *Russia's War*, Richard Overy notes that the Germans found Russian POWs often killed all the Poles when the two groups were shipped to concentration camps together.[496] Lax does recall that the makeup of prisoners changed over the course of months after his arrival in the summer of 1944 as different nationals and groups were annihilated in "quarantines" or through extermination-and-labor. "The Hungarian Jews I'd entered with were replaced by trainloads of Poles, both Jewish and Gentile, by Republicans from Spain, by Bulgarians, Greeks, French, Russians, Ukrainians, and German criminals, prisoners from all over Europe speaking languages I had never heard before."[497]

While prisoners' recollections vary, all describe the camp as a hell. To try to determine the reality, one must balance on the one hand the 50,000 square meters dug out with pneumatic drills, shovels, and bare hands (26,000 square meters in four short months), and on the other hand the nine thousand deaths recorded at Gusen II, not to mention the unrecorded deaths. According to Constant Reuter-Cajot, survivor of the Betonkommando (Concrete Command), nobody cared if a prisoner were buried in concrete. The other prisoners were simply told to continue working.[498]

---

[493] Littner, npag
[494] Personal Interview, 21 October 2004
[495] Kileich and Mills, 43
[496] Overy, 82
[497] Lax and Lax, 98
[498] Letzeburger, 373

When he arrived at Gusen II at the beginning of April 1945, Dusan Stefancic, having survived Natzweiler, Dachau and Gusen I, was shocked at what he saw:

Escorted by SS, we walked one morning to the gates of Gusen II and after the guards completed the formalities of our transfer, we were led to our Block. I do not remember the number of the block but I remember very well the shocking look at the barrack. Right in front of the barrack was a stack of naked corpses each with his number written in dark on his chest and powdered with hydrated chlorine lime. The stench of the bodies and the lime was unbearable. Entering the Block there was another number of dead prisoners scattered here and there all over the place, apparently having died in the night. I never entered another barrack at Gusen II without it looking the same: corpses and corpses... From the very moment I entered Gusen II it was clear why the camp had such a horrible reputation: Everything in Gusen II was a shabby unfinished improvisation. Only the extermination of prisoners was brought to full perfection.[499]

Daily life in Gusen II was filled with routine horrors. Karl Littner recalls his first impression of Gusen II was of a "sleazy, dirty" camp much more crowded than any he had been in before. "The camp was packed full with confused, sickly-looking 'Muselman' for whom there was no assigned place in the few existing barracks."[500] When the detainees were bullied out of bed at 04:00 a.m., by all accounts beaten by capos and constantly abused verbally,[501] some recall being able to wash, but others report having gone for months without once being able to clean themselves. Littner and Lax both report never having been allowed to shower in the camp, and Lax relates how he risked his life to wash himself with a hose used to mix cement weeks after soiling himself during a severe beating. This enforced filthiness was part of the torture, as Lax recalls,

---

[499] Stefancic, 15
[500] Littner, npag
[501] Lax and Lax, 83

At home I had been taught to clean myself every time I touched the family dog, but in Gusen, I learned to live not only with violence, death, and hunger but with incredible filth as well. Not once during that year could I brush my teeth or change my clothes. I wore my uniform always, waking and sleeping. I stained it with my feces, urine, sweat. Everyone smelled and the barracks stank of defiled humanity. Our smell followed us everywhere.[502]

The clothes of the dead were stripped from them and given to the living without so much as a delousing.[503]

Since four shared one bed in the overcrowded barracks, they were infested with fleas and lice. Prisoners rarely slept well. Many prisoners who belonged to a "good" command (on the assembly line rather than tunnel excavation) preferred their work place in St. Georgen to the unbearable conditions in Gusen II. At "breakfast," they stood in line for their half litre of "hot" water, colored black and amusingly called "coffee." Often it was their only "warm meal" for the day. Lax recalls trying to get at the back of the line so he could receive coffee grounds as well, just to have something to eat.[504] After roll-call, many were loaded into the open box cars standing ready.

Some do not recall all the details about how they got to work.[505] Perhaps the memory is lost in more dreadful ones, or perhaps it is the more dreadful memory. Others say the short train trip to the wooden loading platform near the Schleppbahnbrücke (Railway Bridge) at St. Georgen ended in another beating as they left the box cars, verbally abused the whole while. Those who missed the privilege of riding the "Schleppbahn" ran along its rails for the two kilometers from CC Gusen II to St. Georgen.[506] They then joined prisoners unloaded from the train in one hundred rows of five on the meadow between the railway embankment and the Farthofer's farm house, which was surrounded by a high fence. An "Oberkapo," accompanied by other capos and

---

[502]   Ibid., 110
[503]   Ibid., 107, Littner, npag
[504]   Lax and Lax, 111
[505]   Lax, Personal Interview 21 October 2004
[506]   Littner, npag

SS men, chased the "Fünfhunderter" (formations of five hundred prisoners each) from Farthofers´ farm over Bahnhofstrasse (Road) to the Mariengrube Sandpit and into the underground plant's entrances.[507]

If one of the five prisoners in a row was unable to run, the other four had to carry him along without losing speed. This early morning run at top speed was only possible because the SS and capos continuously beat the prisoners, threatening them with the crematorium at CC Gusen I. Many detainees, unable to keep up with the "march," were dragged along by their comrades and thus able to survive one more day. Prisoners too weak for this "march" were not allowed to operate the machinery lest they slow the production. Together with detainees who collapsed at work, they were stored, without medical attention, until the return march at the end of the shift or simply thrown onto the "cart for dead bodies" while still alive. Prisoners able to finish the march to Bahnhofstrasse (Road) in front of the tunnels were counted again. From there they were led to their underground work stations through a tunnel opening next to the former brewery or through a small tunnel into the Mariengrube Sandpit.[508]

For prisoners on the Kommando "Bergkristall-Fertigung," (aircraft assembly) like Littner, the twelve-hour shift began at 6:00 a.m. and ended at 6:00 p.m. with only one fifteen-minute break during which the prisoners were allowed to eat. They received a clear soup, usually cold, with the occasional turnip or potato. In the evening, prisoners who survived the day were replaced by thousands on the second shift. At work, they were treated like machinery. The civilian foremen and tradesmen and the SS guards ignored them, pretending they did not exist. Except for a few civilian workers, SS guards and capos, everyone was forbidden to talk to or to approach the detainees. Even for ordinary SS guards a minimum distance of six steps was obligatory. The prisoners themselves were forbidden to speak a single word to one another. Detainees facing each other on the workbenches along the tunnel walls were not even allowed to look in one another's eyes. Littner recalls:

---

[507] Interview 881127. Transcript in the possession of the author.
[508] Maria F. Personal Interview 20 September 2000, Johanna B. Personal Interview 21 September 2000, various survivor testimonies in possession of the author.

The half-moon shaped tunnels were big enough to accommodate an airplane body without its wings. All around the center, the tunnels were numbered. Nine Jewish slaves and I worked in Tunnel 7 welding steel brackets for Messerschmitt airplanes. I hardly knew any of the other workers. It was forbidden to socialize or speak to each other. An Austrian civilian was our supervisor (Meister), but he spent most of his time in his office cubicle. At work, we were seldom bothered except when we had to replace the oxygen cylinders. Passing the guarded gate into the mountain yard, the SS guard, just for the pleasure, used to stick us with his bayonet or the butt of his rifle every time we passed him.[509]

Figure 27: Finished fuselages fully equipped with cockpit and antennas waiting for delivery in one of the Bergkristall tunnels, 7 July 1945 Source: Dennis Mills, AFHRA

---

[509]   Littner, npag

When interviewed, Littner did not recall how he acquired the position on the welders' command. Because of a blow to the head while at CC Mauthausen, his memory of his arrival at Gusen II and his first weeks in the tunnels are not complete. He does not recall if his registration, which noted that he was a welder, was used to determine what job he would have in the tunnels or if he volunteered in the same manner as Joe C. and Victor Kielich had.[510] Martin Lax recalls that the SS were still asking the general slave population for volunteers for skilled labor jobs after he arrived at Gusen II in summer 1944. "They would ask for carpenters and people would volunteer. Then they would be taken to do a job which had nothing to do with carpentry."[511] Apparently the use of Hollerith cards or other registration material was not exact at Gusen II even when exact information was available.

Even on a construction command, however, those who could survive long enough to gain experience found better treatment. Lax recalls that the civilian foreman would only "admonish" prisoners for mistakes. "Unlike the capos and SS, they appreciated experienced workers. Their task went more smoothly when they had workers who knew what needed to be done. The SS by contrast would lash a prisoner indiscriminately. The length and severity of the beating would depend on the mood."[512] Here, too, prisoners were expected to count the number of blows or the beating would begin again.

To further confuse matters, orders in the tunnels were given in German, which few prisoners understood, but the capos used whips to keep the prisoners working. Survivors report whips made out of rubber tubes,[513] 2 x 4 pieces of boards and even out of the abundant electrical wiring available inside the underground plant stripped to expose the wire.[514] This "management" method, seldom used even on animals, allowed the production plant overseers to get the maximum effort out of exhausted and weak workers. The smallest mistake put detainees completely at the capos' mercy, often resulting

---

[510] Personal Interview, 15 September 2004
[511] Personal Interview, 21 October 2004
[512] Lax and Lax, 89
[513] Ibid., 89
[514] Littner, npag

in the prisoner's death. Lax recalls a capo who beat prisoners brutally with the least provocation.[515] Lax wrote in *Caraseu,*

> One of the capos was a short Polish man named Vladek, who was especially feared and hated. He often worked with my team. Vladek was a killer and a sadist. He always picked out the weak or crippled prisoners as his victims and took pride in his savage style of beating, which often left his victim dead. First he would drive his fist into a prisoner's solar plexus, hard, leaving the man gasping for breath. Then he brought his knee up and smashed the prisoner in the face. As the man groaned and straightened up, Vladek let him have another blow to the man's exposed gut. As the prisoner staggered, Vladek raised both his fists above his head and brought them crashing down on the back of the man's head and neck. The man sprawled on the ground dead or unconscious. If the man still breathed, Vladek's pride demanded that he finish him off. There was no predicting when Vladek would indulge his twisted desire to show his cruelty.[516]

This not only shows that capos could act with impunity, but that at least Vladek had adopted something of the SS guards' focus on eugenics when he selected the "weak and crippled" for extermination. No prisoner, however healthy, could have resisted Vladek, so his hatred for the weak had nothing to do with disciplining the will. Rather, the focus of punishment was on the body for possessing unwanted physical characteristics. Despite the professionalism brought to the work site by the presence of civilian Meisters, Kammler's organization could never change the SS's priorities, and murder continued to be the result of their rule and influence within the tunnels.

Those operating machine tools like Littner were the "lucky" ones whose skills were much more likely to be noticed by a foreman who had more influence over a man's working conditions. Littner's recollection, cited earlier, of his civilian foreman mixing up the welded parts to save workers from being hanged illustrates another aspect of life in the Gusen camps – the unexpected act of generosity or kindness. Gusen I survivor Dr. Leszczynski, in his speech

---

[515] Personal Interview, 21 October 2004
[516] Lax and Lax, 106

at the 2004 Gusen Memorial, reflected on the "helping angels" that each survivor had in the camps. Dr. Leszczynski recalls four fellow prisoners: (Michal Roczniak, who helped him survive the quarantine at Mauthausen; Tadzio Woytowicz, who shared his bread; an unknown prisoner who helped him down from the cart for the dead; and Piotr Naruszewicz, who helped him in the hospital). "Each of the comrades here [at the 2004 memorial] had such a helping angel. They too made this soil sacred," Dr. Leszczynski said. Littner's story of the foreman mixing the parts to save lives shows there were "helping angels" even at CC Gusen (even among the civilian managers). Lax found a most surprising "helping angel" in an SA man (Sturmabteilung – unusual among guards in any camp) who carried him to the hospital after a machine crushed his leg. The fate of the SA man, who violated the rules separating guards and prisoners, isn't known.[517]

Few found such mercy, however. Building the tunnels was dangerous work for the 6,000 detainees in the "Kommando Bergkristall-Bau" (construction command).[518] Cave-ins during tunnel construction increased the high mortality rate even among civilian workers in summer 1944. After the concrete-work commands, harshly driven by capos, dug into the sandstone using compressed-air drills, a second group of detainees would carry the resulting sand to small railroad lorries. Yet another group would then pull the lorries out of the tunnels. Finally, workers built concrete walls.[519]

People unused to manual labor and Jews were the worst treated prisoners. The weak and injured were declared "arbeitsunfähig" and were sent directly to the crematorium instead of the camp hospital, even though still alive.[520] After only four months, between November 1944 and March 1945, the plant doubled in size,[521] an impossibility without the terror of the SS and the capos' continuous bullying of prisoners. The pace of construction for commands in

---

[517] Ibid., 112

[518] Even, J. P. (survivor „L" 62855 of Gusen II), Letzeburger, 362.

[519] Lax and Lax, 88

[520] Malgaroli, Diario. Lax and Lax, 89

[521] On 30 November 1944 the area of the tunnels was 21,000 square meters, whereas on 31 March 1945 it was about 50,000 square meters.

the tunnels was so brutal that many prisoners lost their lives in workplace accidents or were harassed to death.[522]

The six thousand prisoners in the construction command rotated in three eight-hour shifts because the jobs were so much more demanding than assembly work, which meant there were a total of 6,000 prisoners working on tunnel construction. On average, about four detainees died every day from June to October 1944, but deaths increased to about forty per day after work on the extension for the jet assembly plant began in late 1944. Prisoners were completely exhausted within a few weeks.[523] Variation in the daily death toll can also be attributed to the moods of the capos and the guards and the weather conditions. In the summer of 1944 Lax recalls struggling to breathe as he used an air hammer in the poorly ventilated tunnels. That winter, the cold was so unbearable he risked a beating and perhaps death to line his thin uniform shirt with a concrete bag for insulation.[524]

Those who survived such a workday with enough strength to walk back to CC Gusen II carried the dead bodies to the washrooms next to the barracks, according to some survivors. Others report that the dead were placed on top of concrete trash containers, naked, with their Mauthausen numbers[525] written on their chests.[526] All agree the sanitation facilities were nearly non-existent. Those who remember washing also report that the water itself was dangerous. Anyone who drank it risked dying of diarrhea within a few days.

Littner recalls arriving back at the barracks thus:

---

[522] Again and again people talk about a feared SS murderer who stalked the tunnels with a course wire. He either hanged prisoners he disliked on the machines, or he forced prisoners to commit suicide with the wire. Survivors say that the „executioner of Bergkristall" killed about 12 detainees in the tunnels every day.

[523] Haunschmied, 99 and Stephanie Vitry, „Les morts de Gusen, camp de concentration Autrichien – a partir du depouilement d´un registre de morts Avril 1943 – Mai 1945" (Maitrise d´histoire, Universite de Paris I – Pantheon-Sorbonne, 1994)

[524] Lax and Lax, 87

[525] The first Mauthausen numbers were assigned to Gusen inmates not earlier than 23 January 1944. This date marks the final melding of CC Gusen into CC Mauthausen. In the years before this date CC Gusen had its independent numbering system for its inmates.

[526] Littner, npag.

After 12 hours with barely any food, the capos chased us first into the barracks where every bed was already occupied by the sick and nearly dead. Under the lice-filled, filthy cots, dead people were being stored. To find any place to sleep, I had to push the dead lying on the floor farther under the cot to clear a space for myself.

Selections for murder of the weak and sick continued in the evening. Some recall lethal heart injections prepared in a tub in the barracks. Another method was to drown the inmates in barrels. Hans van Loosen (the camp elder of CC Gusen II) is said to have invited inmates into a dark washroom one by one, only to crush their heads with an axe, reportedly killing 245 inmates in one night.[527] Thus, the camp management ensured only the best "human material" was available for the next day's work and saved the bread a weakened man required to survive a few more days or even weeks in the "hospital." Every night, special commands took dead prisoners piled up by day in front of each of the twenty barracks to CC Gusen I's crematorium. So many prisoners arrived at the crematorium that the dead at the bottom of the piles were smashed beyond recognition. Before cremation, dying or half-dead detainees were placed at the bottom of the heap to be crushed to death under the weight of those already dead.[528]

After the selection, some prisoners recall a "lice check" after which everyone was given a forced shave. In this manner, the "work day" often lasted twenty hours, leaving inmates only a few hours to rest during the night. Bread was only distributed at night. In the beginning, six detainees shared one kilogram of bread daily. Later, twelve would share one kilogram of bread. Terrible fights, sometimes ending in serious injury, broke out for the inedible mixture of brown bread, mold, sawdust, and a vegetable powder. In spite of the horrible taste, it was the only daily "meal" and might have kept more prisoners alive if enough had been provided.[529] The prison bakery (begun

---

[527] Osuchowski, J. quoted in Orski, 41 and Kielich and Mills, 70
[528] Summarized rendering of aspects of the life in the camp of Gusen II and of the mobilization of labor in Bergkristall. Malgaroli, Diario and Letzeburger, 362 ff.
[529] Summarized rendering of aspects of the life in the camp of Gusen II and of the mobilization of labor in Bergkristall.

in 1943 in Lungitz before Gusen III was established there) was not put into operation until spring 1945.[530] The SS had other priorities.

Figure 28: The Crematorium at Gusen, 2007
Source: Rudolf A. Haunschmied

Living conditions in Gusen II were so bad that a well-fed, completely healthy man, on being assigned to work in the tunnels of St. Georgen, could expect to die within 4 months. Surviving six months was unusual. To this day, since "Bergkristall" was a top secret project, very few outside the camp understand the fate of thousands sacrificed at St. Georgen. From the first five months of 1945 to the war's end, 9,000 prisoners were officially recorded as having died in CC Gusen. Most of the dead were probably inmates of CC Gusen II

---

[530] Reichl, 157

but were sent to CC Gusen I's crematorium. In the whole period of existence of the Concentration Camps Gusen, around 35,725 detainees were "exterminated by labor" or murdered.[531] In the period between 28 February 1945 and 30 March 1945, 2,937 unfit inmates of Gusen II were sent to the "Sanitary Camp at Mauthausen" where most of them died after a few days. These victims were attributed to the mortality rate of Mauthausen, although they actually died as a result of Gusen II.[532] Establishing CC Gusen II's existence is also important because it accounts for the higher death toll in the Gusen camps than that of CC Mauthausen.

---

[531] Marsálek, Gusen, 41
[532] Choumoff, Pierre. Letter to the author, 19 December 1996. In the possession of the author.

Liberation and Final Days of the War

American and British historians' discussion of the last two months of the war in Europe often focus on Eisenhower's controversial decision to abandon Berlin as a military objective in favor of preventing German forces from gathering in the National Redoubt.

Typical of American historians, Stephen Ambrose describes as "alarmist" and "imaginary" the Supreme Headquarters Allied Expeditionary Forces (SHAEF) intelligence reports of underground factories and storage facilities there.[533] While Bergkristall demonstrates Eisenhower's concerns were not entirely baseless, an examination of top secret incoming and outgoing messages of SHAEF General Staff Divisions, G-3 (Plans and Operations) from March and April 1945 show no evidence that Patton's Third Army (part of the Twelfth Army Group under General Omar Bradley), was sent into Austria specifically to seize the technology hidden in the tunnels, as some believe.

However, recent findings of Dieter Oeckl and Hans-Günther Richardi draw attention to Dr. Ernst Kaltenbrunner's influence on Eisenhower's concerns about SS troops massing in the south. Oeckl and Richardi report that Kaltenbrunner, who had continued to gain influence with Hitler after taking over the RSHA in 1943 and whose star rose even further as Himmler's fell, contacted Allen Dulles in the Berne Office of Strategic Services (OSS) on 9 March 1945. Kaltenbrunner proposed a peace deal to President Roosevelt via Dulles on the condition that the western Allies accept German forces and the SS as new allies in the a war against the Soviets.[534] Indeed, enough confidence was put in these plans of Kaltenbrunner that the SS at CC Gusen I revealed them to prisoners.[535] Kaltenbrunner also threatened the Americans with a bloody final battle with elite SS units in Southern Germany, Austria and the "Alpine Redoubt Area" which he explained had been in preparation since

---

[533] Ambrose, Stephen. The Victors: Eisenhower and His Boys (New York: Simon and Schuster), 139-140

[534] Dieter Oeckl and Hans-Günther Richardi, Die Alpenfestung – Letztes Bollwerk der SS, broadcasted on 6 October 2004 by Austrian National Television (ORF)

[535] Letzeburger, 350

late 1943 (referring to the "Steyr Works," which of course had underground facilities at CC Gusen).[536]

According to Oeckl and Richardi, Kaltenbrunner's strategy failed in the end because he had an important rival on the other side of the Alps in the person of SS-Obergruppenführer Karl Wolff, the Higher SS- and Police Leader of the Nazi occupied territory in Italy. As luck would have it, unbeknownst to Kaltenbrunner or other high ranking Berlin officials, Wolff offered Roosevelt the surrender of German troops in Italy on the same day, 9 March.

According to Peter-Ferdinand Koch, Himmler and Pohl were party to the peace strategy Wolff offered to the Americans. To save their lives and to play key-roles in post-war Germany, in competition with Kaltenbrunner's threatened final battle for Hitler's empire, Himmler and Pohl offered to arrange a surrender to the Western Allies and sweetened the deal by offering to gather information and contacts regarding key German technology in Bavaria – the planned American occupation zone – in hopes of preventing the Soviets from invading too much of Germany. Koch asserts that this may have been the reason why Hitler condemned Himmler shortly before the end of the war, and why Patton was not allowed to go farther east into Czechoslovakia.[537] Oeckl and Richardi believe that it was Kaltenbrunner's attempt at blackmail that first drew the attention of the Allied Supreme Command to Southern Germany, Austria and the Alpine Redoubt with its numerous fortified plants. At this late date, Oeckl and Richardi say, the Americans had no clear picture of the armament and defence potentials there and were just beginning to piece together information from disparate sources.[538]

Interestingly, the Chronicles of the St. Georgen Parish also mention Himmler's and Pohl's efforts to secure a deal. In a memo regarding the final key events of the war, the local parson wrote that Himmler offered the Americans and

---

[536] Dieter Oeckl and Hans-Günther Richardi
[537] Koch, Peter-Ferdinand ed., Himmlers graue Eminenz – Oswald Pohl und das Wirtschaftsverwaltungshauptamt der SS (Hamburg, Verlag Facta Oblita, 1988), p. 177 ff
[538] Dieter Oeckl and Hans-Günther Richardi

British surrender via Count Bernadotte in April 1945 – an offer that was rejected because it did not comprise peace with the Russians.[539]

In addition to strategic concerns, the Allies prepared for the large number of displaced persons liberated by their advance across Europe. Dr. Malcolm J. Proudfoot served as a Lt. Colonel in charge of operational reports for Displaced Persons Branch, G-5 Division, SHAEF. In a post-war article, he explained that plans to deal with displaced persons were drawn up in the winter of 1943-44 by Anglo-American military authorities in London. "The most exact knowledge possible of the magnitude of the problem was required so that food, clothing, medical supplies and other necessities could be requisitioned to meet the need of caring for these foreign workers and deportees from the time of their liberation until they could be repatriated."[540] "Exact knowledge" at the time could not have included the underground tunnel construction at Kellerbau which commenced as the invasion plans were completed or Bergkristall which began soon after. Later intelligence does not appear to have affected the requisitioning of food and medical supplies for displaced persons or prisoners-of-war in concentration camps in Austria.

The intelligence objectives of the "Operation Freeborn" plan drawn up in November 1944 for the invasion of Austria were: 1) to secure Allied forces, 2) to bring about a political and cultural separation of Austria from Germany and 3) the denazification of Austria. The assumption was that British and American forces would enter Austria through Italy.[541] Section III of the Allied Force Headquarters Office of Assistant Chief of Staff, G-2 [Intelligence] file "Ostmark" contains a list of 18 concentration camps, including Mauthausen, Gusen, Sankt Georgen [presumably Gusen II], Ebensee, and Steyr, as well as a "List of SS Units and Establishments by Type" and a "List of Formations and Units with Personalities by Locations".[542] In addition, the report contains an

---

[539] Chronik der Pfarre St. Georgen, Tom. I, p. 226.

[540] Proudfoot, Malcom J "The Anglo-American Displaced Persons Program for Germany and Austria." The Journal of Economics and Sociolgy. Vol. 6, No. 1 (October 1946) pp. 33-54

[541] Carafano, James Jay "Waltzing into the Cold War". Contemporary Austrian Studies, ed. Bischof, Guenter. (Edison, Transaction Books, 1999), 16

[542] Ostmark: Section III, The SS Allied Force Headquarters, Office of Assistant Chief of Staff, G-2. In possession of the author. Although undated, the file bears illegible innitials and the dates 28/4/45.

assessment of SS Economic Enterprises, which explains, "The Concentration Camps gave [sic] the SS a virtually inexhaustible source of cheap, expendable labour, which could be used for many and varied enterprises. Where it was not expedient to set up an SS enterprise, the camp labour could be farmed out to private firms or used in subcontract work. The work thus directly or indirectly carried on by the SS ranges from tailoring to armaments, and from quarrying to aeroplane construction."[543] This is a clearer picture of SS use of slave labor in Austria than would appear in English for many decades.

As commander of the forces originally slated to invade Austria, Field Marshal Harold Alexander shared Eisenhower's concerns regarding the possibility of fierce fighting there. But Alexander was also able to imagine the impact large concentration camps would have on Allied invasion plans.

On 15 March 1945, Alexander sent a cable to the War Department's Adjutant General for the Allied Combined Chiefs of Staff as well as the British Chiefs of Staff expressing concerns that a "high proportion of SS troops, fanatical Nazis and war criminals may be in Austria or about to concentrate there."[544] Alexander also stated concern that taking "effective action to protect and evacuate prisoners of war will necessitate the introduction of substantial forces into Austria. If inadequate forces are introduced <u>not</u> only are they likely to be overwhelmed but the enemy may be provoked to action against POWs."[545][emphasis in original] He suggested airlifting a sizeable force, given the difficulties of quickly introducing and maintaining two divisions across the Alps. He also recommended dropping supplies, medical equipment and arms into POW camps, but doubted that the POWs could be sufficiently armed to counter any attacks provoked by the arms drops themselves.[546] Of all the predictions regarding the end of the war in Austria, only Alexander's (about a massacre of POWs and the need for a large number of troops and supplies) would turn out to be true.

It was read again on 5/11-5/19/45 by WSK.
[543] Ibid.
[544] Field Marshal Alexander to Agwar for Combined Chiefs of Staff and for British Chiefs of Staff, Cable FX-4426915 March 1945 NARA RG 331/290/7/11/3
[545] Ibid.
[546] Ibid.

On 19 March 1945, in "Operation Sunrise," Dulles met Wolff in Ascona, Switzerland, to discuss the surrender of German troops and SS in Italy.[547] Apparently unaware of these negotiations, on 29 March Alexander again cabled the Joint Chiefs of Staff, two weeks after the first cable, saying that "We must look ahead to occupation of Austria and Northeast Italy. Without another British Div. I shall be short of troops."[548] That same day, Eisenhower directed General Devers' Sixth Army to protect Bradley's right flank as the Twelfth Army Group occupied the Ruhr until the opportunity presented itself to go into Austria. The plan was to link up with the Russians along the Elbe to the east and Linz to the south.[549] Alexander expressed his approval of this plan and encouraged the Americans to occupy the British zone if the alternative would be Soviet occupation.[550] Unfortunately, Alexander's concerns about the occupation, particularly about the danger to inmates if too few troops were provided, were never effectively communicated to the American generals who would ultimately be responsible for the liberation of the Mauthausen/Gusen concentration camp complex. Bradley and Patton's biographers seldom mention Nazi concentration camps in Austria but focus on these generals' decisions to direct most of the Third Army's divisions toward Czechoslovakia in an attempt to halt the Soviet advance into Prague. As a result of this decision, however, a single platoon of 23 Americans would inadvertently liberate 40,000 inmates at CC Mauthausen and Gusen I and II. One division, the 11th Armored Division, would have the responsibility of administering the three largest camps in Austria along with the city of Linz itself in the critical weeks after liberation without warning or adequate food or medical supplies.

As historian Forrest C. Pogue points out, the occupational zones, agreed upon by the Allies at Yalta in September 1944 (which placed CC Mauthausen/Gusen under Soviet occupation after the war) were understood to

---

[547] Dieter Oeckl and Hans-Günther Richardi

[548] Field Marshal Alexander to AMSSO for BCS and Britman Washington for US Joint Chiefs of Staff SHAEF FWD FX-5159029 March 1945, NARA RG 331/290/7/11/3

[549] General Eisenhower to Bradley and Devers, 29 March 1945, Cable FWD 18302 NARA 331/290/7/11/3

[550] Alexander to Combined Chiefs of Staff and for British Chiefs of staff 9 April 1945 NARA 331/290/7/11/3

be unimportant when making military plans directed toward victory over Germany. As Alexander notes in his cable, having each ally in its respective zone would, of course, be convenient, and checking Soviet expansion was a consideration for the Americans and the British. However, the American, British, and Soviet agreement allowed troop positions to be adjusted where necessary after the war. Pogue argues that Eisenhower's decision to stop troops at the Elbe was a military rather than political one intended to bring about a swift end to the war by splitting German forces and allowing Allied troops to head north toward Lübeck and south toward the "National Redoubt." After Berlin surrendered on 2 May, Churchill wanted American forces to occupy Prague (which he felt would "do the Russians some good"),[551] but Eisenhower again did not want to use American troops for political ends. At the request of the Soviets, Eisenhower agreed not to enter Czechoslovakia beyond the Budejovice-Pilsen-Karlsbad line, but said he would continue an advance to the area around Linz, which would be in the American zone.[552]

Mauthausen and Gusen were 15 kilometers east of Linz, in the Soviet zone. In the face of Eisenhower's decision about Prague, Patton and Bradley argued vehemently for permission to cross into the Soviet zone towards the Czech capital.[553] But they adhered strictly to the occupation zone at Linz, avoiding the humanitarian crisis at CC Mauthausen/Gusen despite attempts, even by Eisenhower, to communicate its severity to them. As Alexander feared, the resulting chaos in Upper Austria caused thousands of deaths when US troops liberated the camps without warning or preparation.

Proudfoot, in his 1946 article, states that the conditions uncovered in concentration camps and the difficulties in providing health care and in repatriating thousands brought "Anglo-American military authorities too much unjustified criticism."[554] He also notes, however, "by far the worst problem was presented by displaced persecutees found in concentration camps. Such camps as Dachau, Belsen, Mauthausen, Gusen, Ebensee, and Buchenwald

---

[551] Pogue, "Halt at the Elbe" http://www.army.mil/cmh-pg/books/70-7_22.htm
[552] Ibid.
[553] Ibid.
[554] Proudfoot, 45

were heart-rending sights, and contained health problems that beggared description."[555] It is not clear from the text if Proudfoot is making a distinction between "diplaced persons" and "displaced persecutees" and exempting the later from his assessment of the Anglo-American programs for the former. The fact that three of these camps were in Austria indicates the desperation Proudfoot himself was charged with investigating in mid-May 1945. Another cause for the lack of preparation for displaced perecutees and persons in Austria might be the fact that the May 1944 chart "Estimated Displaced European Population"[556] drawn up by SHAEF G-5 provides no separate estimation for Austria except where displaced Germans in Austria are concerned. The estimates and plans were drawn up by "L.W. Cramer (American) and M. MacDonald (British), SHAEF G-5 Division (Civil Affairs/ Military Government) with the active collaboration of the entire staff of the Branch."[557] Proudfoot evaluates the plan drawn up in the seven months before D-Day as "essentially adequate."[558]

However, Proudfoot acknowledges that in the first year of the invasion the "problem of displaced persons was completely overshadowed"[559] by the task of caring for one million French, Belgian and Netherland refugees and the difficulties of repatriating the small number of displaced persons in Western Europe even where they were "a robust lot, reasonably well nourished and clothed, and possessed a happy and co-operative spirit."[560] SHAEF G-5 assumed that local authorities in the liberated countries could provide for the medical needs and welfare of the displaced, but Civil Affairs soon found this too be less than true when such work had to be carried out under fire. As the invasion progressed, some began to understand the enormity of problems posed by millions of refugees and displaced persons awaiting liberation in "Germany."[561]

---

[555] Ibid., 44
[556] Ibid., 37
[557] Ibid.
[558] Ibid., 38
[559] Ibid.
[560] Ibid., 39
[561] Ibid.

G-5 Civil Affairs was organized to deal with problems of displaced persons, food supply, and transportation in liberated areas, such as France, as opposed to occupied enemy territory. It was understood that tactical commanders were responsible for ensuring that stable conditions existed in territories which came under their command so that military operations could continue. They were, in fact, responsible for maintaining control and providing aid to the population until a civil government could be revived or established.[562] As Proudfoot noted, this was problematic in liberated Allied countries.[563] In fascist Italy and Germany one could not simply leave the local government to operate as it had before the Allied occupation. Nazi mayors had to be replaced, ideally, with non-Nazi mayors. G-5 Civil Affairs was created within the military chain of command to assist military commanders in assessing and preparing for liberating or occupying territory in a manner which furthered the military objective. SHAEF G-3 Plans and Operations was responsible for planning operations and issuing orders and operational directives for military activity during the conflict, as well as for the post-war period as well.[564]

Proudfoot states that from spring 1944 on SHAEF Administrative Memorandum Number 39 placed "full responsibility for the care and eventual repatriation of displaced persons on the military commanders in the field."[565] However, as the Allies approached Austria the exchange of memos and cables between SHAEF and the Twelfth and Sixth Army Groups and between SHAEF G-5 and SHAEF G-3 reveal confusion, if not conflict, over the enormity of the problem and over who bore the responsibility for the welfare of inmates at CC Mauthausen/Gusen. In discussing the decision to integrate United Nations Relief and Rehabilitation Administration (UNRRA) with the Displaced Persons Branch staff, thereby also integrating the civilian UNRRA welfare teams into the army, Proudfoot notes that there was opposition from those "who considered the displaced persons program a postwar problem." Although Proudfoot writes that "farsighted leadership at the command

---

[562] Pogue, "Halt at the Elbe" http://www.army.mil/cmh-pg/books/70-7_22.htm
[563] Proudfoot, 39
[564] Ibid.
[565] Proudfoot, 37

level"[566] allowed recruitment, training and placement of UNRRA teams to continue, the possibility remained that some commanders in the army would continue to see the welfare of displaced persons as a postwar problem.

After the liberation of Buchenwald earlier in April, SHAEF G-5 (for which Proudfoot wrote operational reports) attempted to avoid repetition of "last-minute massacres of prisoners by their German guards."[567] An 18 April 1945 memo from Lieutenant General Grasett, Acting Chief of Staff, SHAEF G-5, to SHAEF G-3 stated,

> It is requested that action be taken by the G-3 Division to drop "SAARF" [Special Allied Airborne Reconnaissance Force] teams at these places imme-diately following liberation in order to establish two-way radio communica-tions with Supreme Headquarters A.E.F. [Allied European Forces] to facili-tate emergency remedial action. (Major Proudfoot of the Displaced Persons Branch G-5 Division is designated to render all possible assistance furthering the requested action.)[568]

The memo also referenced Brigadier General S.R. Mickelson, Chief, Displaced Persons Branch within the G-5 Civil Affairs Division who was then Major Proudfoot's superior.[569] Both Mickelson and Proudfoot appear throughout the "Twelfth Army Group-Mauthausen Camps" file attempting to warn the US generals about the impending crisis at CC Mauthausen/Gusen and attempting to induce SHAEF G-3 to take action.

But errors in critical information hampered the first efforts to communicate the situation in Austria. Attached to the 18 April memo is a list "where critical conditions exist among United Nations political prisoners." Titled "German Concentration Camps At Which It Is Recommended That SAARF Teams be Dropped From The Air," and described as an "up-to-date compilation from

---

[566] Ibid., 40

[567] Brig. Gen. McSherry to Divisions G-1,G-2,G-3,G-4, A-2,A-3, 25 April 1945, NARA 331/290/1/13

[568] "German Concentration Camps at which it is Recommended that SAARF Teams be Dropped from the Air" 18 April 1945, NARA 331/290/1/10/13

[569] SHAEF/g-5/2711/7.2 12th Army Group-Mauthausen Camps, NARA 331/290/1/10/13

reliable military and French Intelligence sources," the list cites Mauthausen as having only 3,000 prisoners.[570]

Additionally, on 18 April 1945, SHAEF G-5 Displaced Persons Branch sent a secret cable, FWD-19395, to the 21st Army HQ Military Government, as well as General Omar Bradley's G-5 12th Army Group and Lieutenant General Jacob L. Devers G-5 6th Army Group requesting preparations be made to "meet known critical situation[s] among United Nations prisoners held at the following concentration camps which come into the area of your advance."[571] Mauthausen is listed, but three days later a follow-up memo was sent directly to the 12th Army Group's G-5 Displaced Persons Branch stating, "Attached is a list giving known details concerning the concentration camps cited in referenced cable [FWD-19395]." On this list Mauthausen is again said to have only 3,000 prisoners.[572]

By 20 April, Patton had regrouped in Bavaria, according to his biographer Ladislas Farago, and turned toward the suspected "National Redoubt" along the Danube.[573] Presumably, CC Mauthausen/Gusen would be in the Third Army's "area of advance," but CC Mauthausen is not present in a 23 April SHAEF G-5 study forwarded to the SHAEF Ground and Air Intelligence and Planning offices requesting that "all possible aid to United Nations political prisoners" held in the camps be provided. Major Proudfoot is again given as the contact.[574] The study discusses six concentration camps, including Dachau and Flossenbürg, where "recent intelligence reports confirm serious condition[s] among an estimated 38,000 prisoners."[575] Twice that number of prisoners awaited aid at CCs Gusen, CC Mauthausen, and CC Ebensee – three

---

[570] Signed Lt. General A.E. Gasset, ACof S, G-5 to SHAEF G-5, Displaced Persons Branch NARA 331 290/7/10/13, Location of Known and Possible Prisoner of War Installations in Germany and Occupied Countries as Known to PWX-GI-Division, SHAEF, 18 March 1945, [AFHRA] 670-616-1

[571] SHAEF FWD, Signed SCAEF to HQ 21 Army Group Rear for Mil Gov, CG 12 Army Group Rear for G-5, CG 6 Army Group Rear for G-5 Cable FWD-19395 NARA 331 290/7/10/13

[572] Brigadier General A. G. Salisbury Jones, Deputy Chief, Displaced Persons to 12th Amry Group, Rear, G-5, Displaced Persons Branch, NARA 331/290/7/10/3

[573] Farago, Ladislas, Patton: Ordeal and Triumph, (New York: Ivan Obolensky, 1963), 783

[574] Lieutenant General A. E. Grasset to SHAEF Divisions G-2 G-3 A-2 A-3, 23 April 1945, NARA 331/290/10/13

[575] Ibid. The camps which do appear are Dachau, Regensburg, Lübeck, Aschendorramoor, Neusustrum, Borgermoor

of the worst camps by Proudfoot's postwar account – not to mention other satellite camps throughout Austria. But the camps are not mentioned in a 25 April memo discussing plans to provide airborne aid to prisoners of war in concentration camps, either. In fact, Mauthausen does not appear in communications again until 1 May.[576] While Linz was Patton's "ultimate objective on the anti-redoubt drive," as Farago describes it, Patton and Bradley's real interests lay in stopping the Soviets in Czechoslovakia.[577] The concentration camp complex fifteen kilometers east of the Linz would not become a consideration in their plans.

The International Committee of the Red Cross (ICRC) provided the first assistance to prisoners at Concentration Camps Mauthausen and Gusen in April of 1945. Unbeknownst to Hitler or Kaltenbrunner, Himmler had approached the ICRC on 19 February 1945 in an effort to negotiate a peace settlement with the Allies. Swedish Red Cross Official Count Folke Bernadotte told Himmler that concentration camps needed to be turned over first, but Himmler only agreed to allow non-Jews and Slavs to receive food in the first round of negotiations.[578] In the last months of the war, however, Himmler lost Hitler's favor, which was transferred to Kaltenbrunner, who gained so much power even Himmler feared him. In March 1945 Kaltenbrunner moved his office to Altaussee, which was part of Gau Oberdonau (Upper Austria, although it is now in Styria again) to prepare and coordinate the final battle of Nazi Germany against the Allies. Ironically, when Himmler's peace negotiations became known in April 1945, Hitler fired him and replaced him with Kaltenbrunner, who was himself negotiating at the time with the Allies.[579] While Kaltenbrunner would also turn to the ICRC in a last ditch attempt to gain influence, as late as 27 April he told Himmler's deputy at CC Mauthausen (Kurt Becher) that "at least a thousand men must still die every day in Mauthausen."[580] On 29 April, the day after Italian Dictator Benito Mussolini's death, "Operation Sunrise" (the negotiation between Wolff and Dulles) re-

---

[576] 25 April 1945 from Brig. Gen. McSherry, April 23 1945 Lt. Gen. A.E. Grasset, NARA 331/290/1/13
[577] Farago, 784-788
[578] Gilbert, Martin. The Second World War, (New York: Henry Holt, 1989), 643, and Pike, 16
[579] Dieter Oeckl and Hans-Günther Richardi
[580] Gilbert, 674

sulted in the surrender of all German forces in Italy at Caserta.[581] In Berlin Hitler, whose spirits could not even be buoyed by the model of the planned reconstruction of Linz brought to him earlier that month, shot himself.[582] According to Oeckl and Richardi, the surrender in Italy freed Eisenhower to direct resources to deal with Kaltenbrunner's threat of an Alpine Redoubt. However, while it is obvious that 29 April 1945 was a key date for World War II, correspondence between Eisenhower and his generals from mid-March on reveals that his interest in the Alpine Redoubt predated the surrender in Italy. What the top secret cables from March and April 1945 do reveal is the failure of attempts, even by Eisenhower himself, to alert Bradley and Patton of the impending humanitarian disaster awaiting them in Upper Austria.

At Gusen II in the spring of 1945, Karl Littner saw a strange truck parked near the administration barracks. He recalls:

> The SS men began to separate the Jews from the rest of the column. Other prisoners gathered around like vultures. Where, I wondered, would I store food if I received it? After a while the capos guided our small group inside the administration building. As we approached, the Swiss or Swedish men [presumably from the ICRC] watched the SS make holes in the canned food. Realizing who they were dealing with, the foreign men made no attempt to stop the SS but watched in disgust as the SS officers took the best food for themselves, destroying the rest before throwing the leaking cans of condensed milk, sardines, and other products to us. Laughing, an SS man threw leaking cans and some dry crackers at me. I dropped them right there, only stuffing a few dry crackers in my mouth before I left to face the crowd of prisoners waiting to steal from us.[583]

The ICRC also arranged for the release of several French and Czech prisoners on 22 and 24 April. On 1 May 1945 LCdt. Villaret, Liaison Officer, 3rd Section, HQ French National Defense, notified Brig. General Mickelsen, Chief of the Displaced Person Branch at SHAEF, that he had left CC Mauthausen on

---

[581] Oeckl and Richardi
[582] Gilbert, 674
[583] Littner, npag

April 22 and that Mauthausen had 80,000 prisoners. Villaret strongly urged protective action be taken.[584] General Mickelsen, who was referenced on the SHAEF interoffice memo on 18 April recommending to G-3 that plans be made to drop SAARF teams immediately after liberation, called the Twelfth Army Group to advise them of LCdt. Villaret's report.[585]

Throughout the spring of 1945 CC Mauthausen/Gusen's population had grown as it became a destination for Death Marches from the smaller sub-camps. Subcamps at Peggau, Leibnitz, Hinterbrühl, Floridsdorf, Vienna-Saurerwerke, St. Aegyd, Hirtenberg, Melk, Amstetten, Wiener-Neustadt, and Wiener Neudorf closed, followed by Loibl-Pass, Klagenfurt, St. Lambrecht, St. Valentin and Redl-Zipf were evacuated to CC Mauthausen-Gusen. Hundreds were shot along the way as prisoners were marched through the late spring snow.[586]

In mid-April 1945, three American POWs (Willard Elliot, Olin Brown, and Stanley Vaugn) were being marched from Stalag XVII-B near Krems, Austria through Mauthausen and then St. Georgen. All three report Hungarian Jews being shot by SS.[587] Vaughn recalls, "While we were marching along the road near Mauthausen and St. Georgen we passed a group of about 800 Hungarian Jewish Political prisoners who were being marched in the opposite direction along the road. These prisoners were in horrible condition. They were very weak from starvation; their clothes were in rags, and only about one in ten had shoes. They were dressed in black with a yellow star and the word "Jew" over their breasts. As we passed this group of Jewish political prisoners, I saw some of our men throw cigarettes to them. The Jews went crazy to get these cigarettes and their German guards clubbed them to prevent them from picking them up. I saw the bodies of at least fourteen who had been shot and killed. They had been shot in the head and their bodies lay uncovered at the side of the road."[588]

[584] LCdt. Villaret. Chief, Headquarters of National Defense, 3rd Section to Chief, g-5 Division, Displaced Persons Branch, SHAEF 1 May 1945, NARA 331/290/1/10/3
[585] Brigadier General S.R. Mickelsen to A.C.O.S., G-5 Division (undated), NARA 331/290/1/10/3
[586] Horwitz, 144-145
[587] Record Group 153, Entry 143 270/1/14-15/6-1 Box 8 Vol. 1, NARA
[588] 9SC-WC-1209, 20 August 1945

Hungarian Jews working on Vienna's fortifications and in factories there were also marched toward Mauthausen and kept in tents outside the fortress, swelling the number of inmates awaiting liberation by 8,500 – although three thousand would be corpses by the end of April.[589] At Gusen I, Victor Kielich recalls:

> The thousands of prisoners streaming into the Gusen camps in early 1945 from other camps in Austria and from as far away as Auschwitz had little chance of survival. The SS could hardly feed the 23 to 25,000 or so regular Gusen prisoners. Nor could the crematorium cope with the influx of corpses. Pile upon pile of naked bodies lay around the crematorium barracks. At the beginning of April 1945 Camp Commandant Fritz Seidler ordered Barracks-Chiefs Amelung and Liesberg, and Hospital Capo Sommer to execute 700 sick people from the camp hospital by gassing them in Barracks 31 at Gusen I.[590]

This gassing at Gusen I is well documented. Survivor Marius Colin describes it in Exhibit 26 of US Army Major Eugene Cohen's "Report of Investigation of Alleged War Crimes Mauthausen – Gusen – Ebensee."[591] But there are reports of gassings at Gusen II as well. To the end, the SS continued to select only the best "human material." At Gusen II, Martin Lax was returning to the hospital barracks from an open air shower (given the prisoners there to counter the threat of typhus) when the tall intern and a committee of SS men stopped him. While others were directed to enter, Lax was sent to another barracks. Hearing screams that night, Lax looked out to see the SS shooting prisoners trying to escape from the windows of the gas-filled hospital barracks. The next day he and five to seven thousand others were marched from CC Gusen II to CC Gunskirchen, another subcamp of Mauthausen/Gusen.[592] CC Gusen inmate Lodovico Barbiano di Belgiojoso was also sent to

---

[589]   Horwitz, 144-145
[590]   Kielich and Mills, 69
[591]   NARA Group 238 World War II War Crimes Records, International Military Tribunal Exhibit 249; Le Chène, 209
[592]   Lax and Lax, 119-121

Gunskirchen to work in the construction of that new concentration camp.[593]
The 71st Infantry Division, Third US Army would arrive, without prior warning, on 4 May.[594]

Figure 29: *Gassed inmates at CC Gusen, 1945*
Source: NARA

CC Mauthausen and Gusen I survivor Pierre Serge Choumoff recalls that
"800 other inmates were beaten to death in Gusen II. We heard them crying
in the night and saw their broken bodies brought to Gusen I to be burned in
the Crematorium."[595] Reports of attempted gassings ending in brutal murders
with axes are confirmed by two Czech inmates who left CC Mauthausen on

---

[593] Lodovico Barbioano di Belgiojoso, Notte, Nebbia – Racconto di Gusen (Parma: Ugo Guanda Edi-
       tore S.p.A., 1996), 100 ff.
[594] Lax and Lax, 121
[595] Choumoff, Pierre Serge. Address to the Eleventh Armored Division at Cincinnati on 11 September
       1998. The Thunderbolt, Volume 53, December 1998.

April 24 with the ICRC. Their 3 May report, which was forwarded to SHAEF G-5 states, "On the 23rd of April during the extermination of a group of about 100 people by gas, the gas supply ran short and the partially gassed victims were killed by SS men who finished the job using axes."[596] Along with many cases of typhus and "great shortages of medical supplies," the Czech survivors also report:

> At the beginning of April several transports of deportees arrived in the camp and they were exterminated in the gas chambers. On the 22nd of April the order was given by the camp commandant to exterminate, in the gas chambers, a further 7,000 inmates and it was the intention to exterminate the remaining inmates before liberation so as to cover all traces of criminal activities.[597]

Inside Gusen II, Littner's civilian foreman was ordered by the SS to select half of the welding command to "go to Switzerland." Littner, disappointed that he was not selected, questioned his supervisor, who assured him he had made the selections "at random."

> My supervisor thought seriously for a while, then said, "You know the existing situation here at Gusen II, but you don't know the situation in the place where the Jews selected are going, do you?" Not really convinced he had done me a favor, I thanked him and left. After the liberation, I heard from Austrian farmers whose fields were along the Danube that barges were dumping corpses in the river. I heard that Jews were thrown below deck, sealed into a small area, gassed and then thrown in the river.[598]

The presence of barges intended for mass murder was confirmed by a Colonel Guivante de St. Gast, who left CC Mauthausen on 22 April, in a phone call received by Wing Commander Dehn of the SHAEF Mission France on 3

---

[596] Letter from Major L. Reiger, Chief Czechoslovak Liaison Officer to SHAEF G-5 Displaced Persons Branch, 3 May 1945, NARA 331/290/7/10/3
[597] Ibid.
[598] Littner, npag

May.[599] That same day, Eisenhower, the Supreme Commander of Allied Expeditionary Forces, cabled Bradley and Devers as well as the entire SHAEF Division Commands (G-3 included) quoting almost verbatim the transcript of the phone conversation between St. Gast and Dehn and referencing cable FWD-19395 from 18 April 1945:

> There are satellite camps at Gusen, Sement [sic], Linz, Wells [sic], Loeblepass [sic], containing 80,000 PWs and political deportees of mixed nationality, including women. He [French survivor de Gast] stated the Germans then planning to exterminate these completely. Gas, dynamite and barges for drowning had been called forward and received. Massacres had started when officer left the camp. Officer stated that the prisoners had few arms.[600]

Also on 3 May, Brig. General Mickelsen reported that a Colonel Lash from G-3 Plans and Operations told the Senior Commander of G-5 Civil Affairs that "the Third Army had been instructed to slow the pace of its advance toward Linz."[601] Apparently unaware of Eisenhower's cable, Colonel Lash suggested "action for the relief of the concentration camp at Mauthausen should be requested of the Chief of Staff [G-3] by the ACOS of G-5 Division, omitting the usual slow procedure of a staff study." The memo ends with a recommendation that Mickelson's acting chief of staff "confer at once with G-3, with a view of taking such remedial action as is practicable and advisable."[602] But Mickelsen did not wait for Gen. Gasset to act. A note on the memo in what appears to be the same handwriting as Mickelsen's signature reads, "<u>Spoke G.3</u> (Gen. Whiteley) explains that an operation was considered on 2 May but not put into operation as it was considered that camps would be in our hands before an operation could be staged. 3rd Army ..." [The remaining is scratched out. Emphasis in the original].[603] British Maj. Gen. J.F.M. Whiteley was the Deputy Chief of Staff for G-3 Planning and Operations. Further research will have to determine what G-3 did in this regard.

---

[599] Transcription of phone call from Lt. de Gast, Signed by Wing Commander Dehn, 3 May 1943, Memo SHAEF G-5/DP/2711/7 Mickelsen to A.C.O.S, G-5 Division, NARA 331/290/1/10/3

[600] SHAEF FWD, Signed SCAEF to CG 12 Army Group G-5, 3 May 1945, NARA 331/290/1/10/3

[601] Brigadier General S.R. Mickelsen to A.C.O.S., G-5 Division (undated), NARA 331/290/1/10/3

[602] Ibid.

[603] Ibid.

On 4 May, the day the 71st Infantry Division came across CC Gunskirchen and the day before Sgt. Kosiek and the First Platoon of Troop D, 41st Cavalry Reconnaissance Squadron, Mechanized, of the Eleventh Armored Division happened upon the camps without warning, Major General John Taylor Lewis, the liaison between SHAEF and the Allied forces in France, cabled SHAEF G-5 FWD [at Reims] and SHAEF G-5 Main with very specific information about Mauthausen, Gusen, Ebensee, the Hermann Göring Works in Linz and Loible Pass [sic: Loibl-Pass]. He provides coordinates and accurate numbers of prisoners for each camp. But it is addressed to SHAEF G-5 where the problem was already known.[604]

Pogue notes that Allied forces were cautioned to slow their approach when nearing areas where they might encounter Soviet patrols to avoid shots being exchanged in the confusion.[605] When Eisenhower gave Patton the order to turn toward Czechoslovakia on 4 May, the day after his office cabled the Twelfth Army Group about the camps near Linz, Patton had 540,000 men at his command. "From where he sat, Czechoslovakia looked like a cinch," Farago writes. He also reports that Bradley doubted Patton's ability to turn so quickly north, but also points out that the Third Armies "dispositions were now paying off." Patton's desire to cross the northern limit to the Allied advance into Czechoslovakia and Bradley's efforts to convince Eisenhower to allow him to enter Prague are well known. Most of Patton's troops were positioned to achieve this objective.[606] Less attention has been paid to the effects of decisions not to direct more divisions to assist in the liberation of the camps that lay just beyond his objective at Linz.

Patton did not tour the Mauthausen or Gusen camps after their liberation on 5 May 1945. In his diary on September 15, 1945, he reports having travelled to Munich to meet Eisenhower. While waiting, he met Mickelson (Proudfoot's superior at SHAEF G-5) who showed him a report from a State Deparment official named Harrison about the unsanitary housing affored to displaced persons in Europe and the fact that they were being kept in camps under

---

[604] Major Gen. John Taylor Lewis to SHAEF FWD G-5, 4 May 1945, NARA 331/290/1/10/3
[605] Pogue, "Halt at the Elbe" http://www.army.mil/cmh-pg/books/70-7_22.htm
[606] Farago, 784-787

guard. The report was enclosed in a letter from President Truman to Eisenhower. As Commander of the Military Government of Bavaria (and the American zone in Austria) Patton bore the responsibility for the conditions in the camps as he had born the responsibility for any area his troops liberated during the war. Patton was furious at Harrison's letter. In his diary, he explained his opposition to Harrison's suggestion that German civilians be removed from their homes to make room for displaced persons.

First, when we remove an individual German, we punish an individual German, while the punishment is not intended for the individual, but for the race [sic]. Furthermore, it is against my Anglo-Saxon conscience to remove a person from a house, which is a punishment, without due process of law. In the second place, Harrison and his ilk believe that the displaced person is a human being, which he is not, and this applies particularly to the Jews, who are lower than animals. I remember once at Troina in Sicily, General Gay said that it wasn't a question of the people living with the dirty animals but of the animals living with dirty people. At that time he had never seen a displaced Jew.[607]

Had Patton toured Gusen, he certainly would have been accompanied by the press. Lack of media coverage is further explained by a memo Proudfoot kept of his conversation with a Lt. Col. Brewer. Major Proudfoot notes that Brewer called on 10 May to tell him that the Third Army had uncovered Concentration Camp Mauthausen "approximately two days ago."[608] Lt. Col. Brewer assured Proudfoot that "Full special preparations were made for the situation anticipated there."[609] While Brewer does not request Proudfoot to provide any supplies or medical teams, he does have one request:

Brewer was most anxious that we use all possible influence to control and reduce to absolute minimum the number of visitors to Mauthausen. The

---

[607] Patton, General George S. Diary, Library of Congress Control # MM 83035634
[608] Mauthausen Concentration Camp: Conversation with Lt. Col. Brewer 10 May 1945, NARA 331/290/7/10/13
[609] Ibid.

personnel on the ground are so busy performing necessary work that they have no spare time to conduct tours for visiting dignitaries.[610]

The personnel of the Eleventh Armored Division who liberated the camps had a brief previous experience with concentration camp prisoners in late April. As they approached Austria, they overtook the death marches from Flossenbürg. Staff Sergeant Ray Buch, Combat Command A (CCA) Company 56th Armored Engineer Battalion, Eleventh Armored Division recalls:

> On April 23, my guys...we caught up with them. We'd been passing shallow graves and we didn't even know what was in them because we kept going. Then we came to a place where the graves were just dug and they were getting ready to throw people in and we overwhelmed the SS guards and the inmates took the guns away from the guards and shot them and threw the SS in the shallow ditches and then took off. We took off, too, because we had a destination, but we were amazed at how skinny these people were. When we saw hundreds of them we were dumbfounded.[611]

When asked about the lack of training and information GIs received when approaching these camps, Lyle Storey explained, "We were still fighting a war at that point. It was inconceivable that they could have pulled us out of the field for a seminar on the proper nutrition and care of concentration camp inmates."[612] Given this, the tremendous initiative demonstrated by the American ground troops who discovered the Mauthausen and Gusen Concentration Camps is a testament to their courage and ingenuity. From their position on the road to Linz, they were unable to see the larger picture their superiors had of the war's progress or of the concentration camps they were about to encounter.

Except for those men still fighting fierce battles, the war seemed to be coming to a swift conclusion in the first week of May. Marshal Zhukov accepted the surrender of Berlin at three in the afternoon on 2 May. That evening,

---

[610]   Ibid.
[611]   Personal Interview, 28 August 2000
[612]   Personal Interview, 24 December 2000

Churchill announced that one million German troops had been arrested in northern Italy and Austria. Oberammergau surrendered. On 4 May, three German armies surrendered to the Russians and Salzburg and Innsbruck surrendered to the Sixth Army Group.[613]

On 2 May, Commandant of Mauthausen Ziereis received a delegation of the International Committee of the Red Cross (ICRC) in accordance with an order from Kaltenbrunner, who, having exhausted all other avenues of power, resorted to attempting to appear benevolent. Arriving from Switzerland, Mr. Louis Häfliger negotiated the release of more French, Dutch and British prisoners.[614] Pierre Serge Choumoff was transferred from CC Gusen I to CC Mauthausen with most of the French prisoners, but when he arrived the Red Cross truck was full, so he remained behind. He is among the inmates in the famous picture taken on May 5 of a group of prisoners pulling down the Nazi eagle over the gates of Mauthausen.[615]

Häfliger reports having learned from SS officers that Berlin had ordered Ziereis to blow up the inmates of the Gusen Camp complex along with the local population in the night between 5 May and 6 May 1945 in the tunnels which were loaded with 24.5 tons of dynamite,[616] an extermination plan that is often confused with "blowing up" CC Mauthausen.[617]

However, in an affidavit given by former DEST plant manager Paul Wolfram at the Mauthausen trials in Dachau, Wolfram claimed to have prevented the mass murder by explosive charges of the Gusen inmates. He claims to have first given this account to the CIC at Vöcklabruck, Austria, in June 1945. Wolfram stated:

---

[613] Martin Gilbert, The Second World War, (New York: Henry Holt, 1989)
[614] Marsálek, Mauthausen, 326.
[615] Personal Interview 7 May 1998
[616] „Bericht eines IKRK-Delegierten über seine Mission in Mauthausen" Die Tätigkeit des IKRK zugunsten der in deutschen Konzentrationslagern inhaftierten Zivilpersonen (1939 – 1945) (Genf: Internationales Komitee vom Roten Kreuz, 1985), 136.
[617] Yehuda Bauer, „The Historians" The Liberation of the Nazi Concentration Camps 1945 – Eyewitness Accounts of the Liberators (Washington, D.C.: United States Holocaust Memorial Council, 1987), 93

In early April 1945 I was ordered to the room of commandant Seidler where I met Ziereis, Seidler and SS-Obersturmführer Schuettauf. In this meeting, Ziereis announced a secret order given by Himmler via Kaltenbrunner and Gauleiter Eigruber. According to this order all inmates of Mauthausen (including the satellite camps) should have been exterminated to prevent the enemy to make use of their workforce (100.000 slaves) and to eliminate all witnesses of the events within the camp[s].[618]

Ziereis's orders, under the code name "Feuerzeug" (lighter) were to be top secret under penalty of death for Seidler, Wolfram and Schuettauf and their families. Wolfram claimed that most of the inmates of Mauthausen and Gusen I and II would have been killed in the underground plants at Gusen and St. Georgen after a false air raid lured them into the tunnels. The entrances would then be blasted shut, suffocating them all. According to Wolfram it was Seidler's responsibility to initiate the air raid alarm and to move all inmates (including the Revier) into the tunnels. Schuettauf's task was to secure the entrances with machine guns to prevent any inmates escaping from the tunnels. Wolfram, the only explosives expert nearby, was to personally place all the available explosive material of the DEST quarries in the tunnels. Wolfram claimed to be unwilling to carry out his task from the start and to have purposefully stalled Ziereis by discussing different problems arising from the plan with Ziereis. To delay the operation Wolfram first calculated 3 times as much explosive as was actually necessary. But in response, Ziereis ordered Wolfram to close 2 tunnels of Kellerbau with double walls to save explosive material.[619] This was actually done.

To compensate for lack of explosive material, Ziereis also added 20 to 24 aircraft bombs for which Wolfram claimed to have hidden the detonators. In response to being foiled in this attempt, Ziereis commandeered 2 truckloads with 120 marine mines, but these were also delivered without detonators. Ziereis wanted Wolfram to extract the explosive from these mines with the help of inmates but Wolfram refused because of the danger. Wolfram also

---

[618] Vol. 45 (ETO Case No. 000-50-5-) U.S.A. vs. Paul Wolfram, Box 50 Exhibit D-1 Statement of Paul Wolfram (German)

[619] Ibid.

stated that he told Ziereis that this order of Himmler, Kaltenbrunner and Eigruber should not be carried out since the area had recently been subordinated to Hitler's Plenipotentiary for Jet Planes, Kammler. In charge for only a few days, Kammler would never give approval to destroy these important production facilities. After this, Ziereis never mentioned the plan to Wolfram again. From this time on, perhaps the 27 or 28 of April, 1945, Wolfram stated that Ziereis was drunk much of the time. Wolfram also ordered his wife and his son to flee from the area. Two days later Wolfram ordered his younger son and daughter to flee. That afternoon he fled to the Alps as well by car – claiming to have first thrown the keys to the storage facility that contained the bombs and the mines into the Danube River.[620]

The seriousness of the scheme to blow up the tunnels was confirmed by Col.Rtd. Edward R. Ardery in a 2005 interview. A week after the liberation, then Captain Ardery, Company Commander, 56th Engineers Battalion, was ordered to Bergkristall:

At Gusen they had an underground factory or manufacturing plant where they were assembling Me 262s. The reason why I went in there was because at the end of the town at Gusen there was what looked like a Trolley Track that went to St. Georgen the end of the town that was covered with camouflage. Raised up above it, high above it there was a camouflage net hung from the top of tall buildings which hid the entrance of the tunnels. A platoon or a squad went in with us into the tunnels. Me 262s were inside the tunnels. They couldn't have been flown out of there so they would take them off by train.

There were a lot of explosive in there that people who went in there before us and they had seen it was wired for explosives. I went in there to take them out so that it couldn't be blown up. Delayed fuses were there to delay an explosion up to 28 days. There were definitely charges in there. We spent a lot of time cutting wires and were making a lot of educated guesses about which wires to cut. The explosives were lined up. If they were trying to blow

---

[620]   Ibid.

the thing up they would put them at the best places they could to cause the thing to collapse.[621]

Clearly Wolfram had made more progress towards blowing up the tunnels than he cared to reveal at his trial.

After the war Red Cross Representative Louis Häfliger claimed that the civilians from local communities were to be blown up in the towns as well. But survivor Pierre Serge Choumoff who met Häfliger at the Dachau trials when both were testifying there has suggested that Häfliger added the risk to civilians to protect himself. As a representative of the International Red Cross, he should not have interfered with military operations *unless* civilians were at risk.[622] Complicating discussions of the threat to the local population are the very different uses of the Kellerbau and Bergkristall tunnels during air raids. Mr. Choumoff's doubts that civilians were at risk are partly supported by his experience at Kellerbau: having never seen civilians use the tunnels as air raid shelters, he doubts local people could have been persuaded to use them, especially since the SS methods of driving inmates into and out of the tunnels was bloody and deadly. Different behaviour by either the SS or civilians would have created suspicion among the inmates.[623]

However, the impossibility of communication between prisoners of Gusen I and Gusen II, despite their close proximity, is made apparent by the fact that Mr. Choumoff was not aware that civilians from St. Georgen, like Johanna B. and her children,[624] were regularly sent into the Bergkristall tunnels during alarms. At Gusen II, during an air raid the absence of civilians in the Bergkristall tunnels would have alerted prisoners of danger. While Mr. Choumoff points out no civilian community that had witnessed Nazi atrocities elsewhere in the Third Reich was murdered en masse, the possibility remains that the SS may have contemplated the necessity of driving civilians into the tunnels in order not to alarm the prisoners.

---

[621] Personal Interview, 28 October 2005
[622] Personal Interview, 8 May 2005
[623] Ibid.
[624] Personal Interview, Johanna B., 18 September 2000. Translation by Martha Gammer

What is clear is that Häfliger succeeded in attaining a passenger car and contacting the American Army. Again Choumoff suggests that Ziereis and any SS of influence had left by the day of liberation, 5 May 1945, and so both prisoners and civilians were out of danger. In any case, Häfliger's intent was clearly to contact the Americans – who had a large presence in the vicinity of Linz by that time – and to persuade them to liberate the camps.[625]

Inside Gusen I, Kielich also recalls hearing rumors that Ziereis had ordered Commandant Seidler to blow the prisoners up in the Kellerbau tunnels. Kielich believed that Seidler's fears that inmates would resist going into the tunnels made him more dangerous. He recalls a 2 May confrontation between Seidler and Second in Command SS-Hauptsturmführer Jan Beck:

> Now my friends Stefan, Joseph, Kazik, Tony, Stan, and Edek and I waited, watched, listened and whispered, careful not to disturb the night's stillness. What luck, what a miracle that after so many years we seven might come out of this hell in one piece? In Barracks 3, everyone whose bed faced Roll Call Square sat on the floor to avoid being shot through the wall by machine guns if the SS should try to make a last stand and enter the camp shooting. We could hear Seidler and his SS cronies drinking and singing in the canteen late into the night. Hundreds of others in the barracks at the front of the camp waited with all sorts of weapons such as sticks, chairs, and table legs, anything that could be used to defend ourselves against an attempt to murder us all. A few even had guns smuggled out of the Steyr factory. From the noise that was coming from the Jourhaus we could only guess what transpired on the other side until the gate suddenly opened. Hand on his sword SS-Hauptsturmführer Jan Beck stopped the Commandant, telling Seidler and his drunken pals, "Over my body you enter the camp." When the confrontation moved to our side of the Jourhaus, we could not believe our eyes. In the bright lights, in full view of our barracks, Jan Beck drew his sword and Seidler backed down! It must have been the first time in Seidler's long career that he gave in to a person of lesser rank. With the collapse of his empire, we felt safe. Jan Beck stood on duty for the rest of the night. In

---

[625] „Bericht eines IKRK-Delegierten über seine Mission in Mauthausen" Die Tätigkeit des IKRK zugunsten der in deutschen Konzentrationslagern inhaftierten Zivilpersonen (1939 – 1945), 136 ff

the morning, to our delight the watchtowers were manned by older men not in SS uniforms. The SS guards just disappeared overnight. Were Seidler and his gang also gone? No one knew.

On the morning of 5 May (a Saturday), residents of St. Georgen and Langenstein saw prisoners healthy enough to escape jump over the wall. Johanna B. also recalls these prisoners went into farmhouses and ate everything they could find. Unable to digest it, however, they bled internally, causing them to have bloody diarrhea. "The Americans had to collect them and take them into the hospital. This was the main work in the first days," she recalls. "Even those who could jump out and run away were ill afterwards. They vomited and vomited."[626]

Since the next day was a Sunday, the people of St. Georgen were also surprised to find hundreds of "former"[627] CC Gusen inmates lying on the floor in the St. Georgen parish church. Hundreds of them used their last energy to drag themselves to church and thank God for having survived the "Hell of Hells" at St. Georgen and Gusen. The parish priest wrote in the church chronicle that "there were touching scenes of thousands of believing Poles" in his church.[628]

History shows that women and children are the most vulnerable in such an unstable situation. Maria F. says that she was very afraid, living alone with her young children. She recalls 5 May 1945:

> At nine or ten o'clock I looked out the window and lots and lots of prisoners came out in the morning. They came up the stairs. I was very frightened. The SS had always told the people that if these prisoners would get out everyone would be killed. Some prisoners had killed a horse and took the liver out and asked me to fry it. I put some onions with it. They were awfully anxious.[629]

---

[626] Personal Interview, 18 September 2000
[627] Chronik der Pfarre St. Georgen, Tom. I, p. 224
[628] Ibid., 224.
[629] Personal Interview, 21 September 2000

At four a.m. that morning, in Walding, Austria, Staff Sergeants Leander Hens, Ed Bergh and Robert Sellers, 3rd Platoon, A Company, 55th Armored Infantry Battalion, 11th Armored Division, were told by their Commanding Officer Lt. Henry B. Kieling to check all roads, bridges and enemy forces on the way to Linz.[630] When they found the bridge at Linz mined, Sergeant Ray Buch, CCA 56th Engineers spent the rest of 5 May clearing the bridge of explosives.

> We got a lot of fierce fighting several miles from Linz and Mauthausen around Wegscheid. They held us back for a couple of days and we finally eliminated that problem. The Eleventh Armored Division was headed east along the Czechoslovakian border and we were supposed to stay on this side of it. As we came closer to Linz at Wegscheid we had a lot of opposition from the SS who were making the German soldiers fight back. They were trying to keep us stable so their people to the east could get to us. That was around April 28 or so. We advanced toward Linz, taking our time because we knew the war was almost over. So we decided to save the bridge at Linz. Captain Edward R. Ardery from the 56th Engineers (he was commanding the 56th at the time), he and I and my squad went out on the bridge and he was warning us to watch out for booby traps which was pretty scary. The bridge was not guarded from Urfahr where we came in on the southern side of the Danube. So we spread out looking for dynamite. We weren't supposed to go over the bridge. We found several tons of dynamite under the bridge. We got that taken care of and dumped it in the river.

Hens, Sellers, and Bergh continued on to "clear the area." At around 8:30 a.m. they entered St. Georgen where, by chance, they met Häfliger before he went on to take Sgt. Albert Kosiek to Gusen and Mauthausen. Hens was certain, however, that it was Sgt. Kosiek and the First Platoon of Troop D, 41st Cavalry Reconnaissance Squadron, Mechanized, who uncovered Concentration Camps Mauthausen and Gusen I, II, and III.[631]

---

[630] Hens, Leander. „Liberation of Mauthausen" Speech given on May 6, 2000 at Gusen Memorial
[631] Hens, Speech May 6, 2000;, Albert Kosiek, „Liberation of Mauthausen" Thunderbolt – Bulletin of the 11th Armoured Division Association, Vol. 8, No. 7 (May – June 1955). In the possession of the author.

The surprise with which Kosiek's 23 men and the 1,800 camp guards who surrendered to them were greeted when they reached Gallneukirchen at 1:30 a.m. on 6 May is well documented. The courage and clear thinking of Kosiek and his men is well remembered by the survivors and residents of St. Georgen. Kielich recalled:

> An American army tank with five soldiers rumbled into Gusen I. Sergeant Albert J. Kosiek from Chicago climbed atop and announced in English, "Brothers, you are free."

> A representative of the Red Cross Committee from Mauthausen translated Kosiek's words into many languages and the long years of suffering in German concentration camps ended. Inmates of many nationalities were free human beings again. No sooner was our liberty declared than the sea of heads swayed in all directions. All nationalities sang their national anthems while soldiers in the American tank stood to attention, saluting. The Americans ordered the Austrians and Germans to lay down their weapons. Jan Beck handed his sword to Kosiek, but not before Stanislaw Nogaj handed a special note to Kosiek. Then the mostly Austrian fire fighters and Volkssturm and Beck were marched off in the direction of Linz.[632]

As is well known, CC Mauthausen, and to a lesser extent CC Gusen I, had prisoner organizations which could maintain a semblance of order in the absence of any outside authority. According to J.A.G.D. Liason Officer Major Harold W. Sullivan, after the liberation British civilian John A. Carter was in charge of prisoners.[633] Carter had arrived at Gusen in early 1944. According to his report, he had been arrested for being "in charge of an organization the purpose of which was to locate, feed, shelter, clothe and then get away to Spain; Allied Airmen hiding in France."[634] Carter himself writes in a statement forwarded by Sullivan to War Crimes USFET Main that he remained

---

[632] Kielich and Mills, 83
[633] Sullivan to War Crimes Branch USFET Main, 23 August 1945, NARA RG 549 Entry 290 59.12.3 JAG War Crimes Cases Tried Box 336
[634] Carter to Commanding Officer USFET Main, NARA RG 549 Entry 290 59.12.3 JAG War Crimes Cases Tried Box 336, 1

in charge of Gusen for three weeks at the request of Lt. Colonel Milton W. Keach who confirms this in a later report.[635] Immediately after the Americans left, however, Carter doubted his ability to maintain control.[636]

Victor Kielich recalls a shot was fired as soon as the Americans left Gusen I and a violent struggle ensued which left many capos dead. While there were revenge killings in CC Mauthausen as well, the violence cannot be compared to what occurred in Gusen II, where no order existed at all. Mr. Littner wrote:

> To us, the surviving zombies, when the Americans motioned to us to stay behind, it was a great disappointment. They ordered the guards to put their rifles down on a pile, and told them to form a column. The Germans followed their orders. After that, the American soldiers poured gasoline over the pile of rifles, and set them on fire. Then they continued with their military duties. The crazed well-fed Russian prisoners ran toward the burning pile of weapons, pulling out some not yet on fire and started shooting, killing some of their own brethren.[637]

Dusan Stefancic has similar recollections of the liberation of Gusen II. He estimates that perhaps 500 murders, mostly revenge killings of capos, took place in the Gusen camps after Kosiek and his men left. As Maria F. and Johanna B. also report, Stefancic said thousands of prisoners left the camps despite being requested to remain until the American troops returned:

> Many of these prisoners ate whatever they could find and became immediately ill. Many died. The Americans were not seen for some days. This delay became fatal for many prisoners because many of them took in food in an uncontrolled manner with disastrous consequences. After the disappearance of the Americans the vast majority of the camp prisoners started home on foot. It is clear that a great number of them were physically unfit for such

---

[635] Carter, 1; Memorandum No. 2 Concentration Camp at Gusen, Austria from Major M.J. Proudfoot to Executive, Displaced Person Branch, G-5, 8 June 1945, NARA 331/290/7/10/3
[636] Carter, 1
[637] Littner, npag

a task. Some of those reached their destinations, some simply disappeared, and some were later returned to Gusen I or Mauthausen by the Americans in a completely exhausted condition.[638]

Carter writes that on 6 May 1945 he and Dr. Tony Goscinski, the chief prisoner-physician in the camp, went to Linz...

> for the purpose of obtaining military support as I feared not being able to keep the Camp under control. Owing to our late return – traffic difficulties – the news had got about that "Toni" and I would not return! That we had also fled as had done 12,000 inmates! The truth was, I discovered shortly after my return that there was grave fear of trouble cropping up between the Polish and the people of another Nation, equal in number, and among whom there had always been some strife. Checked the second day after your [U.S.] liberating the Camp, we found that of the 7.000 – approximately – inmates who remained, the number of the former was about 2.600 and about 2.400 of the latter. In spite of that, I really never had the slightest trouble with either during these three weeks while I remained to help "carry on", and I felt rather proud of this![639]

Evelyn Le Chène calls the 11th Armored Division's arrival at CC Gusen as a "cursory" visit. She then describes a "resistance committee led a popular uprising"[640] which liberated the camp on the next day by breaking through the fence (no battle is described). She does not, however, mention Carter. From all accounts, the first month of liberation was confusing. If Lt. Col. Keach of the 11th Armored Division asked Carter to "stay an extra three weeks to 'help carry on'"[641] as both Sullivan and Carter write, perhaps not all prisoners or prisoner-national-committees recognized Carter's authority.

Carter was apparently unaware that members of Kosiek's platoon had been asked to return to CC Mauthausen with members of the Signal Corps on

---

[638] Dusan Stefancic, e-mail to author, 21 January 2000
[639] Carter to Commanding Officer USFET Main, 12 September 1945 RG 549 Entry 290 59.12.3 JAG War Crimes Cases Tried Box 336, 5
[640] Le Chène, 218
[641] Carter, 4

the same day he traveled to Linz for assistance. The famous photographs of the American GIs entering Mauthausen under a banner greeting them as liberators in Spanish were taken by Corporal Donald R. Ornitz on 6 May.[642] A lesser known photograph was also taken that day of six men bludgeoned to death at Mauthausen and left in a barrack, bearing the caption:

> When the town of Linz, Austria, was taken by the Eleventh Armored Division, Third Army, on 5 May 1945 another of Hitler's Labor and Concentration Camps was liberated. Malnutrition, ill-treatment, etc. was responsible for many daily deaths. After the Americans came into the camp and disarmed the guards, some of the infuriated inmates who were still able took up guns and hatchets and proceeded to work on the guards. Six dead men in this one room barrack that was used as a morgue, five were prisoners and the one in the foreground was a guard.[643]

The photo's use was restricted by Lieutenant Janowiak of "Public Info" until 7 July 1947.[644] Such restrictions contributed to the obscurity of the camps and lack of information about the conditions after liberation.

Photographic evidence of Gusen is often mistakenly used to illustrate "Mauthausen," despite it being identified clearly as having been taken at Gusen. The now famous series of photos [46578 – 46112] taken by Signal Corpsmen Ignatius Gallo and Sam Gilbert carry an original master caption that explains the terrible conditions these men found at the camp seven days after liberation:

> The 35 pictures in this series were made 12 May at Gusen Concentration Camp at Mulhausen [sic], Austria, near Linz, Austria. When it was opened, total killed there and maximum held in it are facts not now known. But even after arrival of men of the 3rd US Army, inmates continued to die at the rate of 100 per day. Inmates told investigators the camp primarily was for political prisoners from all over Europe. Investigators learned, however, that at one

---

[642] Still Picture 111-C 206395, NARA
[643] Still Picture 266502-W, RG 319 Entry CE Box 2, NARA
[644] Ibid.

time an unknown number of American fliers were killed there. Men were worked in nearby quarries until too weak for more, then killed.[645]

Furthermore, film footage shot by the US Signal Corps on 11 May 1945 at Gusen I and II is still being used to illustrate the liberation of Mauthausen six days earlier.[646]

The initial violence, much worse at Gusen I and Gusen II, was followed by disorder that inevitably resulted from the liberation of so many prisoners without sufficient ground troops to establish order. Operating in this chaotic environment, the many US Army and Intelligence organizations that converged on the camps and on the installations at Kellerbau and Bergkristall in the following weeks worked tirelessly to document the brutal conditions in the camps or gather technical information. However, misinformation about the locations and numbers of camps as well as the camps' – information which Mickelsen and Proudfoot had tried so unsuccessfully to correct in the weeks before the liberation – would be perpetuated for decades through the reliance on reports written at this time.

Confusion continued well into June, as reported by Captain Samuel G. Wilson the engineering officer attached to the 34th Disarmament Squadron [formerly the 34th Bomb Squadron], 17th Bomb Group, 1st Tactical Airforce. Tasked with discovering technical intelligence about the Luftwaffe at Bergkristall, Wilson wrote in his diary on June 24 after a visit to Mauthausen and Gusen:

> Camp Gusen was similar [to Mauthausen] but if possible even worse. People were dying at a high rate every day in the hospital. One doctor (American)

---

[645] Still Picture 111-C 264919, NARA

[646] "Mauthausen." United States Holocaust Memorial Museum. November 10, 2007. http://www. ushmm.org/wlc/article.php?lang=en&ModuleId=10005196. Film footage of CC Gusen actually forms a major part of the following NARA motion picture holdings.: NWDNM(m)-111-ADC-4319: Concentration and Death Camp Mauthausen, Austria, 05/11/1945 (LIB 1222), NWDNM(m)-111-ADC-4326: Kesselring Meeting, Zell am See, Austria; Field Marshal Kesselring, Berchtesgaden, Germany; Concentration Camp Mauthausen, Germany, 05/08/1945 (B1221) and NWDNM(m)-111-ADC-8571: Prosecution Exhibit No. 230, Nordhausen Concentration Camp; Mauthausen Concentration Camp. Especially the scenes from Gusen are used worldwide to illustrate the Holocaust – but never reference is given to the Gusen camps and its victims.

told me he had seen every disease he'd ever studied in medical school. Someone showed us a room of the crematorium. For an unexplained reason it contained a half-dozen bodies in an advanced state of decomposition with flies and odor to match. We moved on rapidly.[647]

On 29 June 1945 he wrote:

We were advised that the Russians were going to occupy all of Czechoslovakia; I suppose we will move and operate elsewhere. And we had just got started. This is a confused mess, organizationally and about everything else...I suspect the confusion will continue. We seem to be in a competition with the U.S. Infantry, the Allied Military Government and the U.S. Technical Intelligence people. The AMG cooperation ranges from zero to 100%; we don't know the ground rules and there is too much duplication effort.[648]

The US Army controlled the tunnels until 27 July 1945 when they were turned over to the Soviets. The circumstances described by Wilson nearly two months after liberation helps explain the absence of details about the Messerschmitt factories or their use of slave labor from the extant exhibits in the 17 June 1945 report by Major Eugene Cohen. Patton appointed Cohen Investigator Examiner for the War Crimes Branch, JAGS, Third Army on 6 June 1945.[649] While Cohen distinguishes between Gusen I and II in his summary, little information about Gusen II, if any, appears in the surviving exhibits dated from 9 May 1945 to 17 May 1945. Many of these exhibits have been lost or misfiled,[650] but one can find copies of them in other postwar files. For instance, it is possible that Cohen Report Exhibit 205, a statement by Wolfgang Sanner, can be found in a file in the Records of U.S. Occupation Headquarters, Adjutant General Office titled "Detention and Internment Camps." "Appendix M" in this file, titled "Forced Labor" contains a "List of Firms where prisoners of Mauthausen or of the outposts of this camp

---

[647] 34th Bomb Squadron (M) AAF, APO 374, June 1945, AFHRA SQ-Bomb-34-HI
[648] 34th Bomb Squadron (M) AAF, APO 374, June 1945, AFHRA SQ-Bomb-34-HI
[649] Record Group 238 World War II War Crimes Records International Military Tribunal Exhibit 249, Exhibit #1, NARA
[650] Ibid., 5

were worked against payments turned over to the SS."[651] Dated 10 May 1945 and written by Wolfgang Sanner, Manager of A.E.G. Berlin, Secretary of the Labour Drafting Department at the CC Mauthausen, the list contains the following under subheading "Gusen":

Deutsche Erd und Steinwerke G.m.b.H. St. Georgen a. d. Gusen
Quarry and arming [sic] plant Aerplane factory Messerschmidt [sic] and underground mines for arming purposes

Steyr-Daimler Pusch [sic] A.G. (Georgenmuehle)
War Plant

SS Feurgungsstab B 9 [sic] Dip Ing. K. Fiebinger Wien IX Marokannergasse
Building below the surface for secret war material plant

SS Feurgungsstab B9 [sic] Dr. Ing. Kammler (Diploma. Ing. K. Fiebinger Wien) Underground buildings for a secret war-plant[652]

Here it must be said that despite the grueling work conducted by Cohen and his investigators from May 6 when the work "commenced,"[653] and especially the five days from 9 May to 15 May when the statements taken at Mauthausen and Gusen are dated (statements dated 17 May deal with Ebensee), the errors made on the post-war reports would cause confusion for many years. The Mauthausen and Gusen concentration camps are often not differentiated, or reports about Gusen are labeled Mauthausen, and vice versa.[654] The pressure Eugene Cohen and Jack Nowitz were under was immense. No one can fault them for mistakenly identifying Mauthausen as being in "Germany"[655] on occasion. But such errors persist. The OSS Report about "Concentration Camp Mauthausen" contains information about Gusen, but gives no loca-

---

[651] Ibid.
[652] AG 254 Detention and Internment Camps USGCC, RG 260 39.40.17.02, NARA
[653] Cohen Report, 5
[654] Cohen Report, 2
[655] Ibid., Exhibit 23

tion for this camp.[656] The post war trial Altfuldisch et al is known as the "Mauthausen" trial although many of the defendants are charged with crimes committed at the Gusen camps or in association with "Granitwerke Mauthausen" which was actually in St. Georgen.

While the truth about underground factory space built at St. Georgen an der Gusen by slave labor under the direction of Kammler and Fiebinger would sadly be lost for many years to come, the first priority of the regular US troops arriving on 7 May 1945 with the 11th Armored and the 26th Infantry Division, XII Corps, 3rd US Army would be saving the lives of the thousands of prisoners too weak to walk home.

According to the 25 May 1945 report of the 11th Armored Division's Office of the Surgeon General, a surgeon arrived on the 8 May and "sanitary teams from the Army and Corps began surveys and recommendations."[657] In fact, on 8 May, the public health team established on that date made these recommendations and requested an evacuation hospital be established. The "medical soldiers"[658] mentioned in the Surgeon General's report were perhaps the GIs from the 11th Armored Division who organized the removal of tons of "trash and filth."[659] Ray Buch recalls receiving orders to drive bulldozers to Mauthausen on 8 May. He arrived on 10 May with Al Salzman, also from A company 56th Armored Engineers. Buch remembers piles of garbage ten feet deep.[660] CC Gusen II was so filled with vermin and disease that to control epidemics, the wooden buildings were set afire around 16 May 1945 with phosphorous mortar grenades.[661]

---

[656] OSS Inspection of Mauthausen-Gusen May 1945, RG 549 Entry 290 59.12.3 JAG War Crimes Cases Tried, NARA

[657] Sanitary Report, Camp Mauthausen, 11th Armored Division Headquarters, Office of the Surgeon, 25 May 1945, NARA 112/31/1337

[658] Ibid.

[659] Ibid.

[660] Personal Interview, 28 August 2000

[661] Letter from Major Rtd. Charles R. Sandler [Deputy military commander of the liberated Gusen Concentration Camps in May 1945, 21st Armored Infantry Battalion, 11th Armored Division, 3rd US Army] to the author, 12 July 1998.

Karl Littner recalls leaving Gusen II before the Americans burned it. He and his friend Beniek "supported each other" and walked slowly out of the camp for the last time. They looked to the right, and then to the left, and wondered which way to go:

> Reasoning K.Z. Lager Mauthausen was to the left, we decided to go to the right: We had had enough camps for a while. About 500 meters down the road, we saw an SS barracks, now empty. Hungry, weak, weary, tired, and undecided to go anywhere, we went in, and started to investigate this unfamiliar place. The fleeing SS left behind all the furnishings and some raw food stuff, a paradise compared to Gusen II. My sore behind needed to heal [Littner had been beaten with a 2 x 4 for sitting down on the job in Tunnel 7] and we needed to find food. We found blankets to keep us warm during the cold Austrian nights and enough food to keep us going.[662]

They remained in the barracks for some days, undisturbed, taking longer and longer walks as their strength returned. One day, as they paused on the small bridge over the Gusen River, they encountered American soldiers fishing with grenades:

> From a nearby house two little blond haired boys, about 7 and 9 years old, collected the injured fish floating on top of the water into a wicker basket. We volunteered to help the little boys catch more fish before they recovered from the shock and swam away. Still dressed in our louse-filled, shabby camp uniforms, with our heads shaved with the "lice street" (the two finger wide strip down the middle), we must have looked abnormal. The boys' father, Mr. Mayr, looked out his window and noticed the strange people in the company of his boys. He became naturally very concerned about their safety and came out to take a look. After we exchanged a few words, he realized we were harmless, despite our shabby attire, and allowed the boys to continue playing in the river with us present. Mr. Mayr went back to his house to assure his wife that everything outside was fine. After a short while he came out again, and handed me his only white Sunday shirt. I hesitated to take his

---

[662] Littner, npag.

shirt, knowing that it is his only Sunday shirt. He did not have another to give to Beniek.[663]

Figure 30: Burning of CC Gusen II by US troops, 11 May 1945
Source: Museu d´Història de Catalunya

One of Eleventh Armored Division's first priorities was making potable water available from Army sources and organizing three kitchens, one equipped to cook appropriately for "the starved."[664] This done, the supply officer set about trying to find food.[665] But for those prisoners who would never make it home, there was the urgent matter of a burial. Before Tech. Sergeant Ray Buch arrived with bulldozers on 10 May, local people were required to dig graves. Maria F. recalls that the first day the Americans returned people in

---

[663] Ibid. More than fifty years later, in 1999, Littner returned to St. Georgen with his son, Eli. The elder Mr. Mayr had passed away, but the Littners met a younger brother of the two boys, Dr. Friedrich Mayr.

[664] Sanitary Report, Camp Mauthausen, 5

[665] Ibid., 5

town had to dig graves. "They had to walk to Gusen and the mayor of St. Georgen, who was a butcher and a party member, had to carry the corpses. His jacket was taken and put over the dead corpses. Local school children had to attend the mass funerals." Some days later some liberated prisoners whom she recognized told her, "Don't go down to Gusen for the funeral because you have always been a good woman. Stay here with your children."[666] The Americans made exceptions, as well, and told Johanna B. she didn't have to bring her small children.[667]

For many decades the men and women of the 11th Armored and the 26th Infantry Division who first arrived at St. Georgen, Gusen and Mauthausen received such faint praise that they remain reluctant to acknowledge their accomplishment. When the family of a Polish survivor thanked Lee Hens at the 2000 Gusen Commemoration, his eyes filled with tears as he said, "Well, it's what we were here for."

What Buch recalls most after he arrived on May 10th at Mauthausen is not the looting of the SS community, but the bodies.

> I was helping them dig the graves by that time because I was an engineer. We had a bulldozer from the battalion headquarters and Al Salzman and I were working the bulldozer to dig these six-foot deep trenches one hundred feet long in the soccer field where the SS had built a platform out of rocks and made a soccer field. It was so hard to dig with a bulldozer. We had to get somebody to dig the bigger rocks out by hand. We tried dynamiting a couple of them but granite is the hardest rock there is. This was around May 11 or 12th. They tried to get people in head to foot, head to foot to get more in the grave without piling them on top of each other. 500 in each heap. One wagon-load had two hundred bodies in it. The bodies were so thin it was hard to tell how many were in them. The reason it wasn't smelling as bad as it could have was because the weather was so cool.

---

[666] Personal Interview, 21 September 2000
[667] Personal Interview, 18 September 2000

We buried 1800. 1800 altogether. Found 1400 had been gassed in one lot and 400 in another. There were three big heaps of them in between the hospital and the camps. And the local Germans [sic] had buried ten thousand of them in shallow graves and then had to dig them up because it was too shallow.

Figure 31: *Mass Grave at Gusen (Background: CC Gusen II), May 1945*
Source: NARA

On Buch's return to Mauthausen in 1995, he was surprised that the graveyard he and the other Engineers had built was gone. "We built a wall around the graveyard of granite blocks and put up crosses. We put a few extra humps in it [the wall] to make it less monotonous. At this point [after the liberation] the German [sic] civilians were being paid. But now they took the stone walls and memorials that we had built and put in a parking lot. Now instead of the graveyard they have a parking lot."[668] Buch is referring to one of the visitor parking lots at the Mauthausen Museum.

Louise Birch, a nurse with the 131st Evacuation Hospital who arrived at Gusen I on 16 May, said that (given the magnitude of the problem at the camps) she doesn't think the Third Army could have prepared for it.

> When we were there they finally came up with blankets for them. They were all naked. Men would wrap blankets around their heads so they couldn't be seen. Men would look at the ground in shame and fear. As nurses, we weren't allowed to touch them. We gave no nursing care. People in town had to bathe them. We couldn't speak their language and we were so young, we couldn't take in the magnitude of it. We didn't go behind the walls at Gusen. The hospital was along the road [in the former SS barracks]. All I remember of our wards is that there were around 200 in a ward and we had at least 8 if not more. Over the night anyone who died, usually between 8 or 12, were carried out and we would get more immediately [from behind the camp walls]. They had to be de-loused first. We never had an empty space. Never.[669]

In fact, Mrs. Lehner was one of the first Red Cross volunteers from St. Georgen to assist prisoners. Unlike the American nurses, she was not restricted from touching prisoners and entered the camp as soon as the guards left.[670] Prisoner Aldo Carpi recalls seeing a Red Cross nurse and an Austrian doctor the day of liberation.[671] The reticence of the US Military to allow the nurses contact with prisoners was based upon the real health danger. One farmer in the nearby village of Frankenberg died of dysentery after giving an inmate food in the days after liberation.[672]

---

[668] Ibid.
[669] Telephone Interview, 23 July 2000
[670] Personal Interview, 18 September 2000
[671] Carpi, Aldo Diario di Gusen, (Torino, Einaudi Tascabili, 1993), 162-163, translated by Martha Gammer
[672] Chronik der Pfarre St. Georgen, Tom. I, p. 224.

Records of the 131st Evacuation hospital show that they left Sanderstsdorf Germany for Austria on 9 May.[673] The 11th Armored Division Sanitary report puts their arrival at 10 May, and says they were ready to take 228 patients on 12 May and were in operation for a month. The SS barracks were first set up for 1,000 women prisoners.[674] Mrs. Birch recalls that the men of the 131st left for Gusen first and the 34 female nurses followed, arriving on 16 May from Oberstein to set up for patients. "The men didn't want us to come. They tried to get us to go home," she said, but she remembers they stayed until 21 June, her birthday.[675]

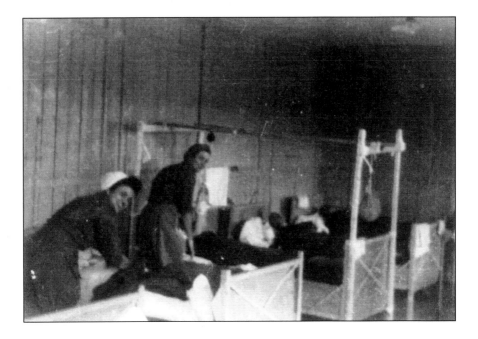

Figure 32: Nurses of the 131st Evacuation Hospital at Gusen, 1945
Source: Louise Birch

On arriving, the 131st Evacuation Hospital report says, "The supply problems were staggering."

---

[673]   Report 131st Evacuation Hospital, NARA 112/390/17/25/7, 4
[674]   Sanitary Report, Camp Mauthausen, 5
[675]   Telephone Interview, 23 July 2000

We arrived only a few days [5] after the liberation and the medical situation was desperate. Nearly three hundred bodies were awaiting burial;* scores were still dying; there was no food, no drugs, no medical supplies, no sanitary facilities. Filth, disease, and starvation were rampant. In four days, eight large SS barracks had been completely cleaned, de-loused, and the hospital already had a census of 2000 critically ill patients. The immediate need was for cleaning up the camp, and obtaining food and medical supplies. Both American and captured stocks were used. Displaced personnel, volunteer Austrians, and German prisoners were used in large numbers. Nearly 4000 patients of twenty-two nationalities were hospitalized and records maintained in a month of operation.[676]

In a signed interview, Mary Traub, a surgical nurse with the 131st Evacuation Hospital, reported the men left for France two weeks before the nurses and "cleaned up everything before we arrived ... Most of the work done in the surgery was repair work and there was not a lot of that to do because the boys had done a lot before we got there." When asked if she recalled if they were generally busy, she said that she only remembers one amputation performed while they were there. Other than this single surgery, she recalled helping women who had been impregnated by the SS. These women also reported that the SS killed their babies immediately after they were delivered.[677]

The 130th Evacuation Hospital arrived on 15 May and was able to set up tents three miles north of Mauthausen at Castle Marbach by May 17, with 515 patients. By 25 May, 1,793 patients would be admitted.[678] Mrs. Lehner, the local member of the Red Cross, worked there for months. Her mother didn't want her to walk the three miles to Castle Marbach every day because it was still so dangerous, but she did. Her late husband was still considered

---

* When asked about the discrepancy between this report of three hundred bodies awaiting burial on 10 May 1945, and his own recollections, Ray Buch said that it is partially explained by the fact that the bodies of the dead were so thin a pile that looked like 300 might actually contain twice that many.

[676] Report 131st Evacuation Hospital, 4-5.

[677] Personal Interview, Signed on 30 March 2005. Mrs. Traub was billeted with Mrs. Birch in Gusen Memorial Committee member Willy Nowy's house.

[678] NARA Record Group 407 Entry 427A, 270/50/24/05 MDEH-130-0 and 0.1, Box 21518

missing-in-action, and she hoped someone, somewhere was taking care of him as she was caring for liberated Allied POWs.[679]

Important documents were still being discovered, and lost. One is confirmed by a 30 May 1945 report by French survivor Lt. Col. P. G. de St. Gast. He arrived with Lt. Veith at Mauthausen on the 15 May, as well, to assist in the investigation. Confirming Major Wilson's statement, de St. Gast states that competing demands by representatives from the national committees of prisoners as well as the U.S. Judge Advocate [Cohen], Review Board [see the 14 June report above], and the American Security Service [presumably the OSS] were confusing the investigation and causing files to be misplaced. "These organizations work in such a way that they are largely shut off from one another. On the other hand, they get in each other's way and try to monopolise [sic] the secretarial staff of the Research Bureau. In short, there are so many conflicting orders given that the carrying out of any logical and constructive work is extremely difficult." Lt. Col. De St. Gast says that important files, such as the registry of prisoners "from No. 18,527 to 43,000" – which he himself saved from being destroyed by the SS – were missing.[680]

Indeed, the seven-page OSS report on Mauthausen and Gusen, also dated 15 – 16 May 1945, makes no mention of any other US organization present. Agents "Golf" and "Pleurisy" report on methods of murder at Mauthausen and Gusen, medical experiments, and conditions in the camps. Ironies such as the fact that trained medical personnel were used as slave labor while untrained criminals dispensed medical treatment to prisoners is noted along with many other details about medical experiments conducted by the SS. Absent from the report are details about Bergkristall. While Mauthausen is said to have had ten to twelve thousand prisoners, the population of Gusen is not mentioned.[681] It is unknown if the OSS officers, Cohen's team of investigators, or the other visitors, like Sullivan, were actually allowed within the walls of Gusen I or near the compound of Gusen II to investigate or if, like the nurses, these men were

---

[679] Personal Interview, 18 September 2000, translated by Martha Gammer
[680] 12 Army Group Mauthausen Camp, Record Group 331 Entry 17 290/7/21/7 Box 50, NARA
[681] OSS Inspection of Mauthausen-Gusen May 1945, RG 549 Entry 290 59.12.3 JAG War Crimes Cases Tried Box 335, NARA

kept at a distance from the remaining prisoners kept behind the walls. Such distance might account for the lack of information about the armament plants. All teams were also, of course, active duty military and so their reports would be subject to censorship and constraint imposed by their superiors.

Information provided by Lt. John "Jack" Taylor, a US Navy Lieutenant and OSS officer whose statement appears in the Cohen Report as Exhibit 3. Taylor's estimation of the total number of prisoners at Mauthausen at liberation, 18,000,[682] is actually fewer than the figure given in his Dupont Mission Report, date 30 May 1945, for Gusen alone at liberation: 24,000. The number Taylor would give for the entire Mauthausen Camp Complex was 91,000.[683] Unfortunately, this document was classified as Top Secret until 1976 and so perhaps was unavailable to Cohen when he completed his report to the Judge Advocate, Third US Army, in December 1945.

Another important description of conditions before and after liberation was supplied by Carter in his 23 August 1945 report to War Crimes USFET Main. Carter was also unfortunately unavailable to make a statement for Cohen because, as Sullivan explained to his superiors at USFET, "Mr. Carter was busily engaged in the administration of the camp and did not have time to give a statement."[684] Because of his duties, Carter was unable to provide Cohen with the list of prisoners (like Dr. Goscinski) whom he believed would be most knowledgable about the camps. Nor could Carter provide Cohen the list of most culpable prisoner-functionaries that he wrote at Keach's request. In his statement, Carter explains that the number of Gusen prisoners at liberation was 22,000 and that Gusen II was built 400 yards from Gusen I. He also explains the use of slave labor by Messerschmitt and Steyr.[685]

Although Mr. Carter's statement would be filed in the exhibits for the "Main Mauthausen Trial" (US vs. Altfuldisch et al), its accuracy would not be reflected in the history of the Gusen camps for many decades. Another expla-

---

[682] Record Group 238 World War II War Crimes Records International Military Tribunal Exhibit 249, Exhibit #1, NARA
[683] NARA RG 226 Entry 190 7/2/04 Box 4, Section III, 15
[684] Carter, 1
[685] Carter, 3

nation for the lack of detailed and accurate information about the Gusen camps may be found in the decision by William Denson, Chief Prosecutor at the Dachau Trials, to rely on the personal testimony of eye witnesses rather than documentary evidence. Denson's biographer Joshua M. Greene writes that Denson believed the world needed "a memorable end to the Nazi catastrophe."[686] To achieve this, "Denson would continue to stress the experience of living victims over the mute data of paper documents." One unfortunate result of this decision was that documents, such as Carter's statement or even SS documents regarding the camps and armament plants used in post-war intelligence summaries[687] were not entered into the public record through the trial proceedings, if indeed they were made available to prosecutors at all.

The investigations were being conducted in the midst of heroic efforts by the 11th Armored and 26th Infantry Divisions to cloth, feed, and provide medical care to survivors. But the situation at St. Georgen, Gusen and Mauthausen threatened to become an international scandal. A report was received by the Deputy U.S. Political Advisor, Donald R. Heath, on 1 June 1945 that stated:

> 27,000 inmates of Mauthausen [sic] Camp have been left virtually to fend for themselves. The majority is in most critical condition, three to four hundred dying daily due to severe under-nourishment, typhus, and T.B. Only American combat units are in the area, possessing no adequate facilities or personnel to handle the situation. No use is reported to have been made of conditions in this camp to further illustrate Nazi criminality. On the other hand, failure to bring prompt succour is reported to be used by Russians for anti-American propaganda in the area which they control.[688]

Of course, Lt. Col. Brewer had asked Proudfoot to discourage visitors, which would have included the press who might well have exploited the conditions

---

[686] Greene, Joshua M. Justice at Dachau (New York: Broadway Books), 54

[687] Esche II Work Plan, 4 April 1944, (Figure 9c), J.I.O.A. Final Report No. 1, Part 1, Section III, Appendix A. Washington, DC, Joint Intelligence Objectives Agency, September 1945. NARA, RG 319, Army Staff, „P"-File, Location: 7/23/42/5, Box T169.

[688] Donald R. Heath, Deputy, United States Political Advisor for Germany to Lieutenant General W. B. Smith, Chief of Staff, SHAEF 1 June 1945, NARA 331/290/7/10/3

there. On 6 and 7 June, Major Proudfoot himself visited the camps to report back to Brigadier General Mickelson, Chief of Staff, Displaced Persons Branch regarding Mr. Heath's concerns.

Figure 33: Prisoner formation of thanks to liberators on Roll Call Square of CC Gusen I (pay attention to the side-gate by which inmates were sent to the quarries and war industries for years), May 1945
Source: Major Charles R. Sandler

At CC Mauthausen, Major Proudfoot met with the Commanding Officer, Lt. Col. Seibel who reported that his operations began there on 7 May, two days after liberation. When Proudfoot asked if the 11th Armored Division had received preliminary warning of the camps, Seibel said that neither he nor the division was given any notification and as a result, Proudfoot writes that contrary to what Lt. Col. Brewer had told him on 10 May "no special preparations had been made to relieve conditions at the moment the camps were uncovered." This lack of preparation was confirmed by Lt. Col. H. W.

Decker and Captain W.S. Morton, Chief and Deputy Chief Military Government Officers of the 11[689] Armored Division stationed at Linz.[689] Proudfoot also visited Gusen I, under the authority of Lt. Colonel A. C. Keach of the 11th Armored Division.

While Proudfoot's visit was made more than a month after liberation, it remains a valuable source of information about CC Mauthausen/Gusen. However, survivors and witnesses agree that not all of Seibel and Keach's assessments of the situation are entirely accurate. Both told Proudfoot that on their arrival thousands of prisoners had left the camps and presented a danger to the local population.[690] Keach reported of the Gusen camps:

> The camp when uncovered was in a chaotic condition. Of the some 8,000 [sic] former prisoners, only 1,000 sick and disabled were on the premises. The remainder were roaming throughout the vicinity, pillaging and looting. A Mr. Carter of the British Intelligence Service had taken charge in the camp and was attempting to keep some semblance of order. The SS food warehouse on the premises had been entered and damaged as had been done to most of the buildings. Troops of the 11th Armored Division began rounding up the former residents scattered around the vicinity; within a few days the population of the camp again totalled 8,000 prisoners.[691]

Marsálek also notes that prisoners took revenge, lynching former capos, guards as well as innocent German and Austrian detainees. As a consequence innocent people were placed in protective custody by the Americans on 8 May 1945.[692]

---

[689] Major M. J. Proudfoot. Memorandum No. 1 Concentration Camp at Mauthausen, Austria from Major M.J. Proudfoot to Executive, Displaced Person Branch, G-5, 7 June 1945, NARA 331/290/7/10/3

[690] Memorandum No. 2 Concentration Camp at Gusen, Austria from Major M.J. Proudfoot to Executive, Displaced Person Branch, G-5 8 June 1945 NARA 331/290/7/10/3

[691] Ibid.

[692] Marsálek, Gusen, 43

Survivor Dusan Stefancic is adamant that Keach exaggerated the danger prisoners presented. He recalls:

> The landscape was strewn with sick and exhausted prisoners who had to be brought back to camp. This was the extent of any "rounding up" by the Americans. This seems to be the group Keach is referring to, but this number was not more than 1,500. I do not exclude some sporadic harassment of the population, but never by 7,000 prisoners. The reasons for such sporadic excesses can be explained by the simple fact that the behaviour of the Austrian population was in no way different from the one in Germany. Therefore any terrorizing of the local population should be understood as an act of revenge.[693]

Although the police records of St. Georgen do not reflect criminal activity in the days immediately following liberation on the scale that Lt. Keach described, a concerted effort by local police forces on 25 May resulted in the arrest of 180 former CC inmates known as "greens" for the green triangle they wore designating them as German career criminals. Equipped with automatic rifles in some cases, these criminals had hidden in the forest and carried out hold-ups in the vicinity. On arrest by local authorities, they were returned to CC Gusen and held there by the American forces. After the Soviet occupation, these criminal prisoners, prevented from returning to their countries of origin by their police records, remained in the SS barracks and, along with the Soviet occupational forces, continued to harass the local population, the record shows.[694] Maria F. recalls that ordinary prisoners "had robbed some things from the SS village. I remember some bath towels they had taken from the SS village and they gave them to me. I had them for a long time. Some of the prisoners brought me a box of light bulbs from the stores inside the tunnels to exchange for food. Some farmers took generators from the tunnels for their private use. But nobody ever harmed me. From the SS houses everything was taken."[695] Of course, prisoners knew where the SS lived because they had built their homes.

---

[693] e-mail to author, 21 January 2000
[694] Chronik des k.K. Gendarmeriepostens Sankt Georgen an der Gusen.
[695] Personal Interview, 21 September 2000

In defense of Lt. Col. Keach, Ray Buch said,

> He was D company. 21st Infantry. He was in charge of the guards stationed
> in the camp. Keach did a pretty good job but they were dying from lack of
> food. What could he do? They were all over. Some of them starved to death
> before they could crawl to the next town or to the farmhouse. If they were
> nude, you could dress them again. But what could you do?[696]

Figure 34: *SS village at St. Georgen, 1942*
Source: AHDG; Collection Franz Walzer

Indeed, Major Proudfoot's conclusions sound a similar note. "In view of
the exceedingly difficult problem which confronted the military personnel,
who had no previous experience in operating an installation of this type,
it is felt that the work done justifies high praise."[697] Carter also expressed

---

[696] Personal Interview, 28 August 2000
[697] Major M. J. Proudfoot, Concentration Camp at Mauthausen, Austria, 7 June 1945, NARA
331/290/7/10/3

"entire admiration" for Keach's ability to negotiate difficult situations.[698] In his 1946 article published a little over a year later, Proudfoot would describe the conditions at Gusen, Mauthausen and nearby Ebensee as three out of six of the worst camps in terms of health-related problems in Europe.[699]

Yet another team of investigators would arrive on 17 May 1945. In a 9 June 1945 Report on Buchenwald and Mauthausen Concentration Camps sent to Commanding General 12th Army Group ATTN: G-5 Legal Office, Col. Allen B Michell, Acting Chief, Prisons Branch, GSG states that his group, consisting of a Major Marye, Lt. Taracouzio, and a Lt. Sturgis, received orders on 15 May 1945 to inspect all the concentration camps falling in the Third Army's zone of occupation. At Mauthausen Col. Seibel assured them that all assistance would be given to them. However, when they began their search for SS documents they were told that the SS had destroyed them all. "This did not seem likely, and a barrack to barrack search was conducted which resulted in our finding the Haftlings-Personal-Karte [sic]." Michell says that these were for all the camps in Austria.[700] He estimates the number of prisoners to have been 16,500 at Mauthausen and 6,000 at Gusen. This number more closely approximates those too weak to leave after liberation as well as the estimate Taylor offered in his unclassified statement for Cohen. It is possible that Cohen, like Michell, was told by Seibel that all SS records had been destroyed, which would account for the lack of documentation from the camps themselves in his report and his reliance on personal testimony.

Five days after Michell wrote the report "Buchenwald and Mauthausen," in a "Review of Activities in the US First and Third Armies 27 April 1945 to 1 June 1945" sent to Commanding General, HQ, US Army Group CC [combined commanders], Michell deleted his estimation of the number of prisoners from his entry for 17 May 1945. However, Appendix P states the number of nationals released[701] from Mauthausen to be 12,684 and from Gusen to be only 3,765.[702] These numbers resemble the erroneous intelligence reports

---

[698]   Carter, 4
[699]   Proudfoot, 44
[700]   AG 254 Detention and Internment Camps USGCC, NARA RG 260 39.40.17.02, 26
[701]   Ibid., 6
[702]   Ibid., 2

from April 1945 more than the reality faced by the 11th Armored Division and 26th Infantry Division.[703]

Perhaps in response to the possibility of an international scandal, the official reports, even by a single officer, reduced the number of prisoners at both Gusen and Mauthausen considerably. At the same time, they did not report the existence of the Me 262 underground factory. Further research will perhaps discover how and why the information available to the 34th Disarmament Squadron on its 19 June 1945 tour of Bergkristall was not made available to Major Eugene Cohen for evidence of War Crimes, or to "Golf" and "Pleurisy" of the OSS. But Captain Wilson of the 34th Disarmament Squadron reports that "the plant was under heavy American guard and even though we had passes we experienced trouble getting in."[704]

The arrival in June 1945 of Captain Wilson's squadron signalled one of the final chapters of the war for local residents. Wilson and the squadron left Dijon, France on 12 June 1945 for Linz where they were tasked with discovering technical intelligence regarding the former Luftwaffe at Bergkristall. In a special report attached to their unit history, George Stowell recalls seeing the demolition charges the SS had placed, but never used, at the tunnel entrances. As a bomb squad member, he could not help but admire the camouflage and construction that made "the place practically impervious to our bombs."[705]

An important account of Bergkristall is given in Captain Wilson's unpublished article, "Disarming the Luftwaffe." On 19 June 1945 Sam Wilson visited Bergkristall. In his diary he wrote,

> This morning Major Gurkin (Sq Commander), Capt Fenchel (Sqdn Bombardier), Capt Peters (Sqdn Armament), Capt Fahs (Sqdn Communications), Capt Krumm (Sqdn Armament), Capt Wooten (Sqrn Navigator) and I went out

---

[703] Signed Lt. General A.E. Gasset, ACof S, G-5 to SHAEF G-5, Displaced Persons Branch NARA 331 290/7/10/13, Location of Known and Possible Prisoner of War Installations in Germany and Occupied Countries as Known to PWX-GI-Division, SHAEF, 18 March 1945, [AFHRA] 670-616-1
[704] 34th Bomb Squadron (M) AAF, APO 374, June 1945, AFHRA SQ-Bomb-34-HI, 7-8
[705] 34th Bomb Squadron (M) AAF, APO 374, June 1945, AFHRA SQ-Bomb-34-HI, 7-8

to see the underground Messerschmidt [sic] ME-262 factory at St. Georgen about 16.5 Kilometers due east of Linz and North bank of the Danube. Messerschmidt [sic] was supposed to be operating the factory for fuselages which were shipped somewhere west for final aircraft assembly. The ME-262 is a jet propelled, twin engine fighter used very effectively in the closing months of World War Two principally in France and West Germany. The plant was under heavy American guard and even though we had passes we experienced trouble getting in. We finally got a guide who was head of the plant technical police when it was operating. Entrance was through any one of 5 portals. Tunnels had been driven horizontally in a grid with same size drifts (at right angles to the tunnels) on about 250 foot centers. Tunnels and drifts were about 20 feet high and 20 feet wide. Walls, floor and ceiling were concrete. The place was lighted by Mercury vapor lamps, walls all painted white. We saw 30 completed fuselages on the production lines. Assembly progressing from rear (or faces) of the tunnels and progressed out horizontally to level outside ground. At the furthest point in on each tunnel were key sub assemblies that were added to as the assembly line progressed toward the tunnel portals. There was an underground diesel generator of 480 KVA used for standby. Normal power was from regional power grid. There were complete testing laboratories. Huge bins were full of everything from rivets, bolts and nuts to instruments ... all to make up complete fuselages as the end product. As much as possible was assembly line production. The units holding the frames for the fuselages were portable and in some cases made of wood. Railroad cars were apparently used for final assembly of the fuselage. There were many different drill presses and even electric riveting machines (something I had never seen ... I was used to air driven riveters). All of the former were like new. There were at least two huge presses of about 6,000 tons capacity. They used a lot of phenolic molds for forming sheet metal. I noticed many of the big machine tools were manufactured in Cincinnati, Detroit, Chicago, etc... this was like getting a jab in the ribs! Big ventilation ducts were made by putting wood sheet ceilings in, they were suspended from the arched ceilings of the tunnels. The intervening space was large enough to get fresh air into all parts of the factory. There were elaborate wash rooms, all large. Trains could back into the main tunnel for the purpose of shipping completed fuselages or to deliver heavy equipment and materials. Most of the ventilation was natural. Main electrical power control panels were "typically German" as every wire and every bus-bar was given a color code. There were many compressed air switches the like of which I'd never seen in my Mining Engineering days. These were to cut off power for the entire plant.

Figure 35: *Hydraulic press inside Bergkristall, 7 July 1945*
Source: Dennis Mills, AFHRA

Labor was of many nationalities. Some of it was said to be slave labor from the concentration camp at nearby Gusen. People when worn out by the work and poor feed were shipped to Mauthausen camp also nearby; they were replaced by people from Camp Gusen.

The airplanes were of excellent construction. I thought comparable to our own factory standards. Some of the work was hand-work and excellent in places used high production techniques. Much of their labor was skilled and most of all might have been plentiful and at nearly zero cost to the manufacturer, Messerschmidt [sic]. Production at the end of the war was ten fuselages per day and there were plans to increase the rate to 50 fuselages per day. Our guide said construction of the plant started in March 1944. In one year and three months they were at a production rate of ten fuselages per day. I doubt if the U.S. could have done much better.

The factory is situated near the infamous Mauthausen Concentration Camp where 142,000 [sic] people were said to have been executed during the war. There were signs in the plant in German, French, Czech and Italian. I saw no signs in English or Russian. The plant was never bombed but it would have been a waste of bombs. As I recall the tunnels were 50 to 100 feet underground and had heavy iron doors for blast protection at the portals.

They said production stopped the same day the war ended. We use 8 May for the end of the war; that is exactly 6 weeks to the day we visited the plant. We knew American technical intelligence had seen the plant but outside of ourselves, only some high brass were the only ones who knew about the plant. It looked like production could start up in a few days. The guide said the last shipment of fuselages from the plant was 5 May 1945. Shipped fuselages were complete with all wiring, canopy, oxygen bottles and plumbing, instruments, seats and safety belts. Even radio transmitters and receivers and antennas were installed. I didn't know where the fuselages were shipped but we heard it was somewhere near Munich. I don't know where wings were manufactured nor landing gear nor where final fuselage was accomplished and test hops made...probably in the vicinity of Munich, but that is conjecture.

Furthermore, in a letter accompanying his memoirs, he stated:

"Given a couple of years of full production, a sane administration in Berlin and an accelerated training program might have seriously, maybe fatally, crippled our bombing effort in 1945 – 46".

After discovering the bodies in their visit to the Gusen crematory on 24 June 1945, Wilson wrote,

Gusen was the infamous camp where the Commandants wife had lamp-shades made of human skin. His son used to climb a nearby hill and shoot into the barracks for amusement. Every day inmates by the dozen threw themselves on the electrified barbed wire. The crematorium at Camp Gusen, like at Mauthausen was nearly full of human ashes and bones. The SS had sterilized all female prisoners. Many had surgery for removal of their breast. The former inmates for the most part just stared at us, just waiting to get their release by dying. The SS was credited with all the executions, torture and medical experiments. At least we left the two camps, badly shaken.

On 2 July 1945 he wrote,

Still at Linz, living in the Urfahr hotel on the banks of the Danube. Again we were told the Russians were going to move up the Danube and all Americans were to head west, in our case to Hörsching Airdrome.

We heard on reliable authority the Allied Military Government is hurriedly stripping our ME-262 plant south east of Linz city limits [St. Georgen]. Everything in the way of aircraft assemblies, tooling, test equipment and other facilities is being shipped to a safe American controlled area (and to the USA). They paid some attention to our recommendation I guess, we thought it all usable.

On 8 July 1945 we hastily loaded trucks at St. Magdalena Barracks and moved all men and equipment to Hörsching A/D. We were told the Russians were taking over our hotel at Urfahr as well as St. Madgalena. We worked at top speed to get out of town and to the safety of the Airdrome.

In an appendix to his diary he further wrote:

As it probably happens after every major war involving large areas and many troops there was a lot of ransacking of Austria by Allied troops. The Russians were like locusts, thorough, cruel and single minded. They wanted slave labor to rebuild Russia and to expand her borders and influence.

253

As I have mentioned elsewhere our relation with the Russians just across the Danube were just short of border warfare. In Urfahr at night you could hear Russian and American troops exchange occasional rifle shoots across a nearby Danube railroad bridge. Matters didn't improve much for shortly after we got to Linz a beautiful Danube steamboat used for sightseeing by Americans disappeared on a trip up the river. In a few hours straggling passengers walked to Linz. The Russians in small armed motor-boats had stolen our steamer at gunpoint. Our American men were not armed so there was no risk of World War Three starting up!

William Zettelmoyer, also of the 34th Disarmament Squadron, reported that he felt the "disarmament program"[706] was not popular with local people. "I felt that civilians still on the scene feel haughty and arrogant toward us for removing some of the material and equipment...I hope we can do a good job disarming her and teach her to learn the ways of democracy so that we may help prevent this happening again."[707]

Nevertheless, General Tedder of SHAEF MAIN sent a routine (as opposed to classified) cable to the Twelfth Army Group on 25 June 1945 stating, "Steps will be taken to ensure that no factory or similar installation in the future Russian occupation zone is destroyed or dismantled; furthermore no machinery or component parts will be moved therefrom save for military necessity." [708] Although she says she can't recall if it was during the war, or during the American occupation, or after, Maria F. recalls equipment being taken out of the tunnels by the truckload.[709]

There is no question that the material in the tunnels was strategically important, even though the Allies had captured Me 262s. The British, and to a lesser degree, the Americans had worked on jet-propelled planes at the beginning of World War II. Although their propulsion technologies were superior from the beginning, their efforts failed due to aerodynamic problems. The Germans

---

[706]   34th Bomb Squadron (M) A AF, APO 374, June 1945, AFHRA SQ-Bomb-34-HI, 10
[707]   Ibid. When liberated by the Americans, CC Gusen II was filled with vermin and disease.
[708]   SHAEF Main signed Tedder to EXFOR: Twelfth Army Group 25 June 1945, NARA 331/290/7/11/3
[709]   Personal Interview, 21 September 2000.

had problems as well with these planes in the take-off and landing phases, but the American design was not able to take off. Prof. Messerschmitt solved the problem by optimizing aerodynamics and with a sophisticated system of leading edges which were produced at St. Georgen and Gusen along with fuselages. It took the Americans until 1947 to discover, even with captured German technology, the critical technology of jet-plane aerodynamics that helped them to safeguard their leading position in the field of jet-fighter production.[710]

Figure 36: Partly destroyed tunnel at Kellerbau, 2001
Source: Reinhard Kaspar

After the Americans stripped the tunnels of what was presumably the most important equipment and left the Mühlviertel region on 29 July 1945, the Soviets arrived. They, too, shipped equipment, but east rather than west, until

---

[710] Laurence Loftin, Quest for Performance: The Evolution of Modern Aircraft – NASA SP-486 (Washington, D.C., NASA Scientific and Technical Information Branch, 1985), 279 ff.

1947. On 15 November 1947, because the unstable political situation allowed the possibility that the region might not remain in Soviet control, the tunnels were considered too strategically important to risk returning to the west. A poorly-trained Soviet army prison detail attempted to blow them up with 500 kg aircraft bombs, also slated for destruction. However, the explosions only destroyed several tunnel intersections.[711]

The DEST railway was used for the last time in 1955 to withdraw Russian occupying forces without interfering with civilian commuters using the railway stations on the Linz – Ceske Budejovice line. Like many of the barracks in St. Georgen and Gusen, the rails disappeared, dismantled when the tunnels were blown up. In 1948 the "Administration of the Soviet Assets in Austria (USIA)" was located in parts of CC Gusen I and ran the formerly German business concern as "Granitwerke Gusen" until 1955.[712] Exploiting the former DEST installations at Gusen allowed the Soviets to extract reparations from the local economy. In contrast, by the summer of 1947 the DEST installations in the Wienergraben Quarry were scheduled to become part of the Mauthausen Memorial. Pleased with the revenue from Gusen and considering the need for a memorial already fulfilled, the Soviet occupational forces saw no reason to allow the Provincial Government of Upper Austria to erect a proposed memorial at Gusen in 1950.[713]

After Austria regained sovereignty, the remaining German-owned property at St. Georgen and Gusen became public property. In an agreement on 8 June 1956 between the Minister of Finance of the Republic of Austria and Mssrs. Poschacher, ownership of key DEST installations at Gusen was finally returned to the original local firm.[714] The "Öffentliche Verwaltung der Deutschen Erd- und Steinwerke GmbH" (DEST public administration) operated in St. Georgen until the early 1960s.[715]

---

[711] Meldung des Gendarmeriepostenkommandanten von St. Georgen an die Bezirkshauptmannschaft Perg, 6 September 1947, Gemeindearchiv St. Georgen.
[712] Gemeindearchiv St. Georgen a.d. Gusen.
[713] Schreiben der Zivilverwaltung Mühlviertel an das Amt der Oberösterreichischen Landesregierung of 28 February 1950. Oberösterreichisches Landesarchiv, ZVM Präs. 976/55, Schachtel 4.
[714] Grundbuch Mauthausen, TZ 0912/56.
[715] Gemeindearchiv St. Georgen a.d. Gusen.

Figure 37: Residental housing and stone industry at Gusen today, 2007
Source: Rudolf A. Haunschmied

After 1955, the remaining portions of land were given to the local communities, to housing cooperatives and to private individuals by the Republic
of Austria. Since the Third Reich purchased no local land after 1943, the
grounds of CC Gusen II and the territory of Bergkristall always belonged
to the original owners. The Republic of Austria only recently arranged for
control of the tunnels excavated between 1943 and 1945. So the tunnels
have only been the property of the Republic of Austria as a legacy of the
Third Reich since the end of 2000[716]. During this long period of inactivity,
the grounds of the two concentration camps at Gusen were allowed to be

---

[716] Bergkristall is now code-named „Luftschutzbunker OÖ 20" and Kellerbau III „Luftschutzbunker
OÖ 21/1" and Kellerbau I & II „Luftschutzbunker OÖ 21/2". Anlage A.1.2 (ehemalige Luftschutz-
stollen) zu BGBl. I 141/2000 vom 29. Dezember 2000.

developed into residential housing, camouflaging the history of underground systems in suburban neighborhoods for decades.

Epilogue

In the late 1940s and 1950s, sweeping away structural reminders of this dark chapter was a common political practice. The DEST administration and settlement buildings, no longer needed to promote "German identity," became private housing, as did the Jourhaus, the brothel, the two buildings which consisted of Blocks 6,7 and 8, and two CC Gusen I SS barracks buildings.[717] The Camp Gusen Cemetery set up by Ray Buch and other American soldiers between May and July 1945 was dismantled in 1955 and 1956 by the Austrian government. Most of the bodies were dug up and re-buried at the Mauthausen Memorial with the exception of the few taken back to their homelands. When the idea was raised to transfer the CC Gusen I incinerators to the Mauthausen Memorial Museum, too, survivors worried that their stories would be buried as well in the officially recognized narrative of Mauthausen. The international «Comité du Souvenier du Camp de Gusen» formed in Paris. Under the leadership of Dr. Ermete Sordo of Italy and Prof. Roger Heim of France, survivors and their families raised money to buy land surrounding the crematoria in 1962. The Republic of Austria did not contribute any funds. On 8 May 1965 the KZ Gusen Memorial was inaugurated through the private initiative of survivors and their families.[718] Thirty years later, concerned that the Memorial was decaying, survivors transferred responsibility for its maintenance to the Republic of Austria during the local-international commemoration at Gusen on 3 May 1997. This date marks the first time one Austrian Federal Ministry officially took responsibility for any part of the Gusen camps without displacing it to the Mauthausen Memorial.

After 1985, when local people turned toward the legacy of the DEST installations and the concentration camps at St. Georgen and Gusen, a highly effective local-international cooperative evolved. Local people and survivors joined in celebrating the 50th anniversary of the liberation in 1995.

---

[717] Barracks 6,7 and 8 were combined into two buildings
[718] Smretschnig, Christian „Memorial de Gusen" Bautenkatalog zur Gebäudelehre-Prüfung (Vienna: Technische Universität Wien – Institut für Gebäudelehre, 1999)

Much progress has been made toward reviving the memory of the KZ Gusen Camps which had nearly been lost to Austrians and to the German language: information about the camps has been collected and distributed in small local gatherings where survivors and their families have met with local people. Publications have reached a wider audience. Efforts have been made to increase the awareness of local and state authorities. Through these efforts the KZ Gusen Memorial building was renovated in 2001, and structural conservation of the Bergkristall and Kellerbau tunnels began in 2002 – 2004. A new Visitors' Center[719] was built near the KZ Gusen Memorial in 2004 and, since 2007, Audiowalk[720] Gusen leads visitors for the first time since decades directly from the KZ Gusen Memorial to the closed gates of Bergkristall.

Figure 38: *KZ Gusen Memorial, 1996*
Source: Rudolf A. Haunschmied

---

[719] http://www.gusen-memorial.at
[720] http://audiowalk.gusen.org

Figure 39: *Entrance into the remaining parts of Kellerbau at Gusen today, 2007*
Source: Rudolf A. Haunschmied

An in-depth history of the KZ Gusen camps has yet to be written for German speakers, yet there is important literature in Polish, Spanish, Italian, French, and many other languages. The absence of a German contribution reveals another bitter truth: 3,165 Germans and Austrians died in the Gusen camps, but their stories are unknown in their native tongue. The 1989 German version of this text was a beginning. We hope this revised English text may encourage the further study of the Gusen Concentration Camps and their place in the history of World War II and the Holocaust.

In the last ten years, much has opened up as a result of the unprecedented cooperation between survivors and local people. We hope someday the complete story of the Gusen camps will be on display at the Visitors' Center and that the Bergkristall Tunnels will open as well. After all, if plans could be drawn up to make the tunnels a caloric power plant (1959), a depository for nuclear waste (1969 – 1975), an underground army field hospital and air-raid shelter (1975 – 1980), why not a memorial? Open the tunnels and leave them open. Let the lost stories and lost voices of 40,000 fill that darkness as once their hearts filled with the memory of love. Let us breathe in the last exhalations of the dead and then turn, each of us, to the light.

Figure 40: Entrance into Bergkristall today, 2007
Source: Rudolf A. Haunschmied

Acronyms and Abbreviations

#	Number
14 f 13	Euthanasia program originally intended for mentally ill
A4	Medium range ballistic missile (V2 rocket)
A9/A10	Long range ballistic missiles
A/D	Airdrome
AEF	Allied European Forces
AFHRA	Airforce Historical Research Agency
AG	Aktiengesellschaft (stock corporation)
AHDG	Arbeitskreis für Heimat-, Denkmal- und Geschichtspflege St. Georgen
ASKOE	Arbeiter-Sport-Klub Österreichs
AMM	Archiv Museum Mauthausen
ATTN	Attention
B3	Bundesstrasse (Federal Road) No. 3
B8	Artificial underground building No. 8 (St.Georgen – Bergkristall)
B9	Artificial underground building No. 9 (Melk – Quarz)
Ba III	Production Section No. 3 of DEST at St. Georgen (Bergkristall)
BArch	Bundesarchiv Berlin
BDC	Berlin Document Center
BdE	Commander-in-chief for the reserve army
Bürg	Acronym used by Göring to camouflage "Flossenbürg"
CC	Concentration Camp (KL)
CC	Combined Commanders
CCA	Combat Command A
CIC	Counter-Intelligence Corps
CIOS	Combined Intelligence Objectives Sub-Committee
CSP	Christian Social Party
CSM	Company Sergeant-Major
G-2	Intelligence Division (SHAEF)
G-3	Plans and Operations Division (SHAEF)

G-5	Civil Affairs/Military Government Division (SHAEF)
GDP	Grossdeutsche Partei (Greater Germany Party)
Gestapo	Geheime Staatspolizei (Secret State Police)
GmbH	Limited Liability Company
GMC	Gusen Memorial Committee
DEST	Deutsche Erd- und Steinwerke GmbH (German Earth and Stone Works)
FKS	Fertigungskreis (production circle)
FWD	Forward
HAHB	Hauptamt Haushalt und Bauten (Main Office for Budget and Building)
Hausen	Acronym used by Göring to camouflage "Mauthausen"
HQ	Headquarters
HSSPF	Höherer SS- und Polizeiführer (Higher SS- and Police Leader)
ICRC	International Committee of the Red Cross (Geneva)
IKL	Inspectorate of Concentration Camps
JIOA	Joint Intelligence Objectives Agency
KL/K.L.	Konzentrationslager (Concentration Camp)
KLM	KL Mauthausen
Kripo	Criminal Police
KVA	Kilowatt
KZ	Konzentrationslager (Concentration Camp)
Me	Messerschmitt
MG	Machine Gun
MHC	Museu d´Història de Catalunya
MP	Automatic assault rifle
NARA	National Archives and Records Administration
NASM	Smithsonian National Air and Space Museum
NCO	Non-commissioned officer
NS	National Socialist
NSDAP	Nationalsozialistische Deutsche Arbeiterpartei
O´gau	Oberammergau
OFA	Oberbayerische Forschungsanstalt (Oberammergau)
OSS	Office of Strategic Services
POW	Prisoner of War

(R)	Reservist indicator for SS-ranks
RFSS	Reichsführer SS
RM	Reichsmark (currency)
RMfBuM	Reich Ministry for Armament and Ammunitions
RSHA	Reichssicherheitshauptamt (Reich Security Main Office)
SA	Sturmabteilung
SAARF	Special Allied Airborne Reconnaissance Force
SD	Security Service of SS and German Police
SDP	Social Democratic Party
SHAEF	Supreme Headquarters Allied Expeditionary Force
SQDN	Squadron
SS	Schutzstaffel
T.H.	Technische Hochschule (Technical University)
T.Stuba	SS-Totenkopf Sturmbann (SS-guard battalion)
UNRRA	United Nations Relief and Rehabilitation Administration
US	United States of America
USFET	United States Forces, European Theater
USIA	Administration of Soviet Assets in Austria
USSBS	United States Strategic Bombing Survey
WNF	Wiener Neustädter Flugzeugwerke
WTL	SS college of armament technology
WVHA	Wirtschaftsverwaltungshauptamt (Business Administrative Main Office)
ZBL	Zentralbauleitung (Central Construction Directorate)

List of Illustrations

Bibliography

Interviews

Johanna B., 18 September 2000. Translated by Martha Gammer.
Birch, Louise, 23 June 2000
Buch, Raymond S., 28 August 2000
Joe C., 7 May 2004
Choumoff, Pierre Serge, 7 May 1998
Gertraud D., 14 August 2007
Maria F., 21 September 2000. Translated by Martha Gammer
Kriechbaum, Norbert, OÖ Landesarchiv, 6 June 2006
Lax, Martin, 21 October 2004
Lehner, Maria, 18 September 2000. Translated by Martha Gammer
Dennis C. Mills, 23 September 2004.
Willy and Irmi Nowy, September 2000
Interview 861203. Transcript in the possession of the author
Interview 861207. Transcript in the possession of the author
Interview 881120. Transcript in the possession of the author
Interview 881127. Transcript in the possession of the author
Interview 971229. Transcript in the possession of the author
Stefancic, Dusan, 8 May 2000 and 7 May 2004 and e-mail to author, 21 January 2000
Storey, Lyle, 24 December 2002
Traub, Mary, 30 March 2005

Archives Consulted

Airforce Historical Research Agency (Maxwell)
Arbeitskreis für Heimat-, Denkmal- und Geschichtspflege (St. Georgen/Gusen)
Archiv der Stadt Linz (Linz)
Archiv Museum Mauthausen (Vienna)

Bezirksgericht (Mauthausen)
Bundesarchiv (Berlin)
Dokumentationsarchiv des Österreichischen Widerstandes (Vienna)
Gendarmeriepostenkommando (St. Georgen/Gusen)
Institut für Zeitgeschichte (Munich)
Marktgemeinde St. Georgen a.d. Gusen (St. Georgen/Gusen)
Museu d'Història de Catalunya (Barcelona)
National Archives and Records Administration (College Park)
Oberösterreichisches Landesarchiv (Linz)
Pfarre St. Georgen a.d. Gusen (St. Georgen/Gusen)
Smithsonian Air and Space Museum (Washington)
Volksschule St. Georgen a.d. Gusen (St. Georgen/Gusen)

Private Collections

Collection Pierre Serge Choumoff (Paris)
Collection Martha Gammer (St. Georgen/Gusen)
Collection Franz Gindlstrasser (Katsdorf)
Collection Reinhard Hanausch (Regensburg)
Collection Rudolf A. Haunschmied (St. Martin/Traun)
Collection Reinhard Kaspar (St. Georgen/Gusen)
Collection Lars Labitzke (Berlin)
Collection Karl Littner (Los Angeles)
Collection Jan-Ruth Mills (Tucson)
Collection Angelo Ratti (Milan)
Collection Dusan Stefancic (Ljubljana)
Collection Franz Walzer (St. Georgen/Gusen)

Primary Sources

12 Army Group Mauthausen Camp, Record Group 331, Entry 17 290/7/21/7
  Box 50, NARA

34th Bomb Squadron (M) AAF, APO 374, June 1945, AFHRA SQ-Bomb-34-HI

Affidavit Erich Rupprecht, NARA microform publication M890/27/0650.

Affidavit Otto Walther, NARA microform publication M890/27/0047.

AG 254 Detention and Internment Camps USGCC NARA Record Group 260 39.40.17.02

Aktenvermerk für SS-Gruppenführer Fegelein of 14 July 1944. BArch, Film 713

Air Division Headquarters United States Forces in Austria, Intelligence Section, APO 777, US Army, 20 June 1946 506.619B AFHRA

Field Marshal Alexander to AGWAR for Combined Chiefs of Staff and for British Chiefs of Staff, Cable FX-44269, 15 March 1945 NARA 331/290/7/11/3

Field Marshal Alexander to AMSSO for BCS and Britman Washington for US Joint Chiefs of Staff SHAEF FWD FX-5159029 March 1945, NARA 331/290/7/11/3

Field Marshal Alexander to Combined Chiefs of Staff and for British Chiefs of Staff 9 April 1945 NARA 331/290/7/11/3

Aufstellung der von Häftlingen geleisteten Arbeitsstunden für die Luftfahrtindustrie, 21 February 1944. NARA, microform publication M890/9/0707 (1584-PS)

Heinrich B., Bericht. Die Nationalsozialistische Tätigkeit in Österreich in der Zeit 1933/34 bis 1938.

Beglaubigte Abschrift aus dem Handelsregister des Amtsgerichts in Berlin, Abteilung B 53864, Bezirksgericht (local court) Mauthausen, Grundbuch (land register), TZ 586/38

„Bericht eines IKRK-Delegierten über seine Mission in Mauthausen". Die Tätigkeit des IKRK zugunsten der in deutschen Konzentrationslagern inhaftierten Zivilpersonen (1939 – 1945) (Genf: Internationales Komitee vom Roten Kreuz, 1985)

Bericht des Gendarmeriepostenkommandos St. Georgen/Gusen an die Sicherheitsdirektion Linz. Unveröffentlichtes Manuskript für das von der Bundesregierung herausgegebene Rot/weiß/rot Buch 1946, Dokumentationsarchiv des österreichischen Widerstandes (DÖW No. 8359). Vienna, undated

Bericht des Rüstungsstabes über die Besprechung mit Exc. Hollebronth am 20.12.1944 an RLM-Hauptausschuss Flugzeuge (Oberstingenieur Alpers). BArch R3/1757/27.

Bericht „Überprüfung des Bauvorhabens Bergkristall am 21. Januar 1945" vom 2. Februar 1945. Kommission zur Überprüfung des Einsatzes von Bergleuten bei U-Verlagerungen (gebildet durch: Zentralstelle für bergbauliche Sonderaufgaben, OT – Amtsgruppe Bauwirtschaft und Reichsvereinigung Kohle). In the possession of the author.

Bericht „Überprüfung des Einsatzes von Bergleuten beim Bauvorhaben Bergkristall" vom 27. Januar 1945. Zentralstelle für bergbauliche Sonderaufgaben, OT – Amtsgruppe Bauwirtschaft und Reichsvereinigung Kohle. In the possession of the author.

Bezirksgericht Mauthausen, Grundbuch, TZ 535/33

Briefverkehr der Bauleitung Mauthausen/Gusen betreffend Verbrennungsöfen für Gusen. BArch, NS 4/Ma/54

Carter to Commanding Officer USFET Main, NARA RG 549 Entry 290 59.12.3, JAG War Crimes, Cases Tried, Box 336

Chronik der Pfarre St. Georgen (Chronicle of the roman catholic Parish of St. Georgen)

Chronik des k.K. Gendarmeriepostens Sankt Georgen an der Gusen (Chronicle of the Rural Police Command at St. Georgen)

Pierre Choumoff, Letter to the author, 19 December 1996

Pierre Choumoff, Address to the Eleventh Armored Division at Cincinatti on 11 September 1998. The Thunderbolt, Volume 53, December 1998.

Das SS-Wirtschaftsverwaltungshauptamt und die unter seiner Dienstaufsicht stehenden wirtschaftlichen Unternehmungen (NO-1573). Archiv des Institutes für Zeitgeschichte München

DEST-Bilanz 1939, Aufstellung über das Anlagevermögen der Deutschen Erd- und Steinwerke G.m.b.H. Berlin. BArch NS 3/1345/14 ff.

DEST-Bilanz 1939. Aufstellung über erworbene Grundstücke. BArch, NS 3/1345/29.

DEST-Bilanz 1939, Aufstellung über die in den Jahren 1938 und 1939 eingesetzten Häftlinge und Bewertung derselben. BArch, NS 3/1345/58

DEST-Geschäftsbericht 1942. BArch NS 3/1168/51

DEST-Geschäftsbericht 1943, BArch NS 3/1168, NS 3/1231 and NS 3/1239

DEST-Inventur 1939, Bestandsaufnahme der Halb- und Fertigerzeugnisse. BArch NS 3/1345/34.

DEST-Monatsberichte, BArch NS 3/1346

Draft layout of Bergkristall "Magistrat Linz AB. 3" (accompanied by a file card dated with 23 August 1942). In the possession of the author.

Eger, Richard. "Re: Me 262 Production at St. Georgen underground plant". E-mail to the author. 23 June 2004

General Eisenhower to Bradley and Devers, 29 March 1945, Cable FWD 18302 NARA 331/290/7/11/3

Erlass des Chefs der Sicherheitspolizei und des SD – IV A 6 b Allg. Nr. 4344/44g of 3 August 1944. BArch, Z 11 1680 A.1, Stapoleit Düsseldorf.

Erlaubnisurkunde des Landrates des Kreises Perg Zahl: II/G/243-1942 vom 14.4.1943 betreffend den Betrieb einer Werksküchenkantine durch DEST, Gemeindearchiv St. Georgen

Esche II Work Plan, 4 April 1944, (Figure 9c), J.I.O.A. Final Report No. 1, Part 1, Section III, Appendix A. Washington, DC, Joint Intelligence Objectives Agency, September 1945. NARA, RG 319, Army Staff, "P"-File, Location: 7/23/42/5, Box T169.

Fernschreiben vom 7. Oktober 1940 an alle Stapo(Leit)Stellen betreffend Infektionskrankheiten im Arbeitslager Gusen. BArch, Z 11 1680 A.1.

Ing. Karl Fiebinger technical drawing No. 322/L/31 of the sewage treatment plant, designed 18 March 1944 by Ing. Büro Dipl. Ing. Karl Fiebinger are part of J.I.O.A. Final Report No.1, Part 1, Section III, Appendix A

Lt. General A.E. Gasset, ACof S, G-5 to SHAEF G-5, Displaced Persons Branch NARA 331/290/7/10/13

Lieutenant General A. E. Grasset to SHAEF Divisions G-2 G-3 A-2 A-3, 23 April 1945, NARA 331/290/10/13

Gemeindearchiv St. Georgen a.d. Gusen

"German Concentration Camps at which it is Recommended that SAARF Teams be Dropped from the Air" 18 April 1945 NARA 331/290/1/10/13

German Underground Installations: Part One of Three, CIOS Section, Intelligence Division APO 887, September 1945, NARA RG 319, "P"-File, Joint Intelligence Objective Agency, Br. No. 1, Part 1 of 3.

Reinhard Hanausch. Sklavenarbeit für den Düsenjäger. KZ-Produktion und Zwangsarbeit bei den Regensburger Messerschmitt-Werken 1939 – 45 (unplublished)

Louis Häfliger, interview broadcasted on 2 February 1988 by Radio Österreich International.

Donald R. Heath, Deputy, United States Political Advisor for Germany to Lieutenant Feneral W. B. Smith, Chief of Staff, SHAEF 1 June 1945, NARA 331/290/7/10/3

Leander Hens, "Liberation of Mauthausen" Speech given on May 6, 2000 at Gusen Memorial

Interrogation Reports: War Crimes Proceedings at Nuremberg, Speer Interviews, NARA

Interpretation Report No. U.18, Underground activity at Linz/St. Georgen, 22 January 1945. Airforce Historical Research Agency (AFHRA), intelligence reports of the Mediteranean Allied Air Forces´ Files (Intelligence Section – Target Analysis, reel 207, microfilm roll 25194).

Jägerstab-Schnellbericht, 3 March 1944. BArch R3/1756/310

J.I.O.A. Final Report No.1, Part 1, Section III, Appendix A. Washington, DC, Joint Intelligence Objectives Agency, September 1945. NARA, RG 319, Army Staff, "P"-File, Location: 7/23/42/5, Box T169.

Kanzlei-Anmerkung des Landeshauptmanns von Oberdonau Z/RO. I.H. 46/1-1940, XIa of 13 February 1940. Gemeindearchiv St. Georgen a.d. Gusen.

Kaufvertrag abgeschlossem zwischen der Gemeinde Langenstein und der DEST vom 2.10.1940. Bezirksgericht Mauthausen, Grundbuch, TZ 16/41.

Victor Kielich and Jan Ruth Mills, The Way of Thorns, unpublished manuscript

Otto Klinger, Volkschulchronik St. Georgen (Chronicle of the Primary School of St. Georgen)

Kriegstagebuch Rüstungskommando Linz, NARA microform publication T77/744

Labitzke, Lars. Chronologie der Geschichte des SS-Totenkopfsturmbannes KL Mauthausen-Gusen, unpublished

Lageplan "Esche" prepared by "Ing.Büro Dipl Ing Karl Fiebinger", Drawing No. 322/L22, 5 April 1944.

Lageplan Gusen I u. II. NARA RG 549 Box 334

Lageplan RLM GL/C-B 2/I Nr. 16012/43, 1 February 1944

Lageplan der Steinbrüche Gusen, Kastenhof und Pierbauer, 15 June 1943

Liste der Angehörigen der NSDAP und ihrer Wehrverbände und der Personen, die sich um die Aufnahme in die SS (Schutzstaffel) beworben haben, in der Ortsgemeinde St. Georgen a.d. Gusen.

Littner, Karl. Life Hanging by a Spider's Web, unpublished manuscript

"Location of known and Possible Prisoner of War Installations in Germany and Occupied Countries as known to PWX-GI-Division", SHAEF, at 18 March 1945" 670-616-1 AFHRA

LS-Führerprogramm. Deckungsgräben – Korrespondenz A-Z. B0029n. Archive of the City of Linz.

Malgaroli, Felice. (survivor IT 115577 of Gusen II), Diario, (unpublished manuscript)

Mauthausen Concentration Camp: Conversation with Lt. Col. Brewer 10 May 1945 NARA 331/290/7/10/13

Mauthausen Trials, Reviews and Recommendations. Case 000-50-5-11 (US vs Andreas Battermann) and Case 000-50-5-30 (US vs Bernhard Fernikorn). http://www.hhs.utoledo.edu/dachau/mautr&r.html, 6 June 2006)

Mauthausen Trials, US vs. Shuettauf, et al. Case No. 000-50-5-3. NARA Record Group 153 Entry 143 270/1/14-15/6-1 Box 12, http://ecc.pima.edu/~gusen/Schuettauf/Index_to_Schuettauf_Summaries.htm

Mauthausen Trials, US vs. Paul Wolfram. Case 000-50-5-49, RG 338 (new RG 496), Box 423 and 424, Records of the U.S. Army Commands, 1942 – Records of Headquarters, US Army Europe (USAREUR), War Crimes Branch, War Crimes Case Files ("Cases Tried"), 1945 – 1959, NARA.

Mediterranean Allied Air Forces Intelligence Section, APO 650, US Army A-2 Division, 17 November 1944, [AFHRA]

Mediterranean Allied Air Forces Intelligence Section Interpretation Report No U. 11 Austria 1 January 1945; MAAF 25220 1944 1020 995.999, Air Force Historical Research Agency [AFHRA] 510-3665

Mediterranean Allied Air Forces Intelligence Section, APO 520, US Army A-2 Division, 17 November 1944, [AFHRA]

Meldeunterlagen für Georg Bachmayer

Meldeunterlagen für Carl Walter Chmielewski

Meldeunterlagen für Franz Ziereis.

Meldung des Gendarmeriepostenkommandanten von St. Georgen an die Bezirkshauptmannschaft Perg, 6 September 1947, Gemeindearchiv St. Georgen.

Memorandum No. 1 Concentration Camp at Mauthausen, Austria from Major M.J. Proudfoot to Executive, Displaced Person Branch, G-5 7 June 1945 NARA 331/290/7/10/3

Memorandum No. 2 Concentration Camp at Gusen, Austria from Major M.J. Proudfoot to Executive, Displaced Person Branch, G-5 8 June 1945 NARA 331/290/7/10/3

Messerschmitt-Betriebe – Fertigungsübersicht Werk Regensburg. Messerschmitt A.G. Augsburg, Zentralplanung Serie, Blatt 2 von 2. Smithsonian National Air and Space Museum, Captured German/Japanese Air Technical Documents, ADRC/T-2, Microfilm R 2497

NARA Record Group 153, Entry 143 270/1/14-15/6-1 Box 8 Vol. 1

NARA Record Group 226, Entry 190 7/2/04, Box 4, Section III

NARA Group 238, World War II, War Crimes Records, International Military Tribunal, Exhibit 249

NARA Record Group 238, World War II, War Crimes Records, International Military Tribunal, Exhibit 249, Exhibit #1

NARA Record Group 407, Entry 427A, 270/50/24/05 MDEH-130-0 and 0.1, Box 21518

OSS Inspection of Mauthausen-Gusen, May 1945, RG 549, Entry 290 59.12.3, JAG War Crimes Cases Tried, NARA

William Messerschmitt, 11 – 12 May 1945 Interview No. 6 USSBBS 137.315-6 AFHRA

Brigadier General S.R. Mickelsen to A.C.O.S., G-5 Division (undated) NARA 331/290/1/10/3

Mob.-Stärkenachweisung der K.L. durch den Inspekteur der Konzentrationslager vom 12. Februar 1940. BArch, NS 4/Ma/36/22.

Niederschrift der am 11.3.1945 in Bergkristall (=St. Georgen) abgehaltenen Besprechung betreffend 609-Fertigung. Smithsonian National Air and

Space Museum, Captured German/Japanese Air Technical Documents, ADRC/T-2, Microfilm R 3996

Nuremberg Military Tribunal, Volume 5, pages 488, 573 and 1242, http://www.mazal.org/archive/nmt/05/, 10 March 2003.

Ostmark: Section III, The SS Allied Force Headquarters, Office of Assistant Chief of Staff, G-2. In possession of the author.

General George S. Patton, Diary, Library of Congress, Control # MM 83035634

Photographic documentation showing the Turnerbund members of St. Georgen converting the stable into the gym in 1931. Photographic collection. Arbeitskreis für Heimat-, Denkmal- und Geschichtspflege St. Georgen an der Gusen.

Planungsdokument „Bedarf und Bestand unterirdischer Bauvorhaben", 14 April 1944. BArch R3101/31.173/188.

Protokoll aufgenommen am 1. Juli 1945 über Veranlassung der Amerikanischen Militärregierung (Mil.Polz.) in St. Georgen a.d. Gusen wegen der erfolgten Massregelung, Verhaftung und Internierung des Weichenstellers Heinrich B. in das Konzentrationslager Dachau verfügt von Frau Anna K derzeit in Graz.

Ratti, Angelo (survivor Gusen II 57616), and Rigamonti Franco (survivor Gusen II 57617), Memorie di *Mauthausen* – Gusen I e Gusen II (Milano, unpublished)

Letter from Major L. Reiger, Chief Czechoslovak Liaison Officer to SHAEF G-5 Displaced Persons Branch, 3 May 1945 NARA 331/290/7/10/3

Report 131st Evacuation Hospital, NARA 112/390/17/25/7,

Brigadier General A. G. Salisbury Jones, Deputy Chief, Displaced Persons to 12th Amry Group, Rear, G-5, Displaced Persons Branch, NARA 331/290/7/10/3

Sammelbericht des Rüstungsstabes an das RLM, 22 November 1944, 7-22.11. (57). BArch, R3/1757/93.

Sanitary Report, Camp Mauthausen, 11th Armored Division Headquarters, Office of the Surgeon, 25 May 1945, NARA 112/31/1337

Letter of Charles R. Sandler [Deputy military commander of the liberated Gusen Concentration Camps in May 1945, 21st Armored Infantry Battalion, 11th Armored Division, 3rd US Army] to the author, 12 July 1998.

Schatz, Maria, Speech given at 2006 Gusen Memorial, translated and summarised by Siegi Witzany

SHAEF/g-5/2711/7.2 12th Army Group-Mauthausen Camps, NARA 331/290/1/10/13

SHAEF FWD, Signed SCAEF to HQ 21 Army Group Rear for Mil Gov, CG 12 Army Group Rear for G-5, CG 6 Army Group Rear for G-5 Cable FWD-19395 NARA 331 290/7/10/13

SHAEF FWD, Signed SCAEF to CG 12 Army Group G-5, 3 May 1945, NARA 331/290/1/10/3

SHAEF Main Signed Tedder to EXFOR: Twelfth Army Group 25 June 1945 331/290/7/11/3

Schreiben des Landeshauptmannes von Oberdonau vom 20. Februar 1940 an das Siedlungsamt Linz, den Bürgermeister von St. Georgen, den DEST-Werkleiter SS-Hauptsturmführer Spichalsky and Architekt Theer.

Schreiben des Chefs des Rüstungslieferamtes an den Chef des Amtes Bau im RMfRK, 3 March 1944 and 13 March 1944. BArch R3101/31.173/266 and 272

Schreiben Pohls an Himmler betreffend eines diesbezüglichen Fernschreiben von Reichsmarschall Göring, 14 June 1944. BArch, NS 19/3571 (NO-4242).

Schreiben Direktor Walther an den Oberbürgermeister von Linz of 3 May 1944. B0029n, Mappe Stollenbauten – Korrespondenz A-L. Archive of the City of Linz.

Schreiben der Zivilverwaltung Mühlviertel an das Amt der Oberösterreichischen Landesregierung of 28 February 1950. Oberösterreichisches Landesarchiv, ZVM Präs. 976/55, Schachtel 4.

Schreiben des Jägerstabes – Abt. Planung vom 13. April 1944 betreffend „Deckung des Bedarfes an bombensicheren Räumen (unterirdisch und Bunkerbau) – Zellen". BArch R 3101/31.173/186

Brig. Gen. McSherry to Divisions G-1,G-2,G-3,G-4, A-2,A-3, 25 April 1945 NARA 331/290/1/13

Sketch "Gusen II with Airraid Shelter". NARA RG 549 Box 346.

Albert Speer, 15 May 1945 Interview No. 11, USSBS AFHRA

Albert Speer, Interrogation. Trial of the Major War Criminals before the International Military Tribunal. Nuremberg, 19 June 1946.

Stärkemeldung der Granitwerke Mauthausen. Records of the United States Nuremberg War Criminal Trials, United States vs. Oswald Pohl et al. (Case IV), January 13, 1947-August 11, 1948, NARA microform publication M890/13/0968 (NI-541)

Stefancic, Dusan. KL Gusen I and II and the production of Messerschmitt aircraft Bf 109 and Me 262, unpublished manuscript

Lyle Storey, unpublished memoirs

Sullivan to War Crimes Branch USFET Main, 23 August 1945, NARA RG 549, Entry 290 59.12.3, JAG War Crimes, Cases Tried, Box 336

Summary of POW interrogation by American Foreign Service to Air Intelligence, 18 December 1943 AFHRA

Major Gen. John Taylor Lewis to SHAEF FWD G-5, 4 May 1945 NARA 331/290/1/10/3

Transcription of phone call from Lt. de Gast , Signed by Wing Commander Dehn, 3 May 1943, Memo SHAEF G-5/DP/2711/7 Mickelsen to A.C.O.S, G-5 Division, NARA 331/290/1/10/3

"Translation of German Document, Oberammergau," Dipl. Eng. Ludwig Bolkow to von Schultz-Tratzigg, Inclosure 1 [sic], 25 October 1944 AFHRA 512.6259

Transportliste of 2 January 1944, Archiv Museum Mauthausen (AMM) at the Austrian Federal Ministry of the Interior, Vienna, AMM B13/I.

Truppenstammrolle und Bestätigung der Dienstenthebung durch das SS-Personalamt im SS-Hauptamt vom 15. April 1939. BArch (ehemals BDC), SSO, Sauer, Albert, 17.08.1898.

Veränderungsmeldung K.L.MAUTHAUSEN / UK. GUSEN vom 28. April 1945. AMM B/12/14

Verfügung des Luftwaffenwehramtes im Oberkommando der Luftwaffe of 31 August 1944. BArch, NS 4Hi/21/345.

LCdt. Villaret Chief, Headquarters of National Defense, 3rd Section to Chief, g-5 Division, Displaced Persons Branch, SHAEF 1 May 1945, NARA 331/290/1/10/3

Letter of the City of Neutraubling of 23 December 1988 to the author

Vorschlag für die Verleihung des Ritterkreuzes zum Kriegsverdienstkreuz mit Schwertern an Dr.-Ing. Hans Kammler, 20 August 1944, BArch, SSO-Film 151-A, 204 ff.

Wagenkontrollbücher des Bahnhofes St. Georgen für die Güterabfertigung
Captain Samuel G. Wilson, Disarming the Luftwaffe, unpublished (in the possession of the author)

Secondary Sources

700 Jahre Kirche zum Hl. Georg in St. Georgen/Gusen (St. Georgen a.d. Gusen: Pfarre St. Georgen a.d. Gusen, 1988)

Aldebert, Bernard. Gusen II – Chemin de Croix en 50 Stations, ed. transl. Elisabeth Hölzl (Weitra: Bibliothek der Provinz, 1997)

Allen, Michael. The Business of Genocide [Business] (Chapel Hill: The University of North Carolina Press, 2004)

"The Business of Genocide" Business and Industry in Nazi Germany. Eds Francis R. Nicosia and Jonathan Huener (New York: Berghahn Books, 2004)

"The Banality of Evil Reconsidered: SS Mid-Level Managers of Extermination through Work". Central European History 30 (1997)

Ambrose, Stephen. The Victors: Eisenhower and His Boys (New York: Simon and Schuster)

Bauer, Yehuda. "The Historians" The Liberation of the Nazi Concentration Camps 1945 – Eyewitness Accounts of the Liberators (Washington, D.C.: United States Holocaust Memorial Council, 1987)

Belgiojoso, Lodovico Barbioano di, Notte, Nebbia – Racconto di Gusen (Parma: Ugo Guanda Editore S.p.A., 1996)

Bernadac, Christian. Deportation 1933/1945, Vol. 3 (Paris: France-Empire, 1993)

Black, Peter R. Ernst Kaltenbrunner: Ideological Soldier of the Third Reich. (Princeton: Princeton University, 1984)

Black, Martin. IBM and the Holocaust, (New York: Crown, 2001)

Brook-Shepherd, Gordon. The Austrians. (New York: Carroll and Graf, 1996)

Bukey, Evan Burr. Hitler's Austria: Popular Sentiment in the Nazi Era, 1938 – 1945. (Chapel Hill: University of North Carolina, 2000)

Hitler's Home Town. (Bloomington: Indiana University Press, 1986).

Carafano, James Jay. "Waltzing into the Cold War". Contemporary Austrian Studies, ed. Bischof, Guenter. (Edison: Transaction Books, 1999)

Carsten, Francis L. Fascist Movements in Austria. (Beverly Hills: Sage, 1977)

Dobosiewicz, Stanislaw, Mauthausen/Gusen – Oboz Zaglady (Warszawa: Wydawnictwo Ministertwa Orony Narodowej, 1977)

Dwork, Deborah . Ed., Voices and Views: A History of the Holocaust (New York: The Jewish Foundation for the Righteous, 2002)

Edmondson, C. Earl. The Heimwehr and Austrian Politics 1919 – 1936. (Georgia: Athens, 1978)

Esden-Tempska, Carla "Civic Education in Authoritarian Austria, 1934 – 1938." (History of Education Quarterly, Volume 30, No. 2)

Fabréguet, Michel. „Entwicklung und Veränderung der Funktionen des Konzentrationslagers Mauthausen 1938 – 1945". Die nationalsozialistischen Konzentrationslager, Vol. 1 (Göttingen: S. Fischer Verlag GmbH, 1998)

Farago, Ladislas. Patton: Ordeal and Triumph, (New York: Ivan Obolensky, 1963)

Fritsch, E. "KZ-Stollen – ein zeitgeschichtliches Denkmal," Mitteilungen des Landesvereins für Höhlenkunde in Oberösterreich, 1988/1 (Linz: Landesverein für Höhlenkunde in Oberösterreich, 1988)

Freund, Florian Arbeitslager Zement – Das konzentrationslager Ebensee und die Raketenrüstung. Industrie, Zwangsarbeit und Konzentrationslager in Österreich. Vol. 2. (Vienna: Verlag für Gesellschaftskritik, 1989)

Freund, Florian and Bertrand Perz, Das KZ in der Serbenhalle: Zur Kriegsindustrie in Wiener Neustadt. Industrie, Zwangsarbeit und Konzentrationslager in Österreich. Vol. 1. (Vienna: Verlag für Gesellschaftskritik, 1987)

Gilbert, Martin. The Second World War, (New York: Henry Holt, 1989)

Gindelstrasser, Franz. Franz Peterseil – Eine nationalsozialistische Karriere (Grünbach: Buchverlag Franz Steinmassl – Edition Geschichte der Heimat, 2003)

Gostner, Erwin. 1000 Tage im KZ – Dachau-Mauthausen-Gusen (Innsbruck: Edition Löwenzahn, 1986)

Grau, Alfred. "Der Zusammenbruch 1945 wie wir ihn erlebt haben, 1975". St. Georgener Heimatblätter, Folge 55 (St. Georgen a.d. Gusen, September 2007), 15-25

Greene, Joshua M. Justice at Dachau. (New York: Broadway Books)

Grunberger, Richard. The Twelve Year Reich. (New York: Da Capo Press, 1995)

Haunschmied, Rudolf. "Zum Gedenken 1938/1945". 300 Jahre erweitertes Marktrecht St. Georgen a.d. Gusen – Geschichte Buch (St. Georgen/Gusen: Marktgemeinde St. Georgen an der Gusen, 1989)

Heigl, Richard. „Die Messerschmitt AG in Oberammergau (1943 – 1945) – Auslagerung, Projekte, Fremdarbeitereinsatz", Mohr-Löwe-Raute – Beiträge zur Geschichte des Landkreises Garmisch-Partenkirchen – Band 3 (Garmisch-Partenkirchen: Verein für Geschichte, Kunst- und Kulturgeschichte im Landkreis Garmisch-Partenkirchen e.V., 1995)

Heimatverein und Gemeinde Luftenberg an der Donau (ed.), Heimatbuch Luftenberg an der Donau (Luftenberg: Heimatverein und Gemeinde Luftenberg an der Donau, 1997)

Holmes, Blair R. "Austrian Monarchists, 1918 – 1938" Parkinson, F. ed. Conquering the Past. (Detroit: Wayne State University, 1989)

Horwitz, Gordon J. In the Shadow of Death (New York: The Free Press, 1990)

Internationales Komitee vom Roten Kreuz. Die Tätigkeit des IKRK zugunsten der in deutschen Konzentrationslagern inhaftierten Zivilpersonen (1939 – 1945) (Genf: Internationales Komitee vom Roten Kreuz, 1985)

Jaskot, Paul. The Architecture of Oppression, (London: Routledge, 2000)

Keren, Daniel. "Cremation at Gusen: A Timesheet", http://www.holocaust-history.org/gusen-cremation-timesheet/index.shtml, 14 June 2004

Klepp, Monika and Reinhold Eckerstorfer. 200 Jahre Öffentliche Volksschule St. Georgen a.d. Gusen (St. Georgen/Gusen: Volksschule St. Georgen an der Gusen, 1996)

Koch, Peter-Ferdinand, ed., Himmlers graue Eminenz – Oswald Pohl und das Wirtschaftsverwaltungshauptamt der SS (Hamburg: Verlag Facta Oblita, 1988)

Koehl, Robert Lewis. The Black Corps: The Structure and Power Struggles of the Nazi SS (Madison: University of Wisconsin Press, 1983)

Kogon, Eugen, Hermann Langbein, Pierre Serge Choumoff. Nazi Mass Murder. (New Haven: Yale University Press, 1993)

Konrad, Helmut. "Social Democracy's Drift toward Nazism before 1938." Parkinson, F. ed. Conquering the Past. (Detroit: Wayne State University, 1989

Kosiek, Albert. „Liberation of Mauthausen" Thunderbolt – Bulletin of the 11th Armoured Division Association, Vol. 8, No. 7 (May – June 1955).

Lax, Martin with Michael B. Lax, Caraseu: A Holocaust Remembrance (Cleveland: The Pilgrim Press, 1996)

Le Caer, Paul Schlier, 43 – 45 (Paris: Amicale Francaise de Mauthausen, 1984)

Le Chène, Evelyn. Mauthausen – The History of a Death Camp (Ealing: Corgi Book, 1973)

Loftin, Lauren. Quest for Performance: The Evolution of Modern Aircraft – NASA SP-486 (Washington, D.C.: NASA Scientific and Technical Information Branch, 1985)

Letzeburger zu Mauthausen (Luxembourg: Amicale de Mauthausen, 1970)

Maleta, Alfred. Der Weg zum „Anschluss" 1938 – Daten und Fakten. (Vienna: Karl v. Vogelsang-Institut, 1988)

Marsálek, Hans. Die Geschichte des Konzentrationslagers Mauthausen – Dokumentation

Marsálek, Hans. Mauthausen: The History of Mauthausen Concentration Camp. Translated by Max. R. Garcia. (Linz: Austrian Society of Mauthausen Concentration Camp, 2003)

Marsálek, Hans. Konzentrationslager Gusen – Ein Nebenlager des Konzentrationslagers Mauthausen (Vienna: Österreichische Lagergemeinschaft Mauthausen, 1987)

Maislinger, Andreas. "Franz Jägerstätter." Parkinson, F. ed. Conquering the Past. (Detroit: Wayne State University, 1989)

McIsaac, David. Strategic Bombing in World War II: the Story of the United States Strategic Bombing Survey (New York: Garland, 1976)

Murray, Williamson. Strategy for Defeat: The Luftwaffe, 1933 – 45 (Airpower Research Institute, 1983)

Neufeld, Michael. The Rocket and the Reich (New York: Freepress, 1995)

Oeckl, Dieter, and Hans-Günther Richardi. Die Alpenfestung – Letztes Bollwerk der SS, broadcasted on 6 October 2004 by Austrian National Television (ORF)

Orski, Marek. Gusen 2004 – the Past and the Present. (Gdansk: Wydawnictwo Gdanskie, 2004)

Overy, Richard. Russia's War (New York: Penguin Books, 1997)

Pauley, Bruce F. "The Austrian Nazi Party before 1938." Parkinson, F. ed. Conquering the Past. (Detroit: Wayne State University, 1989)

Pauley, Bruce. From Prejudice to Persecution, (Chapel Hill: University of North Carolina Press, 1992)

Perz, Bertrand. Projekt Quarz: Steyr-Daimler-Puch und das Konzentration-slager Melk. Industrie, Zwangsarbeit und Konzentrationslager in Österreich. Vol. 3. (Vienna: Verlag für Gesellschaftskritik, 1990)

Perz, Bertrand and Florian Freund. "Auschwitz neu? – Pläne und Massnahmen zur Wiedererrichtung der Krematorien von Auschwitz-Birkenau in der Umgebung des KZ Mauthausen im Februar 1945", Dachauer Hefte, Nr. 20 (Sonderdruck), without date.

Pike, David Winegate. Spaniards in the Holocaust (London: Routledge, 2000)

Pogue, Forrest. "Halt at the Elbe" http://www.army.mil/cmh-pg/books/70-7_22.htm

Prinz, Johann. Das karge Leben – 80 Jahre Sozialdemokratie in Langenstein (Langenstein: SPÖ Langenstein, 1999)

Proudfoot, Malcom J. "The Anglo-American Displaced Persons Program for Germany and Austria." The Journal of Economics and Sociolgy. Vol. 6, No. 1 (October 1946)

Rädlinger, Christine. Zwischen Tradition und Fortschritt – Oberammergau 1869 – 2000 (Oberammergau: Gemeinde Oberammergau, 2002)

Reichl, Leo. „Das KZ-Lager Gusen III – Beginn und Aufbau einer Grossbäckerei in Lungitz und Abbruch dieser Anlagen" Oberösterreichische Heimatblätter, 54. Jahrgang, Heft 3/4 (2000)

Republik Österreich. Anlage A.1.2 zu Bundesgesetzblatt BGBl. I Nr. 141/2000 vom 29. Dezember 2000

Riedel, Dirk. „Privatunternehmer im KZ: Aufstieg einer Firma im NS-Staat", Dachauer Hefte, Nr. 19 (Sonderdruck), without date

Rief, Silvia. „Wir schmieden das Schwert: Arbeits- und Alltagserfahrungen eines Rüstungsarbeiters im Zweiten Weltkrieg, Steyr-Daimler-Puch AG,

Werk Letten und Konzentrationslager Gusen" (Diplomarbeit, Universität Wien, 1996).

Ross, Stewart Halsey. Strategic Bombing in the United States in World War II. (London: McFarland, 2003)

Sagel-Grande, Irene, et.al. Justiz und NS-Verbrechen. Sammlung Deutscher Strafurteile wegen Nationalsozialistischer Tötungsverbrechen 1945 – 1966. Bd. XVII: Die vom 04.11.1960 bis zum 21.11.1961 ergangenen Strafurteile. Lfd. Nr. 500-523. Ks 1ab/61 Strafverfahren gegen Chmielewski Karl. (Amsterdam: University Press Amsterdam, 1977)

Schausberger, Norbert. Rüstung in Österreich 1938 – 1945, Publikationen des Österreichischen Instituts für Zeitgeschichte und des Instituts für Zeitgeschichte der Universität Wien, Vol. 8 (Vienna: Verlag Brüder Hollinek, 1970)

Schwarz, Robert. "Buerkel and Innitzer." Parkinson, F. ed. Conquering the Past. (Detroit: Wayne State University, 1989)

Schmitzberger, Markus. Was die US Army in der Alpenfestung wirklich suchte – Eine Theorie zum Decknamen der Anlage "Quarz" in Roggendorf bei Melk (Schleusingen: Amun-Verlag, 2001)

Schmoll, Peter. Die Messerschmitt-Werke im Zweiten Weltkrieg. (Regensburg: Mittelbayerische Druck- & Verlags-Gesellschaft, 1998)

Skrjanec, Ivan. "Erinnerungsbericht – Der Abgang nach Gusen II". (France Filipic, Slowenen in Mauthausen. Mauthausen-Studien, Band 3. (Vienna: Bundesministerium für Inneres, 2004))

Singer, Engelbert. Analyse der Pfarrgemeinde St. Georgen/Gusen (St. Georgen a.d. Gusen: Pfarre St. Georgen a.d. Gusen, 1983)

Slapnicka, Harry. Oberösterreich zwischen Bürgerkrieg und Anschluss, 1927 – 1938 (Linz: Oberösterr. Landesverlag, 1975)

Slapnicka, Harry. 550 Stichworte zur Zeitgeschichte. (Grünbach: Edition Geschichte der Heimat, 2000)

Smretschnig, Christian „Memorial de Gusen" Bautenkatalog zur Gebäudelehre-Prüfung (Vienna: Technische Universität Wien – Institut für Gebäudelehre, 1999)

Speer, Albert. Erinnerungen (Berlin: Propyläen Verlag, 1969)

SPÖ Mauthausen (ed.). Der harte Weg. Geschichte der Arbeiterbewegung von Mauthausen (Grünbach: Edition Geschichte der Heimat, 1989)

Steiner, Herbert „The Role of Austrian Resistance with Special Reference to the Labor Movement" (*The Journal of Modern History* Volume 64, Supplement: Resistance Against the Third Reich, Dec. 1992)

Sydnor, Charles. Soldiers of Destruction, (Princeton: Princeton University, 1990)

Thies, Jochen. "Hitler's European Building Programs" Journal of European History, Vol. 13, No. 3 (July 1978), 413 – 431

Trnka, Gerhard. "Das urnenzeitliche Gräberfeld von Gusen in Oberöster-reich", Archaeologia Austriaca, Band 76 (Vienna: Franz Deutike Verlags-gesellschaft mbH, 1992)

Ulrich, Herbert. "Labour and Extermination: Economic Interests and Primacy of Weltangschauung in National Socialism." *Past and Present*, No 138, (Feb. 1993)

United States Strategic Bombing Survey, Aircraft Industry Report

Vilsmeyer, Gabriele. Der Flugplatz Obertraubling (Obertraubling, 1976)

Vitry, Stephanie. "Les morts de Gusen, camp de concentration Autrichien – a partir du depouilement d'un registre de morts Avril 1943 – Mai 1945" (Maitrise d'histoire, Universite de Paris I – Pantheon-Sorbonne, 1994)